THE ISRAEL DEFENCE FORCE
AND THE FOUNDATION OF ISRAEL

The Israel Defence Force and the Foundation of Israel

Utopia in Uniform

Ze'ev Drory
Ben-Gurion University

RoutledgeCurzon
Taylor & Francis Group

LONDON AND NEW YORK

First published 2005
by RoutledgeCurzon
2 Park Square, Milton Park, Abingdon, Oxon, OX14 4RN
in association with The European Jewish Publication Society,
PO Box 19948, London N3 3ZJ

Simultaneously published in the USA and Canada
by RoutledgeCurzon
270 Madison Avenue, New York, NY 10016

RoutledgeCurzon is an imprint of the Taylor & Francis Group

© 2005 Ze'ev Drory

Typeset in ZapfCalligr BT by Taylor & Francis Books
Printed and bound in Great Britain by MPG Books Ltd, Bodmin

British Library Cataloguing in Publication Data
Drory, Ze'ev
The Israel Defence Force and the foundation of Israel
1. Israel. Tseva haganah le-Yisrael – History 2. Military social work – Israel –
History 3. Israel – Emigration and immigration – Government policy
4. Israel – Emigration and immigration – Social aspects 5. Israel – Military
policy 6. Israel – Politics and government – 1948–1967 I. Title
956.9'4052

Library of Congress Cataloging in Publication Data
Drory, Ze'ev.
The Israel Defence Force and the foundation of Israel/ Ze'ev Drory.
p. cm.
Includes bibliographical references and index.
1. Israel–Armed Forces–Civic action. 2. Immigrants–Israel–Social
conditions. 3. Israel–Emigration and immigration–Social aspects.
4. Immigrants–Education–Israel. 5. Ben-Gurion, David,
1886–1973–Contributions in civil–military relations. 6. Civil–military
relations–Israel. I. Title.
UH725.I75D47 2004
956.9405'2–dc22   2003069680

ISBN 0–714–65663–1 (hbk)
ISBN 0–714–68552–6 (pbk)

This book is dedicated to my family – Batya, Maya, Uri, Ohad and Nimrod – who in the past few years have heard continual lectures from me on Ben-Gurion, the IDF and Israeli society.

Contents

Illustrations

Acknowledgments

This book has its genesis in a thesis for the Doctorate of Philosophy at the History Department of Israel's Ben-Gurion University. During the course of my research and writing I received help from many individuals. I give them my thanks and gratitude.

First and foremost, I would like to bestow thanks on my teacher, Professor Zeev Tzahor, who guided me during my doctorate and provided encouragement and assistance throughout.

Professor Ilan Troen offered good advice and enabled me to participate in the researchers' seminar at Yourntown outside Oxford. I learned much at this seminar, especially in conversations with Professor Joseph Gurney.

Professor Yoav Gelber devoted hours to lengthy discussions with me, from which I benefited greatly.

I was privileged to serve as a research fellow at the Ben-Gurion Research Centre at Sde Boker, and the Centre's workers helped me over many years. I wish to thank the director of the Centre, Dr Tuvia Freiling, for his support and help. The dedicated IDF archive staff took great pains in locating and sorting material for me.

Dr Meir Pe'il and Osnat Shiran, senior researchers at the Tabenkin Centre at Efal, and the Centre's archive staff did their utmost to facilitate my endeavours. In addition, the staff of the Central Zionist Archives in Jerusalem placed their good services at my disposal.

Orit Shaham-Guver and Motti Golani, friends and colleagues, read and assisted in editing different sections of the work.

My gratitude is extended to the director of the Ben-Gurion Research Centre, Shaul Shragai.

My partner Dorit Harel knew how to listen, to respond and to inquire, to enlighten and to comment with a cheerful smile.

Abbreviations

AKM	HaKibbutz HaMeuchad Archives
BGA	Ben-Gurion Archives
GHQ	General Headquarters
HALP	Historical Archives of the Labour Party
IDF	Israel Defence Force
IDFA	Israel Defence Force Archives
JFN	Jewish National Fund
Nahal	Noar Halutzi Lohem (Pioneering Fighting Youth)
NOA	Nahal Oz Archives
SA	State Archives
UKA	United Kibbutz Archives
UN	United Nations
ZA	Zionist Archives

Introduction

Immediately following its establishment in 1948, the State of Israel was forced to contend with a number of very complex problems. Foremost among them was the struggle for its existence, which required the mobilization of all human and material resources. However, this did not prevent the fledgling State from opening its gates to massive immigration at the height of its War of Independence and from continuing with this influx of human capital following the cessation of hostilities. During the first year of independence Israel took in more than 100,000 *olim* (immigrants) and by the end of 1951, 700,000 *olim* had entered the country. In the course of its first three years, the State's Jewish population more than doubled. Policies pursued at this time in the immigration and absorption, social and educational fields, and the resultant settlement programmes, gave shape to the geographic, social, economic and security landscape of the Israeli State for years to come.

David Ben-Gurion, acting simultaneously as Prime Minister and Defence Minister of the new State of Israel, stood at the centre of these historical processes and played a leading role in their formulation. He sought to build a new society, an Israeli society possessing unique characteristics, and he awarded the army a special place in the realization of this goal. His visionary utopia was dressed in military attire. The Israel Defence Force (IDF) was envisaged as a state instrument of the first order, fully detached from the political system and party pressures. Preliminary steps toward this objective began to crystallize when Ben-Gurion boldly disbanded the Palmach (a strike force of the Hagana), the very same body he had deployed to break up Etzel (the National Military Guard) and Lehi (Fighters for the Freedom of Israel). According to Ben-Gurion, this instrument was designed to secure not only the survival and safety of the State but also to serve as the standard bearer in the pioneering areas of education, immigrant absorption and settlement.

With the help of the IDF, which was directly subordinate to him, Ben-Gurion sought to circumvent political and party hindrances and overcome bureaucratic obstacles and inter-ministerial squabbles. He set in motion various forces which, by means of indirect enticements, mobilized the younger generation into a succession of national missions and led to the formulation of basic values for the new, immigrant, society in the making.

This book seeks to analyse how the aspirations of Ben-Gurion were converted into practice. It will attempt to survey and examine the early involvement of the IDF in fashioning the contours of Israeli society and respond to the following questions:

- what was Ben-Gurion's personal contribution in activating the IDF's seemingly 'extra-military' national missions, and from which sources did he obtain the power and authority required for such undertakings?
- what gaps occurred between intentions and decisions at the political and governmental level, and in implementation in the field?
- what was the IDF's role in settlement activity during and following the War of Independence?
- what were Nahal's goals, duties, and contributions in the area of settlement?
- what was the IDF's social and educational share in the massive immigration absorption process?
- what was the IDF's place in the educational undertakings and information dissemination programmes directed toward Israeli society as a whole?
- what were the roles and contributions of the Gadna in the areas of education and immigrant absorption?
- what was the IDF's status and what was its contribution to the formation of the society's common national and social value system?

The relevant time frame for this study begins on 14 May 1948, the date when Israel declared itself a State, and ends during the latter part of 1953, with Ben-Gurion's decision to resign from the Government and join Kibbutz Sde Boker in the Negev. The entire period may be divided into three subordinate time frames. First, the period of the War of Independence – from the declaration of Statehood in May 1948 to the opening of negotiations with the neighbouring states on a cease-fire agreement in February 1949. The

IDF was involved in two major non-military missions during this period: the recruitment of immigrant soldiers [Gahal], and settlement activities. Secondly, the period of mass immigration – from the end of the War of Independence to the end of 1952. During this period the IDF was called upon to help residents of the transit camps and various types of immigrant settlements in light of the conditions of distress in which the newcomers found themselves, and took upon itself responsibilities for engineering activities, logistics and medical care. These years constituted the acme of the IDF's socio–educational activity among the immigrants and its assistance to border settlement throughout the Negev and the Arava. Thirdly, the period of consolidation and settlement – from the end of 1952 until the end of 1953. During this time the IDF continued to assist immigrant agricultural settlements and frontier settlements in routine security matters, education and community activities. The deployment of Nahal soldiers on border settlements in the Negev and Arava also began at this time.

In the research which gave birth to this book I have relied mainly upon primary sources located in the following: the IDF archives, the Ben-Gurion archives, the Zionist Archives, the Tabenkin Archives, the Labour Party Archives (the Lavon Institute), and the State Archives. Some of these are personal documents, speeches and diaries of decision-makers written during the period under discussion. I was greatly aided, and not by chance, by contemporaneous newspapers. The press was an active partner in the description of events, in the production of information and propaganda, and, in effect, in the shaping of society. Moreover, leading personalities were prone to write in the newspapers and this material contributed important clarifications. I also interviewed some personalities who were participants in the decision-making processes and their implementation – principally to amplify the knowledge gathered from other sources.

Over the last few years, considerable material on the history of the establishment of the State of Israel has been published, including that concerning the periods of transition from settlement to State and from the Hagana to the IDF. A number of these publications helped me significantly (see Bibliography).

Chapter 1

David Ben-Gurion's Position and Influence in Shaping the State

Since the War of Independence, the Israel Defence Forces have played a central role in the life of the State well beyond that which is most obviously and clearly signified by its designated name. The forces were established amidst the turmoil of war to defend and secure the physical survival of the State of Israel. More specifically, they were authorized to repel the invasion of the Arab armies, obtain as continuous and as large a territorial expanse as possible within the Land of Israel, and protect those borders. Clearly, these tasks are standard military requirements. Yet, from its earliest days, the IDF was involved, directly and indirectly, in the formation of the character and way of life of the society through the inclusion in its sphere of responsibility of civilian tasks in the areas of settlement, education, and immigrant absorption.

This non-military orientation of the IDF was precipitated largely by the constraints of reality. From the very beginning, the geo-political situation made security a national priority. Not only have security and related topics always captured the attention of public opinion and the major protagonists in the political system, but for many years security concerns have also comprised a very healthy proportion of the gross national product. Even more importantly, a decisive majority of the adult population in Israel has passed through the IDF. This was the case with regard to the War of Independence, which was without doubt a most important formative experience of the young State. During the course of the war, 108,000 soldiers served in the IDF – about 15 per cent of the entire population, and this figure carries a much greater weight when measured in terms of the State's qualitative and professional cadre. Following the war, broad-based military recruitment shaped the IDF's composition through a combination of conscription and a reserve system that included all soldiers from the time of their completion of compulsory service until the fourth and fifth decades of their lives.

Under these conditions it was, in effect, a foregone conclusion that the IDF would be tied into various national endeavours that were not purely military in nature. Its influence would be felt in the building of a civilian elite and in the formation of concepts and outlooks in various social arenas. Moreover, there is no doubt that this development was to a great extent influenced not only by external constraints and their implications but also by ideational processes and their translation into practice. These processes were especially linked to David Ben-Gurion, 'the founding father' of the State, in the eyes of many, and unanimously regarded as the dominant personality in State leadership during the first 15 years of independence. Thus it is impossible to understand the extra-military involvement of the IDF during these years – and particularly during the nascent moments of the State – without examining the conceptions and actions of David Ben-Gurion in the arenas relevant to these civilian initiatives.

Anita Shapira defined Ben-Gurion as a leader whose:

> place is preserved as one of the 'monstrous figures' of history, a dominant personality type destined to fashion the fate of peoples and states and leave a mark on history. They are people who have the strength of their convictions, who know at critical moments how to make the right decisions, to select the important tasks and determine priorities, and whose deeds are justified by the test of reality.[1]

Nathan Rotenstreich saw Ben-Gurion as an 'historical personality', a type of individual who can 'sift out the circumstances and conditions and intentionally lead the train of events in such a manner that he invigorates its course and hollows out its contours. In relating to circumstances and directing them, he carves out an historical path.'[2] Shimon Peres portrayed Ben-Gurion as a leader who combined a powerful intellect, a phenomenal memory and an obdurate and determined character, and that his diligence and perseverance blended with his decisiveness and pursuance of goals.[3]

For our purposes, it is important to recall Shlomo Avineri's description of Ben-Gurion as:

> a complex personality … who more than any other Israeli leader was a subject of sharp contention among friends and foes alike … But his thought contains a great deal of continuity and engagement with the same series of basic problems … Any attempt to find an orderly account of 'the social and political philosophy of David Ben-Gurion' is futile. We do not encounter a theoretical system because his teaching reveals a dynamic belonging to a complex and ever changing life … The theoretical foundations of Ben-Gurion's Zionist thought can be encapsulated in two principles: in the first place, Zionism is a revolt against the Jewish tradition; secondly, to carry out this revolution, it is not enough to declare it. One has to seek out the social subject who will be able to carry it out.[4]

It appears that during the first years of the State Ben-Gurion thought that the IDF could function as part of the social subject of that revolutionary base, and would do so through the coining of a new concept – 'statist pioneering'.

Looking back, it is easy to see that in each time period Ben-Gurion preferred to concentrate his activities on one subject, on the assumption that that subject would bear fruit and bring about decisive changes. It is also easy to see that during the course of his life he knew how to transfer all his energy and personal and political power from topic to topic and from area to area. He did this, according to Zeev Tzahor,[5] out of faith in his mission and in his ability to realize it, as well as in his unlimited thoroughness in getting down to details without losing track of the main point.

Ben-Gurion was not willing to relinquish his standpoints easily. Even when he found no support for his direction or opinions, he would put up a fight, exercise his authority and his leadership ability, and use all available means of manipulation and democratic processes to attain his goals. He was in essence a pragmatic leader, who in advancing his objectives knew how to tread a path between 'vision' and practical policy, between stubbornness and readiness to compromise. His strength and originality were not in the formulation of ideas but rather in their political conversion. This found particular expression in the fact that he attributed significant value to those organizational instruments which served his purposes. 'The important thing in my view', he wrote, 'is the economic, political, and social strength of the working people. On this account, I regard it as obligatory to build up the economy, the Histadrut, the State. On this account, I attribute importance to tools and instruments.'[6]

Among the personalities who greatly contributed to the formulation of Ben Gurion's thinking, a central place must be given to Vladimir Ilyich Lenin, the leader of the Bolshevik Revolution. Although Ben-Gurion tended to be very critical about what occurred in the Soviet Union, Lenin and the revolution provided him with a clear-cut example of the conversion of ideas into social and political facts.[7] Ben-Gurion referred to this in his memoirs, and manifest signs of this appear in his desire to build a voluntary movement of sufficient strength to shape the nation's character. It seems that one can also see here the root of his later ideas, which raised not a little criticism from his political opponents, of establishing a para-military regime (for example, organization of immigrant, public works battalions).

From the time of his arrival in Palestine in 1906 to the 22nd Zionist Congress, in Basel in December 1946, Ben-Gurion's involvement in security matters was not especially significant. Although he was prone to recall with pride his part in the defence of Sejera and his participation in military encounters against Arab marauders in 1907 and 1908, in fact he was not accepted into the ranks of the 'Hashomer' (Jewish guard and self-defence organization) at its founding in 1909. Nor was he a party to all the security initiatives that were undertaken within the operative compass of this militia. Moreover, toward the end of the first decade of the twentieth century, he left the farming communities in Galilee for Jerusalem and became involved in political activities that were completely removed from security matters. Afterwards, he set out to study law in Constantinople, returned to Palestine at the outbreak of the First World War, and was expelled from the country in 1915 by an edict of the Ottoman regime. Following his expulsion he arrived in the United States, where he played an active role in organizing volunteers for the Jewish Legion. Ben-Gurion joined the American branch of the Legion and was in its ranks when he arrived in Egypt en route to Palestine; he even attained the rank of corporal, but this was later taken away from him because of a disciplinary violation connected with political party activity. Like a majority of the Jewish Legion members, Ben-Gurion did not participate in any military operations, but according to Tzahor 'his experience as a soldier in the Jewish Legion reinforced his perspective. He was impressed with military hierarchy and the ability of the army to galvanize armed forces and function as a policy-determining instrument.'[8]

In 1919, Ben-Gurion became one of the leaders of the newly formed party, Achdut Ha'avodah (Union of Labour), and one of its senior representatives in the Yishuv's institutions. It was as a representative of Achdut Ha'avodah, the largest workers' party in the Yishuv, that he became involved, during the first two months of 1920, in what would be called the 'Tel Hai Affair'. At a session of the Provisional Committee of the Jewish Community in Palestine on 23 February 1920, he firmly opposed withdrawal from the northern settlements, which at that time had not been included under British jurisdiction. The outlook which Ben-Gurion expressed was to become part of basic strategy almost 30 years later during the War of Independence:

> It is clear to us, that all places in which a Jew labors must be defended. What should we do when they attack us? If we flee from bandits, we will have to abandon not only the Upper Galilee but the whole of the Land of Israel … As long as we have the capacity to defend – it is our duty to defend and not to abandon our locations.[9]

While the genesis of later military strategies found occasional expression in Ben-Gurion's writings and pronouncements during these early years, he was not at the centre of critical military decisions. In the middle of June 1920, when the Achdut Ha'avodah Congress decided to accept 'in recognition of its importance and the Congress's historical responsibility, the initiative placed upon it by the Hashomer organization to attend to security matters, to organize the workers' participation in defence matters, and to ensure national and social planning of national defence in Palestine.'[10] Ben-Gurion was already stationed in London as the party's representative. Within a year he returned to Palestine. Prior to his return, the Histadrut (General Federation of Jewish Workers) had been founded and received responsibility for security matters from Achdut Ha'avodah. From December 1921 until the end of 1935, Ben-Gurion was secretary-general of the Histadrut, its most senior office. By virtue of this position, he also served as the highest authority of the Hagana organization until its Command Council (Ha*Mifkada Ha'artzit* – 41 members who held responsibility for security in the Yishuv) was established under the auspices of the national institutions in 1931. However, most of his energy in this period was given over to non-military matters, principally to the 'conquest of labour' and to building up the power of the Histadrut. He did not refrain from decisions regarding security (including personal initiatives such as appointments) when his intervention was required, but it appears that in general he relied completely upon Eliyahu Golomb and his close associates in their role as supervisors, on behalf of the Histadrut and the party which controlled it, of the Hagana and its daily activities.

A good part of this reliance continued in the next stage of Ben-Gurion's career, in his first years as Chairman of the Palestine Executive of the Jewish Agency and as effective leader of the Yishuv. Now he had responsibilities for a range of activities, such as immigration and settlement, which clearly had security aspects, as well as the task of formulating defence policy but he was still far from being directly involved in security affairs and daily involvement in defence matters.

Changes began to occur on the eve of the Second World War. With the publication of the 1939 White Paper, Ben-Gurion began to wage a militant struggle against the document's obligatory regulations, which would have had the effect of relegating the Jewish population to a minority status in Palestine and of severely limiting the rights of immigration and settlement. This struggle was to be prosecuted, according to Ben-Gurion, by means of different instruments of the Hagana organization and he intended to closely orchestrate the operation of these instruments.

Thus, for example, in the first stage of the struggle against the White Paper, Ben-Gurion gave orders for the establishment of *Aliya Bet* (unofficial immigration) with his confidant, Shaul Meirov-Avigur, appointed its first head. This step was taken after initially he had opposed the idea of illegal immigration for fear of impairing political ties with the British. He rapidly sought a reversal of the policy of underground immigration and turned it into a policy of unconcealed entry into Palestine. This altered programme was called *Aliya Gimmel*. It would operate in broad daylight by bringing many immigrant ships to the coast and disembarking passengers under the protection of armed members of the Hagana prepared to counter British intervention.

In the end, the outbreak of the Second World War, on 1 September 1939, pushed aside plans for launching a flotilla of illegal immigrant ships from Europe to Palestine along the sea-lanes of the Mediterranean. In the meantime, Ben-Gurion introduced a completely different type of security issue. One of his more prominent pronouncements in this vein was voiced on 8 September 1939 in a meeting with a select group of senior Hagana members. He told them:

The [First] World War brought us the Balfour Declaration. This war must bring about the establishment of a Jewish State ... The first condition for a Jewish State is the establishment of a Jewish army, first of all in Palestine and for Palestine. We must establish Jewish military units ... throughout the country wherever we have the possibility of doing so ... Our central strength is in Palestine – and a suitable Jewish military power is likely to determine the fate of the Land of Israel.[11]

Translation of these words into practice was still quite remote and the moment had not yet arrived at which Ben-Gurion's active and direct involvement could bring this about. He participated on various occasions in negotiations with the British for the establishment of Jewish–Palestinian fighting units attached to British forces, but certainly did not stand at the centre of this initiative. He enthusiastically supported placing an emphasis on volunteering for the British army as opposed to entering the ranks of the Palmach. More than once he stated that His Majesty's Armed Forces would supply suitable military training for many members of the Yishuv, and would prove beneficial in the struggles that were to come. Nevertheless, the area of security was not yet the focus of his activity and thought.

The first months of the war made a strong impression upon Ben-Gurion and would be reflected in his future ruminations on security matters. He was present in London from May to September 1940, the height of the Battle of Britain, and was witness to the resilience of the civilian population, especially their mature collective consciousness in the face of heavy bombardment from the air. In 1948 he recalled those days: 'I have seen what a people is capable of achieving in the hour of supreme trial. I have seen their spirit touched by nobility ... This is what the Jewish people could do. We did it.'[12]

It is noteworthy that Ben-Gurion's involvement in the disputes concerning the mobilization of Yishuv recruits into the British army was tied to important developments linking politics and security. By and large, the Palmach enjoyed the protection of the HaKibbutz HaMe'uchad (United Kibbutz) leadership, which was also the leadership of the left-leaning 'B' Faction in Mapai (and afterwards the leadership of the Achdut Ha'Avodah movement) and in many matters was opposed to Ben-Gurion. To a great extent, this dispute was perceived as part of the larger-faceted dispute between Ben-Gurion and his opponents in the Labour Movement. Its echoes were clearly heard in controversies which arose in the War of Independence, including those centring around the building up of forces and the appointment of senior posts in the IDF, and the dramatic episode involving the disbanding of the Palmach.

Several months after the conclusion of the Second World War, in October 1945, Ben-Gurion instructed Moshe Sneh, head of the Command Council of the Hagana, to begin assault operations against British targets within the framework of 'the Jewish resistance movement' – a joint action of the Hagana, Etzel and Lehi. 'There will be no let up in our immigration and settlement efforts', he wrote. 'It is necessary to undertake sabotage and retaliation. Not personal terror … every sabotage operation must carry weight and make an impression … The response must be continuous, daring, and not planned for the short run …'[13] Despite these military initiatives, this must still be gauged as a partial involvement of the political leader in joint security operations. Two clear indications bear this out. In the first place, Moshe Sneh, leader of the Command Council and on the receiving end of instructions, was also head of the Security Department of the Jewish Agency Executive. (In any case, he acted as a buffer between Ben-Gurion and the armed forces of the Yishuv. A 'kind of' Defence Minister beside a 'sort of' Prime Minister). Secondly, the X Committee, which was appointed to supervise the operations of the 'Jewish resistance' on behalf of the national institutions, did not include Ben-Gurion, and this was not contrary to his wishes.

In an additional step, parallel to his 'resistance movement' initiative, Ben-Gurion orchestrated a secret and radical security initiative in the area of military requisitions. Under his instruction and supervision, and with the help of solicited donors, a Hagana mission began to operate on a wide basis in the United States. The mission purchased weaponry, which had made its way to the American market in the wake of the Second World War. At the same time, Ben-Gurion began to formulate a security conception which quickly resulted in his taking over the management of the security apparatus of the Yishuv and the State. On 1 July 1945, he appeared before a group of Jewish high-financiers in New York and, according to his later account (which was affirmed by other witnesses), 'I told those present that in the very near future, after the British leave Palestine, we will be facing, sooner or later, all the Arab armies … Although we are not many – we can stand up against them if we have the required arms.'[14] Shipments of the 'required weaponry' initiated at this time began to arrive in Palestine in the summer of 1946, and was one of the factors which brought about the decision to terminate the 'resistance movement'.

THE SECURITY PORTFOLIO ON THE ZIONIST EXECUTIVE

The 22nd Zionist Congress, the first after the Second World War and the Holocaust, convened against the background of the struggle for the immediate establishment of a Jewish State. Ben-Gurion, in addition to his role as chairman of the Zionist Executive, procured its security portfolio. This was an innovatory step on Ben-Gurion's part; until then, he had not held any portfolio on the executive body of the Zionist movement. But much more than that, it was a total change in the organizational set-up of the Zionist organization, and it came on the eve of major communal disturbances.

During the uprisings of 1936–39, the Jewish Agency had estab-lished a unit called the Security Bureau but its activities were limited to handling the Supernumerary Police Force. It had a secondary status in the organizational structure – subordinate to the Political Department of the Agency Executive (at whose head stood Moshe Sharett). Over a period of time, two fictitious portfolios attached to the Agency Executive were created and two senior members of the Hagana were appointed to fill them: 'Recruitment' headed by Moshe Sneh, and 'Supernumeraries' under the direction of Eliyahu Golomb. These portfolios supplied a legal cover for those operations of the Hagana which diverged from its underground activities. The situa-tion changed to a certain extent in August 1945 following Golomb's death. Sneh, who was head of the Hagana's Command Council, was given a place on the Zionist Executive and in its Political Department. In these roles there was a certain basis for seeing him as holding the Security portfolio of the Executive, and thus neutralizing Ben Gurion's desire to be involved in security matters. However, this situation ceased to exist with Sneh's resignation from all his positions in the Jewish Agency and the Hagana in September 1946.

On 20 April 1947, the Zionist Executive re-affirmed an explicit division of positions which had previously been passed at the conclusion of the Basel Congress in December 1946. This included its primary appointment of Mr D. Ben-Gurion as 'Chairman of the World Congress, Head of the Security Committee, and member of the Political Affairs Committee'.

The absence of a security portfolio possessing a senior and declared status, until Ben-Gurion decided to head it, is connected to the special status of the Jewish Agency Executive as the legitimate governing body of the Yishuv during the British Mandate period. This Agency was supposed to dissociate itself from all underground activities and in no way was it openly to appear as the political–civilian wing governing the Hagana.

The responsibility and supervision of the Hagana was assigned to a Command Council, a civilian body which was first established in 1931 and was reorganized at the end of the thirties and the beginning of the forties. It was a parity organization constituted by two equal factions: the Histadrut and representatives of various public and civilian organizations. By virtue of a combination of circumstances, it enjoyed a considerable degree of autonomy. On the one hand, as was stated, there was a need to guarantee a degree of separation between it and the official leadership. On the other hand, within the Hagana, Eliyahu Golomb, the stalwart confidant of the official leadership, enjoyed a senior and special personal status. In this manner, the leadership was relieved from the fear of standing before faits accomplis. In addition, it was accepted by all parties involved that the head of the Command Council, who was also the determining voice between the two factions in every instance of stalemate, be appointed by the Jewish Agency Executive and the National Executive (the officially-recognized, representative body of the Yishuv), and that he be accountable to both these organizations. This political and personal arrangement accounts for Ben-Gurion's infrequent intervention in Hagana affairs and the formulation of its different programmes.

Shortly after the conclusion of the Second World War, Ben-Gurion began to realize that military and security matters were about to occupy a central place in the country. This was the true ground for his remarks, cited above, which were uttered in New York in July 1945. This was also the reason for his declaration, approximately one and a half years later, at the 22nd Zionist Congress at Basel:

> The primary problem is that of security … Until recently the only question was how to defend against the native Arab population who would from time to time attack Jewish settlements or the Yishuv, but now we face a completely new situation. Israel is surrounded by independent Arab States … who have the ability to purchase and manufacture weapons, to build and train armies … An attack of Arabs living in the land of Israel does not endanger the Jewish community but there is a danger that the neighboring Arab States will send their armies to attack the Yishuv and annihilate it. This danger threatens our very existence.[15]

On the basis of this outlook, his tendency to focus upon what he thought to be the most important subject of the historical moment, and his sense of responsibility as leader of the Yishuv, emerged his resolute claim to create the security portfolio and appoint himself to the post – all this notwithstanding the fact that up to this point he had hardly occupied himself with security matters. If anyone had doubts whether the relationships between the political echelon and the Hagana would remain unchanged, they were quickly removed. Ben-Gurion grasped the reins of power with a strong and firm hand.

Ben-Gurion was 60 years old when, at the end of March 1947, he began his 'seminar' designed to learn about the security problems of the Yishuv. In the coming months most of his time was devoted to inquiries into the situation of the Hagana, and to finding a response to the question whether or not it could hold up in a war with the Arab armies. He carried out intensive meetings with members of the Command Council, members of the General Staff Headquarters of the Hagana, district commanders, commanders of the Palmach and heads of the Information Service – the intelligence branch of the Hagana. He also made field trips throughout the country to inspect at first hand the issues which were raised during these meetings – from the quality of the command and the building up of the rank and file, through training and battle preparation to the problems of armament, equipment and manpower. In the course of his inquiries, Ben-Gurion came to the sombre conclusion that the Hagana, under its present command, would not be capable of turning into an army of regulars. He wrote in his diary:

> Training even at the brigade level [of the Palmach] is not sufficient. There is a shortage of commanders, the commanders we have are not sufficiently qualified, they lack operational experience, planning is faulty, the budget structure is not goal-oriented. The greatest flaw – experience and military manpower have not been appropriately used, the equipment is not suitable. For many years a central idea has been absent – what is its role?[16]

The complaint regarding the inability of the Hagana to exploit available military experience focused first and foremost on the limited integration of Jewish forces demobilized from the British army following World War Two. Their numbers exceeded 26,000 veteran soldiers; many among them had served as battlefield commanders or had acquired specialized military training in different areas, yet most of them were not in Hagana's ranks. Failure to induct them into the Hagana was due to personal considerations (there was a natural tendency for Hagana commanders, including those in the Palmach who did not see service outside the country, not to relinquish their positions) and ideological tenets (unwillingness to adopt doctrines and procedures associated with a regular 'commonplace' army). Ben-Gurion regarded this as a serious error, in light of imminent war, and tried to rectify matters by inducting more and more 'British' officers into the upper echelons of the Hagana. At this point he was forced to compromise in order not to bring about a deep split with senior Hagana members (who on no account were overjoyed about his energetic plunge into security concerns. Nevertheless, he often consulted with veteran Legion soldiers in all matters concerned with the structure of the army that he was planning. A clear-cut example of this occurred when, in the course of the 'Seminar', he asked Chaim Laskov and Shalom Eshet to present their army plans in addition to the plans submitted by Zeev Sheffer (head of Hagana's civilian Command Council) and Yochanan Ratner (head of the Programme Bureau of the organization). He invested great efforts in having the former plans approved.

Another of Ben-Gurion's struggles against the Hagana chiefs concerned arms-procurement matters and was anchored in his outlook with regard to future military developments. The impending clash with regular Arab armies required, in his opinion, military equipment qualitatively and quantitatively different from that acceptable for a military underground. He talked about this in a closed session with senior Hagana staff. Some regarded his words as alarmist but he persevered along the same line. Referring to his own testimony from the session, Ben-Gurion noted: 'It appears to me that there is a need to procure heavy arms: tanks, half-tracks, cannon, heavy mortars for a land army, fighter aircraft as the basis for an airforce, torpedoes, submarines, and other vessels for the navy.'[17]

Almost as an aside in the 'seminar' framework Ben-Gurion began to formulate a line of thought, which would be continued after the War of Independence, oriented towards extra-military operations of the IDF. On 3 April 1947 he wrote in his diary:

> Youth: not to establish a new youth movement in the conventional manner – which formulates its own *weltanschauung* and determines a position regarding current and enduring questions about the nation and society – but rather a framework of youth subservient to the nation. There is no hope that the pioneering youth movements

will embrace all youth. 'Splinter groups' [Etzel and Lehi] recruit [youth] and seek out lower age groups – they begin at age 12. We must do the same. A minimum of military training, field trips, learning about the country, information sessions (on illegal immigration and the like), Zionist education; leaflet distribution by the children, newspaper reporting, contributing to local production – and service in the entrance ranks of the 'Hagana'. It will embrace both working youth and students, mainly in the distressed neighborhoods.[18]

This marked the germination of his Gadna programmes, concerning which pioneering youth movements and their political patrons were less than enthusiastic.

At the conclusion of the seminar Ben-Gurion began, by virtue of his leadership and authority, to work on the construction of the security system. This included the establishment of an infrastructure for a permanent military, the expansion of military requisitioning, independent production in the framework of a locally-developed arms industry, and finally the organization of operational plans. In official instructions issued to the general staff of the Hagana at the beginning of June 1947 he wrote:

> In the instance of an armed attack by the Arabs, the determining factor will perhaps only be power, decisive Jewish military power. Without the organization being trained and able for this task – it will fail in its basic objective, and the very existence of the Yishuv and the Zionist enterprise will be in danger of being destroyed … Training the organization not only to confront this mortal danger and successfully defend Jewish settlements and the Yishuv but … also to defend the land and our national future on it – this is the burning task of this era.[19]

Ben-Gurion goes on to discuss the changes required in the Hagana's structure, equipment and training. He detailed the structure of its military strength, placing an emphasis upon the integration of the Legion soldiers and other veterans of the British army who had acquired experience in the Second World War. In addition, he emphasized the establishment of specialized corps and the need for founding military schools for training knowledgeable and qualified officers. In his memoirs, Joseph Avidar, then Deputy Commander-in-Chief of the Hagana, wrote that 'the month of July 1947 can be seen as the date which marks a major turning point with regard to the prevailing general conception of the Hagana's objective'. Avidar noted that several factors contributed to the revolutionary changes, 'but it appears that these factors by themselves would not have brought about the correct and immediate conclusions regarding the objective of the Hagana had not Ben-Gurion taken over the Security portfolio following the Zionist Congress'.[20]

Chief of Staff of the Hagana, Yaakov Dori, was to relate to another central facet of Ben-Gurion's innovations in 1947. The 'Seminar' led Ben-Gurion to pay overly-stringent attention to the lack of clarity regarding relations governing the subordination of the army to the political echelon and the command structure. It was a most sensitive topic in light of the political involvement built into the very institutional structure of the Command Council. After the 'Seminar', Ben-Gurion was adamant in his opinion that there should be one national authority controlling all the military forces, combining under its authority all the factions and bearers of command. Dori wrote:

> Given the circumstances of our activities then ... these attempts [of the opponents of Ben-Gurion] could have endangered the integrity of the concept of a single and solitary, supreme national authority. In certain known cases, this might have even harmed the high level of dedication to its goals – one of the greatest resources of the Hagana. Undoubtedly, one can point out failures that are due to this deficiency and it can be affirmed that this fact more than once made it hard to impose absolute discipline, which is vital for a fighting force.[21]

Ben-Gurion conducted bitter debates over this matter – within his party, in the upper echelons of the Histadrut, with the Zionist Executive, and later with the Provisional Government. More than once in the wake of these disputes he exercised all his authority and weight, accompanied continually by threats of resignation. In the end it appears that without his aggressive intervention, and without his determination to establish a regular army, the Hagana leadership would not have come to the conclusions and actions necessitated by the threats that hovered over the Yishuv during this period. Without Ben-Gurion's intervention in the building-up of a military force and its preparedness for war, in military procurement activities, and in the integration of veteran officers from the British army, the Yishuv would have been unable to withstand the campaign waged by the invading Arab armies on 15 May 1948.

BEN-GURION'S MILITARY LEADERSHIP IN THE WAR OF INDEPENDENCE

The decision of the United Nation's General Assembly on 29 November 1947, to divide Palestine between a Jewish and Arab State, led to violent Arab disturbances which, in hindsight, were seen as the initial stage of the War of Independence. The first clashes in the mixed Arab/Jewish towns, and the attacks on Jewish vehicles along the various main highways, confirmed the projections of the heads of the Hagana with regard to the anticipated nature of the armed Arab activities. The organization had prepared itself for these eventualities and, in retrospect, appeared ready to cope with them. However, within a few weeks there was an escalation in the scope and intensity of these actions. Organized armed forces from the neighbouring countries joined the Arabs in Palestine and the situation worsened considerably with Israel's declaration of independence on 14 May 1948. In its wake large expeditionary forces of the regular Arab armies invaded the country, exactly as Ben-Gurion had forecast when he had demanded and received the security portfolio in December 1946. Thus, the organization and training of the regular Israeli army, with all its implications, took place during the course of the war.

Ben-Gurion was, in effect, the person who, as the supreme commander of the IDF, managed the War of Independence. This was the result of a combination of factors: Ben Gurion's assertive personality; a lack of clarity with regard to the function of the High Command; the continuing ill-health of the Chief-of-Staff, Yaakov Dori, and the fact that Ben-Gurion relied upon the Chief of the General Staff Branch, Yigael Yadin, enough to place the 'technical' management of the war in his hands.

Ben-Gurion's intervention in military decisions more than once raised objections from senior officers of the general-staff headquarters and generated conflict and frustration. One of its clear-cut results was Yochanan Ratner's refusal to replace the ailing Chief-of-Staff, Dori. Ratner had discerned the relationship between Ben-Gurion and the branch heads at General Headquarters, as well as the former's penchant for delving into operational particulars. In his memoirs, Ratner wrote:

> Ben-Gurion decided, despite my objection (and if my memory serves me, the objection of Yigael Yadin as well), to send one (or perhaps two) of our heavy mortars to the Jerusalem front. If he interferes in specifics of this nature, what other things am I to expect? ... I requested to be relieved of the office of Chief-of-Staff.[22]

The crises reached their peak in a letter of resignation sent by the five Headquarters' branch heads to Ben-Gurion on 6 May 1948. This followed the sacking of Galili as head of the Command Council, and the adamant instruction of Ben-Gurion to cancel this function. The appointments' crisis occurred almost two months later. On 1 July 1948 the generals Yadin, Ayalon and Ben-Hur tendered their letters of resignation against the background of Ben-Gurion's decision to foist a series of senior appointments on the Chief-of-Staff (among them veterans from the British army). Following this crisis, the Provisional Government decided to approve Ben-Gurion's appointments, to freeze additional appointments, to request from those who resigned that they continue in their duties, to appoint a commission comprised of five ministers to investigate what had occurred at General Staff Headquarters and to recommend procedures for authority arrangements and working procedures within it.

The 'Commission of Five' worked at a furious pace – this was the period of the first military truce and there was constant fear of renewed fighting – but nevertheless succeeded in exposing a large variety of problems in the course of its investigation. For our purposes, it is important to point out that the protocol of the five-man commission points to Ben-Gurion's decisive role in managing the war campaign. What emerges is his extensive involvement in the appointment of senior officers, his participation in the planning and implementation of the IDF's operations in all areas, his initiative in the promulgation of direct instructions to commanders of the armed forces and his hand in the allocation of manpower and arms to the different combat arenas.

In retrospect, it is easy to confirm that this involvement stemmed largely from Ben-Gurion's fear of missing one-time opportunities, and from a concern that in the course of the war the political objectives, that seemed to him to be of the utmost urgency, would not be attained. These objectives were determined, as far as Ben-Gurion was concerned, by his basic perception of Arab objectives, their military capabilities and their performance on the battlefield.

According to Ben-Gurion's line of thinking, the first Arab objective was the destruction of the Yishuv. If they failed to achieve this goal, he assumed the Arabs would be content with waging a war to prevent the establishment of a Jewish State, even in a portion of Palestine. If these two objectives were not attained, the Arabs' objective would be a war to limit the size of the Jewish State. In conjunction with this assessment and at a time when most people still spoke of 'the uprising', Ben-Gurion demanded that there be investment of all national efforts in preparation for war. In a speech given on 21 January 1948, he declared: 'This is a campaign which will determine the fate of the Jewish people forever. The campaign in the coming months, perhaps for the next seven or eight months, will be constitutive for all Jewish history.'[23]

Nevertheless, at a headquarters' discussion which took place two weeks prior to this on 9 January 1948, Ben-Gurion expressed an important restriction with regard to the manner of fighting – to avoid as far as possible encounters with the British army and police. 'We most not provoke the Government forces,' he said. 'We must not give a pretext for the Government to attack the Hagana.'[24] This general rule would yield fruit in the army camps, the airports and key strategic points, which were transferred without trouble by the British to the Hagana and the IDF.

Parallel to this, the principle of defending every Jewish settlement was in effect and had already been defined in October 1947, before the United Nations passed its resolution on the division of Palestine. Ben-Gurion wrote in his diary at the time:

> I was asked [in a meeting at Hagana headquarters] about the plan: defence of the State according to borders [decided] by a majority [in the UN General Assembly] – or the whole country? I replied: 'It all depends upon what the UN decides. If it is a favorable decision, we will defend every settlement and exert control only over the state area defined by the decision. If it is not a [favorable] decision, we will defend every settlement, repel every attack, and establish services for every Jewish settlement and for all Arabs who want them. We will not determine territorial boundaries'.[25]

When hostilities broke out as a result of Arab non-adherence to the Partition Resolution, the second war-policy alternative was adopted. It of course embraced the traditional conception of not abandoning settlements, a policy which, as noted above, had its origins in the Tel Hai episode of 1920.

Ben-Gurion deployed this outlook not only in the Negev, where isolated settlements divided and delayed the Egyptian army during the campaign, but also along the Jerusalem front. Wherever settlements were cut off from one another there was a genuine fear for the life of the combatants and the civilian population, who might be unable to withstand the siege and would fall in battle (this fear was realized, and with a heavy price, at Gush Etzion). Nevertheless, all suggestions to shorten lines or evacuate settlements were rejected.

In the first stages of the war, it was the Arabs who took the initiative. The Jewish side found itself on the defensive in the mixed towns, on the highways and in the isolated settlements. This resulted in the dispersion of forces, the confinement of the majority of combatants to static positions in defence of settlements and heavy casualties along the main arteries, especially among the escort convoys. In addition, there was damage to the Yishuv's morale and its stature in the international arena. The recurrent debates in the UN Security Council on the Partition Resolution, and the possible retreat from that decision, constituted a clear and weighty threat to the attainment of the nation's political independence in Palestine. In actuality, the major and decisive turning point in the war came about when Ben-Gurion decided to abandon reliance upon self-defence in favour of a militarily offensive strategy. In accordance with this strategic change, the General Staff devised Plan 'D' in March 1948. Its goal was:

> control over territory of the Jewish State and defence of its borders, as well as blocks of settlements and their Jewish population outside these borders, which were facing continuous threat from regular or semi-regular enemy armies operating from bases both beyond and within the State's territory.[26]

In other words, Plan 'D' was designed to obtain territorial continuity between Jewish settlements, to secure control over the main transportation arteries and to link the Jewish areas located within the mixed cities to the nearby major Jewish population centres. Originally, this plan was to become operative with the departure of the British, but with increased pressure stemming from the circumstances described above, it was begun within weeks of its final formulation. On almost all of the battlefronts, the burden of execution was placed on local forces, in accordance with their capability; the breakthrough to Jerusalem required a different approach and led to Operation Nachshon. This operation called for the concentration of large forces and a great amount of weaponry of unprecedented scope, resulting in a temporary, and dangerous, depletion of forces on other fronts. Ben-Gurion gave the order for this daring step; it signified the supreme importance that he attributed to Jewish Jerusalem and the breach of the siege of the city. This operation took place amid intensive debates with senior commanders, led by Yigael Yadin, who posed arguments to Ben-Gurion with all the weight of their military authority. Moreover, even after they had acquiesced to his principal point of view, Ben-Gurion demanded an augmentation of forces, weaponry and vehicles for the operation. Ben-Gurion wrote in his diary on 31 March:

> I told Headquarters that at this moment there is one burning question and that is the battle for the road to Jerusalem, and the 400–500 soldiers prepared by Yigael is not sufficient. This is currently the decisive battle. The fall of Jewish Jerusalem would be a death-blow to the Yishuv. The Arabs understand this and will concentrate their forces to cut off the transportation routes. All forces which are not absolutely necessary must be taken from the Central and Southern fronts of the country, from Tel Aviv, and from the Southern Command, and sent via Hulda – Bab-el Wad – Jerusalem, and reinforcements must be sent in from time to time. Call up brigade commanders immediately and recruit the best men, and do this immediately – this evening, tonight.[27]

In his testimony before the Committee of Five several months later, Yadin, Ben-Gurion's principle opponent on the issue of the Jerusalem front, was to say:

> Here I come to the first intervention of Ben-Gurion, an histori-cal intervention which was to his credit, and for one reason; it did not encounter any difficulties nor did it become entangled, and it was carried out in a domain in which the Defence Minister should make the decisions. This was Operation Nachshon. I openly confess: prior to Operation Nachshon there were bad experiences. It was difficult to open the way to Jerusalem, it would take courage and a major decision to carry out such an operation, and 90 per cent, perhaps 100 per cent, of the decision belonged to Ben-Gurion. And it is correct – he was responsible for carrying out Operation Nachshon.[28]

During and immediately following Operation Nachson, large supply convoys arrived in Jerusalem, allowing the city to store emergency supplies in anticipation of the possible renewal of the siege. However, on 21 April, the road to Jerusalem was again closed. At the beginning of May, Operation Maccabee was planned in order to reopen the way to Jerusalem. This time Ben-Gurion ordered General Headquarters to seize control of the entire area that commands the road to Jerusalem, including the Latrun constabulary outpost. This demand met with fierce resistance from senior commanders who knew that the fighting forces were not trained for such an undertaking and lacked the required quantity of weapons and ammunition. Ben-Gurion wrote in his diary on 14 May 1948:

> Almost the entire Command opposed my position of launching an assault with a larger force and with a more determined drive in order to seize terrain around the Jerusalem–Tel Aviv road from Hulda to Sha'ar Hagai. The reason given was lack of manpower and lack of knowledge about the enemy's plans. Without a clear-cut decision of the Thirteen – I have not yet got used to saying 'Government' – I did not want to give orders which countered the opinion of the entire general staff, but I feel that we have and are missing the opportunity for territorial gains which will determine the fate of Jerusalem and perhaps the fate of the entire campaign.[29]

In the General Headquarters' discussion of 24 May, which sought to prioritize matters, Ben-Gurion stuck to his position regarding the supreme importance of Jerusalem. In posing the question, he asked which was the main and dangerous front for the Yishuv, and against which army should the full weight of the available limited forces be applied. Yigael Yadin saw the Egyptian army and the southern front as the central problem: 'Our principal enemy is Egypt. Egypt has the largest and most powerful army and occupies almost half the territory of Israel. As long as the Egyptian army is not defeated, we must not tie up all our forces on the Jordanian front.'[30] Ben-Gurion, on the other hand, continued to insist upon breaking through on the Jerusalem road and defending the city against the Arab Legion. The fall of the city, he said, would endanger the Israeli State more so than the penetration of the Egyptian army to Ashdod. Thus it is not surprising that two days earlier, on 22 May, Ben-Gurion had ordered the 7th Brigade, under Shlomo Shamir, to attack Latrun, positioned at the gateway to the Judaean Hills about 20 miles from Jerusalem. Yadin and the senior command objected to this directive on the grounds that most of the troops were still fresh recruits, with only two or three days of basic training, and the entire brigade was in its initial stages of organization. Ben-Gurion, however, did not hesitate to address the brigade commander directly, who, trained in the British army tradition, saw in the direct address of the leader an order which could not be questioned.

The attack failed. The 7th Brigade suffered close to 200 casualties. Yadin regarded the entire undertaking as a catastrophe, but Ben-Gurion remained convinced that he was in the right. From a broad-based perspective he proclaimed that 'a great, although costly victory' had been achieved.[31] The assault on Latrun, he explained, brought about the transfer of the Arab Legion from the Jerusalem front to the Latrun area, thus reducing pressure on the city, and in effect determining the outcome of the campaign for Jerusalem.

Again, years later, Yadin would voice a different opinion. In an interview with Israel radio in October 1971 he said:

> The final responsibility resided with Ben-Gurion and if, heaven forbid, I had been mistaken in my evaluation, and Jerusalem had fallen, it would not have helped him to say 'but Yadin told me such and such'. He who undertakes the final responsibility does so whatever the outcome.[32]

The Negev was a separate front in the War of Independence. The vast expanses and the thinly distributed population made it difficult to maintain links and safeguard the water-pipe and transportation routes. Moreover, the small number of settlements and settlers raised doubts whether it was worth staying in the Negev in light of the anticipated incursion and the capacity to withstand it. By the end of December 1947, as incidents multiplied, and attacks on those guarding the water conduit took their toll, it was suggested to Ben-Gurion that settlements south of the Gaza–Beersheba line be vacated.

Ben-Gurion rejected the idea of withdrawal from the southern part of the Negev and demanded from its proponent, his military advisor, Shalom Eshet, a programme for the defence of the military front. The Negev Committee, headed by Joseph Weitz, was quickly formed and set about attending to the provision of various kinds of assistance to the settlements under siege – fortifications, arms and ammunition, water and other critical supplies.

Behind this outlook was Ben-Gurion's notion that vast expanses of the Negev could serve as necessary constituents of the future State. He said:

> In the fate of the Negev block perhaps depends the fate of the entire country. If there is a chance for greater settlement, of massive settlement in the millions, if there is a chance for Jewish sovereignty which rather than being dependent upon UN

benevolence relies upon internal power, upon the power of the compact, continuous, massive, area-conquering Jewish Yishuv – then that area is what we call the Negev.[33]

He therefore rejected outright every suggestion for exchanging the Negev for western Galilee (an area that was awarded to the Arabs according to the Partition Plan and was apparently regarded by Ben-Gurion as easy to conquer). When the road to Jerusalem was finally secured, the centre of gravity shifted to the relief of the siege on the Negev, and to the creation of new political facts in the field itself. On the morning of 6 October 1948, while visiting the headquarters of Yigael Alon, commander of the southern front, Ben-Gurion raised the matter of the conquest of the Negev. Already, on the same day, the Prime Minister had called in Mapai ministers for consultation as a preparatory step for a suitable decision at the Government Cabinet meeting. In his diary he noted: 'Evening: the Government today made the gravest decision since the proclamation of the establishment of the State.'[34]

On 15 October, Operation Ten Plagues, also known as Operation Yoav, commenced. In scope, it was the largest campaign launched during the War of Independence. The operation took place at a time when there was heavy pressure from the Security Council to declare a ceasefire and to withdraw to the lines existing before the attack, but Ben-Gurion succeeded in coping with the circumstances. He delayed his reply to the demands emanating from abroad until the IDF completed the conquest of the Iraqi–Sudan gendarme post which commanded the route to the Negev and to Beersheba. He then sent reconnaissance forces towards the Dead Sea and Ein Hatzava and thus ensured an Israeli grip over the north-east Negev.

On 22 November 1948, Operation Horev began. The objective of this military action was to bring about the removal of the Egyptian army from the Negev and northern Sinai, and in fact to bring about the complete defeat of this army. The broad-based operation went according to plan despite difficulties in its opening phase. IDF forces, under the command of Yigael Alon, conquered the fortified heights of Temilla and Ouja (Nitzana), and on 27 December 1948 the decisive stage of this campaign came to an end. From this juncture, the Egyptian army, no longer fighting within the boundaries of the Israeli State but rather on Egyptian territory, was close to collapse.

The next day IDF forces crossed the international border. Despite orders from Yadin to the commander of the front, Alon, to halt his advance in the direction of El-Arish, one of the ground-force units continued to move towards Abu Agheila and captured an airport 20 km from El-Arish. Yadin cabled Alon: 'I repeat. You are forbidden to undertake any action north from Abu Agheila without my permission.'[35] In the wake of the cable, Alon flew to Tel Aviv to meet personally with Ben-Gurion. At this meeting it was agreed to launch an attack towards the Gaza–Rafiah line while executing a feint towards El-Arish. Ben-Gurion, who feared an excessively angry British response, told Alon: 'If the English come – we'll return to our borders, to Ouja. If they reach Ouja – we'll fight.'[36]

A short time later, James Macdonald, American Ambassador to Israel, delivered a letter from President Truman to Ben-Gurion and Moshe Sharett which carried an ultimatum for the immediate withdrawal of Israeli troops from Egyptian territory. This letter also hinted at the possibility of British military intervention, sanctioned by the British–Egyptian treaty of 1936. Later research revealed that the British had not considered such a step and that the ultimatum in its entirety was an American initiative. But Ben-Gurion had already pre-empted the American demand and had decided, in co-ordination with Sharett and Yadin, to withdraw the IDF from the Sinai. The order for the withdrawal was issued on 31 December 1948.

Immersed as he was in the conduct of the war, Ben-Gurion's statesman-like posture is apparent from his capacity to see the picture in its entirety, and not from the military perspective alone. He was sensitive to the need for safeguarding relations with the major powers, first and foremost with the United States, and he refrained from antagonizing the British, whose policy was hostile to Zionism. He also saw it as requisite to end the war with the neighbouring Arab states.

On the night of 7 January 1949, Ben-Gurion was informed that the ceasefire along the southern border was to be put into effect. The next day he wrote in his diary:

> During the past year we brought about a great revolution in the history of our people: we founded the Jewish State and exited from slavery to redemption; we created the Israel Defence Forces and fought invading Arab armies – and we overcame them. We liberated the Negev and the Galilee and restored its land for the purpose of massive settlement. In one year we brought more than 120,000 immigrants to the country as the initial step in the ingathering of the exiles. We became a state political actor in the Middle East and in the whole world.[37]

THE BUILDING OF A UNIFIED APOLITICAL ARMY

At the same time, against a background of many problems and difficulties, Ben-Gurion was resolute in his determination to build a
unified army completely subordinate to the civilian authorities. It
would not be tied to any organizational or political foundations nor
to bodies such as those which, before the establishment of the State,
sponsored and supported the Hagana or the splinter organizations,
Etzel and Lehi. For him, this was the basic principle of a statist-
security conception and a test of unequaled importance in the
effectiveness of a system of government in a sovereign state.

Following the establishment of the IDF, a swearing-in ceremony
was inaugurated accompanied by the following oath:

> I hereby swear and commit myself to maintain allegiance to the
> State of Israel, to its constitution, and to its authorized govern-
> ment. To accept without condition and without reserve the
> burden of discipline of the Israel Defence Forces and to obey all
> commands and orders given by authorized commanders, to
> devote all my strength and even to sacrifice my life for the
> defence of the homeland and the freedom of Israel.[38]

These words explicitly obligated every soldier to prefer his/her
attachment to the laws of the state, and the commands of its officers,
above any other allegiance.

If things had run smoothly, the oath of allegiance would have
guaranteed the absolute authority of the government, and the
government alone, over the IDF. But in practice – and perhaps as
expected – it became apparent that the creation of a unified army
brought Ben-Gurion into serious clashes with Etzel and Lehi, and
sometime later into a none-too-simple confrontation with the Palmach
general staff as well. The very fact that the army had been organized
in the course of the war influenced the nature of these events; more
than once Ben-Gurion, in opposition to his declared wishes, had to
compromise and come to an agreement with various bodies which
regarded themselves as stakeholders in the military arena.

When the first military clashes with Arab forces occurred, a portion
of Etzel and Lehi members responded positively to the call-up orders
issued by the institutions of the Yishuv. The headquarters of the two
organizations, however, tried to find a means of arriving at different
arrangements in order to avoid the need for their members showing

up for army induction and thereby exposing their identity and identification. In fact, Etzel and Lehi maintained a completely separate existence until the State was proclaimed and the Arab armies invaded. Ben-Gurion warned against this and opposed the various proposed compromises suggested by the Jewish Agency Executive, but in May 1948 he agreed to a compromise whose principle was induction of members of the two organizations into the State's armed forces, except in the Jerusalem area. Since the city was not included in the territory allocated to the Israeli State by the Partition Resolution, Ben-Gurion refrained, in the meantime, from imposing the rule of the State's provisional institutions there. Along the Jerusalem front, the Hagana, Etzel and Lehi continued to operate in their separate frameworks.

THE ALTALENA AFFAIR

The *Altalena* affair, which took place during June 1948, was a dramatic turning point in the struggle to determine the source of legitimate authority in the young state and to unify the army. The ship *Altalena*, carrying combatants and weapons of Etzel to the country's shores, constituted a challenge to the Government's sovereignty. Etzel commanders made two demands: to transfer a portion of the weapons brought by the ship to Etzel members who had been inducted into the army, in order that they be properly equipped for the military campaign; and to distribute a fifth of the cargo to independent units of Etzel in Jerusalem. Ben-Gurion rejected these demands outright on the grounds that only the Provisional Government had the right to distribute weapons in the State and that no other body had the right to dictate how this allocation should be carried out. Yisrael Galili and Levi Eshcol conducted negotiations with the commander of Etzel, Menahem Begin, but the enormous mutual suspicion between the two parties brought this move to a standstill.

The Provisional Government met with the intention of preventing a civil war. In the ensuing debate, Government ministers spoke of the need to enter into a give-and-take situation with Etzel, but Ben-Gurion stuck to his position:

> What has occurred endangers the State ... and this is an attempt to ruin the army and murder the State. On these two questions, in my view, there can be no compromise. And if to our great misfortune we must fight over this – then we must fight.[39]

By a majority of seven to two, it was decided to deliver an ultimatum to Etzel demanding the transfer of the ship and its contents to the Government. In addition, the same majority decided to employ force against the ship if this was necessary. On 19 June the *Altalena* approached the Tel Aviv coast, on the basic supposition held by the heads of Etzel that they could unload the weapons and ammunition with the help of their organization's supporters in the city and its environs. Ben-Gurion held firm to the ultimatum he had presented to Etzel and ordered Yigael Yadin, the Chief of the General Staff Branch for the IDF, to concentrate military forces in the area where leaders of Etzel planned to anchor the *Altalena*. Violent clashes soon took place between soldiers belonging to the Palmach and the Kiryati brigades (the latter a recently formed combat corps for the Tel Aviv area), and Etzel forces who had deserted the State's army units and had come to help their comrades. At four in the afternoon Ben-Gurion ordered Yadin to shell the ship. One of the shells scored a direct hit. The ship went up in flames, and this brought the battle to an end. The number of dead reached 16, and most of the weaponry on board sank into the sea. Among the last to leave the sinking ship was the commander of Etzel, Menahem Begin.

The IDF's activities in the *Altalena* affair continued for several more days following the sinking of the ship. Many activists from the Herut movement, the new party established by veteran Etzel members, were arrested and held without trial in administrative detention. The organization had met its end. In the meantime, a serious crisis erupted in the Government coalition, and in the fifth session of the State Provisional Council on 23 June 1948, Ben-Gurion was asked to explain how matters had deteriorated to the point of bloody clashes and loss of life. He accused Etzel of not honouring its agreements concerning cessation of the organization's military activities, of carrying out weapons' purchases independently and of failing to transfer its weaponry to the IDF. He declared that: 'the importation of weapons by a national military organization, which constituted a violation of its obligations to the State and a refusal to abide by its laws, was an even greater danger because it endangers the State and prepares the ground for civil war on a large scale.'[40] In the same speech, Ben-Gurion explained at length the danger entailed by the existence of independent armed organizations representing political outlooks. He re-emphasized that only one army under one common discipline and one authority would enable the State to take a firm stand in the face of invading Arab armies.

Begin stuck to his position to the last days of his life, claiming that the responsibility for the tragic development fell completely on the Provisional Government. This Government had avoided reaching an agreement and prevented the disembarking of soldiers and the unloading of weapons in an orderly fashion. In his words, the *Altalena's* arrival in Israel had been fully co-ordinated with the Government's representatives, Galili and Eshcol, who reported directly to Ben-Gurion on what was taking place in the area. Ben-Gurion, according to Begin, preferred to exploit the opportunity, to attribute to Etzel an attempt at rebellion and undermining of the foundation of the legal government and to disband it through this military gambit.[41]

In hindsight, it is clear that the *Altalena* affair allowed Ben-Gurion to establish his exclusive authority as Prime Minister and Minister of Defence, and to disband Etzel units while inducting their combatants as individuals into the ranks of the IDF. Something similar, yet different, occurred in the case of the Palmach.

DISBANDING OF THE PALMACH HEADQUARTERS

Unlike Etzel and Lehi, the Palmach was an integral arm of the Hagana and never deviated from its discipline. On the contrary, in the War of Independence the Palmach supplied the Hagana and the IDF with its best fighting forces, including its best commanders. Nevertheless, in the summer of 1948 Ben-Gurion concluded that the time had come to disband the Palmach as an autonomous body. Two principle reasons, military and political, were put forward. In the first place, the Palmach brigades now appeared to him as outfits that should be made directly subordinate to the command structure of the IDF (that is to say, the General Staff and the headquarters of the various fronts). This meant that no operative function remained for the national headquarters of the Palmach which could justify its existence. Secondly, the strong political links between the majority of the senior Palmach officers and the Mapam leadership (the Party was founded in February 1948 following the amalgamation of Shomer Ha'Tsair with Achdut Ha'avoda – Poalei Tzion), appeared to Ben-Gurion as potentially perilous for developments, adversely impacting upon the image of the army and harming its undivided subordination to the Government, especially in light of the bitter political dispute between Ben-Gurion and Mapam.

Leaders in Mapam and senior officers of the Palmach were quick to respond to these two claims by accusing Ben-Gurion himself of narrow political considerations, and attempting to harm the well-being of the army (which required, in their opinion, the continued autonomy of the Palmach). The dispute quickly spread to matters related to how the army should be organized, the determination of its character, and the preparation of training programmes, structure, procedure and regime.

The concepts that expressed and signified the positions of the two sides were 'statism' and 'political movement' respectively. Statism was interpreted as giving a value to the State in itself and its conversion into a source of inspiration for every important consideration. This orientation could only have the consequence of reducing the status and influence of political movements and party frameworks. Completely contrary to this position, the movement adherents put forward group values and concepts (and in the context of this dispute, values and concepts of the labour movement and the working class – in tandem with the claim that these values were permanent and fixed, while the government of the State might change hands and a new government might bring in its wake undesirable values and concepts.

Conversely, it was easy to interpret 'statism' as a claim to give complete primacy to those who hold the reins of state power, that is Ben-Gurion and his party. Thus, the opponents of Ben-Gurion did not cease to claim that the plan for the disbanding of Palmach headquarters was but the first step in detaching Mapam members from key positions in the defence system in order to replace them with officers loyal to Mapai or, what was perhaps worse, professionals who had no clear-cut political character and would serve as 'mercenaries'.

Ben-Gurion was not deterred by these claims. His party, Mapai, wholly supported him from purely political considerations – a feeling or awareness that its standing among the soldiers was not good and that it was advisable to lessen the influence of Mapam as much as possible. But along with this Ben-Gurion also rallied to his side the General Staff and he did not stop trying to convince the officers of the Palmach themselves.

On 29 August 1948, General Headquarters' staff debated the future of the Palmach headquarters in the presence of the Palmach commander, Yigael Alon (who was at this time Commander of the Southern Front) and the administrative officer of the Palmach, Eliezer Shoshani (himself a Mapai member and among the very few from the highest echelons of the Palmach). At this meeting Alon suggested reducing the size of the Palmach headquarters' staff but not eliminating it altogether. He recognized that this headquarters had no actual operative function but requested that training matters, manpower and education (all of which had political ramifications) remain in its hands. In his diary, Ben-Gurion recalled what followed from an additional discussion, on 7 September, in which Palmach representatives raised the need to establish 'loyalty brigades' in the army. He cited a letter from the Chief-of-Staff, Dori, in which it was averred that 'the Palmach distinguishes itself in several things – although not in everything that it itself believes it excels'. To this Ben-Gurion added: 'But [Dori] does not claim that there is a priori and in principle a basis for setting up 'loyal' armies and regular armies. This step equally undermines the foundations of the state and the army.'[42]

Dori himself now requested that the decision regarding the disbanding of the Palmach headquarters be hastened. After his meeting with Palmach commanders, on 14 September at Kibbutz Naan, Ben-Gurion finally concluded that there was confusion between the professional and the ideological/political demands which the Palmach commanders had put forward. He then asked the General Staff to determine a date for the disbanding of the Palmach headquarters.

On 29 September 1948 Ben-Gurion wrote in his diary: 'I carried out a review of the Palmach and issued orders to the chief-of-staff.' They were clear-cut orders to disband the Palmach immediately. The same document also included a description of all the clarifications concerning the continued existence of the Palmach headquarters; it concluded that 'the unity, discipline and general efficiency of the army have been severely damaged' because of special arrangements which are part and parcel of the Palmach.[43]

Dan Horowitz and Moshe Lissak, researchers of the history of the transition from settlement to State, regard the disbanding of the Palmach as the foundation for an a-political army which shuns political and movement linkages. 'The current political situation and the personal circumstances of Ben-Gurion's decision in favor of disbanding the Palmach', they wrote, 'were secondary in importance to that of establishing the norm of a single army that has no other political or social linkages than those which subordinate it to the government through the Minister of Defence.'[44]

In retrospect, it is clear that the decision to disband Palmach headquarters firmly determined the state-like image of the IDF and the separation of the political party system from the IDF commanders and their units. In the words of the poet, Natan Alterman, who at the time vehemently protested against the intention to disband

Palmach headquarters: 'Time in its flowing streams justified many of the arguments of the framework's destroyer.'[45]

In this connection it is perhaps appropriate to add that on the eve of the Jewish New Year, Ben-Gurion rejected a request from representatives of Hapoel Hamizrahi, the religious Workers' Party, to establish separate religious units in the IDF.

> I told them, a) our army will be unified and without different streams, b) for the sake of unity everyone will be obligated to observe the Jewish dietary laws, c) a Jewish atmosphere will govern the Sabbath, d) mutual respect will be inculcated so that non-observant soldiers will not make fun of religious soldiers who put on their phylacteries.[46]

At the beginning of the 1950s, a debate took place regarding the participation of Mapam in the Government coalition. Ben-Gurion rejected this party's demand for a dominant influence over the army in general and over the Nahal soldiers in particular. In the same session he rejected a request by the Ministry of Defence to set up an advisory committee composed of the socialist parties, and the request to give a free hand for propagating information among Nahal soldiers. 'We must not rely upon 'Cossack villages'. The farmsteads are not the only guarantee of security. The State and not the Party will govern Nahal,' he indignantly retorted to Mapam leaders.[47]

At a festive gathering for intellectuals and writers at Ben-Gurion's residence at the close of the war, Chaim Guri asked the host: 'Why didn't you liberate the whole country?' Ben-Gurion's response points to his pragmatic and realistic leadership:

> There was a danger of our becoming entangled in a conflict with a hostile Arab majority. That would have led to a slaughter similar to what happened at Dir-Yassin and the mass expulsion of Arabs, or to the existence of a million Arabs in the State of Israel. There was also a danger of entering into complications with the United Nations and the Great Powers, and a danger of the State going bankrupt. As it is, we liberated a very large territory, a lot more than we thought we would. We now have work for two or three generations.[48]

The fledgling army, according to Ben-Gurion, would carry out a substantial portion of this work.

THE NEW ISRAELI SOCIETY ENVISAGED BY BEN-GURION

Even before the battles of the War of Independence ended, but at a time when it was already clear that Israel was going to win the war, Ben-Gurion increasingly began to think about and invest a great deal of his energy in matters beyond security. In a December 1948 diary entry, under the title 'Hannuka Reflections', he posed the following question:

> What are the conditions for preserving our independence if we hold to the prior assumption that we will succeed in preserving our spirit of freedom? Military security, the negation of exile, rapid population of different parts of the country in the course of intensive development, a regime of freedom and equality, a pioneering hegemony (education geared to pioneering), scientific government, a policy of peace, government stability (stability of the regime).[49]

At this stage it was clear to Ben-Gurion that the heavy pressure exerted by the United Nations and the 'great powers' would not permit a large military campaign aimed at capturing additional populated territory within the western part of the country. Thus, the task was to work with alacrity in order to secure the hold on areas already captured (especially those territories not included in the Partition Resolution). He wrote in 'Hannuka Reflections':

> Our conquests in the Negev and the Galilee will not be sustainable unless we quickly populate these portions of the country – first of all, all the empty villages, and the establishment of a long line of settlements on the frontier and along the coast. At a distance of ten kilometers from the frontier – only soldiers' settlements. An intentional policy of averting large concentrations in a limited number of places [such as Tel Aviv] – an even distribution of the population throughout the country. A belt of villages surrounding Jerusalem and rapid settlement of the corridor to Jerusalem … Planning will be required not only in development – but also in populating settlements, while protecting individual freedom [freedom of movement]. There will be a need for easy terms and special reductions for settling those abandoned sites which are barren and distant.[50]

From this, two important conclusions were drawn. In the first place, there was a need to drastically increase the Jewish population, and the single source for this was widespread immigration. Immigration now appeared to Ben-Gurion not only as fulfilling a Zionist duty to save Jews and eliminate exile, but also as a central foundation of the utmost importance for national security. Several months later, in consultation with personnel in the Foreign Affairs Department preparatory to the Lausanne Conference, Ben-Gurion noted: 'The principal point is absorption of immigrants, and in this are contained all the historical needs of the State.' At the same consultation he added for greater emphasis: 'We could have perhaps conquered the Triangle, the Golan, the entire Galilee. But our conquest of these areas would not have strengthened our security to the extent that absorbing immigrants might do. Doubling and tripling the number of immigrants brings us more and more power.'[51] According to his perspective there was no possibility of, and no room to acquiesce to, any obstruction to immigration whether out of economic or other considerations.

Secondly, alongside immigration as a national priority, Ben-Gurion requested a substantive reform in the settlement programmes. New settlements were, in his formulation, not only instruments for absorbing immigrants and distributing the population but also part of the education of the young generation in the framework of forming a new Israeli society.

Appearing before soldiers undergoing an officer-training course in May 1949, Ben-Gurion asserted that 'every young boy and girl at a certain age must receive agricultural training in addition to physical and military training.' He went on to say: 'Immigrants looking for a challenge, and bold pioneering spirits among them, would found frontier settlements and security villages which would act as a live defensive wall and first line of defence for the State'. In addition, he did not forget to emphasize at this same meeting that 'as long as war is still possible in this world, we cannot exist without an army'.[52]

Ben-Gurion's orientation to immigration, settlement and education of the younger generation in the new circumstances, engendered by the establishment of the State, was anchored in his previous conceptions and concepts. As a hardcore representative of the second-wave of immigration to the land of Israel, he was an adherent to ideas for the realization of Zionism, not only by transferring the Jewish people from exile to the Promised Land but also through a revolutionary change in the social and economic structure of the people, a change which would bring the masses to a life of labour and creativity, principally in agriculture and possession of the land.

More than a decade earlier he had written about this:

> The realization of Zionism means the bringing about of two basic changes in the life of the Hebrew nation: a) transition of the scattered people through an ingathering of the exiles in their native land, b) transition of a nation detached from its land to a life of labor on its native land. These two changes are intertwined and one cannot exist without the other. The Jewish people will not become a people of the land and labor in a country which is not its own. And the people will not return to its country unless it returns to the land and to labor.[53]

Three years later he expanded upon this theme in another article:

> In essence, Zionism is a revolutionary movement. It is difficult to describe a more profound and basic revolution than that which Zionism sets out to do for the life of the Hebrew nation. This is not just a political or economic revolution – rather, it is a revolution in the very foundations of the personal lives of all members of the nation.[54]

Later he would add that:

> For thousands of years, wandering and dispersion could not uproot the existence of the Jewish people and destroy its special image. But they deformed and distorted it. Dependence upon foreigners deprived us of freedom in thought and spirit, impressed upon us, whether consciously or unconsciously, an inner slavery, and narrowed our horizons. A people given over to the grace of foreigners finds it hard to see itself and others in a proper light.[55]

Throughout his political life Ben-Gurion was animated by thoughts of radical changes taking place in Jewish society in the Land of Israel while that society simultaneously strove for political sovereignty. His efforts to translate these thoughts and the rhetoric accompanying it into a practical language changed from time to time. In the early thirties, when he began to articulate the views in *From Class to Nation*, the central point of which was the transmission of the conceptual outlook of the working class to the entire nation, and the placing of national leadership in the hands of the working class, Ben-Gurion affirmed:

> Building the country as a capitalist endeavour will not bring about the realization of Zionism. In a settlement program in which all are capitalists there will be no Hebrew labor and the land will not be transferred to Hebrew hands. Without Hebrew labor and without Jewish-held land Zionism will become a fraud and a false vision.[56]

In 1938, as chairman of the Zionist Executive, that is, in a national rather than a class role, and a very senior one at that, he explained:

> I believe in the working man whether he is a member of the Histadrut or a member of the Revisionist movement. I believe in every worker; it does not matter so much to me what he thinks, what he says – it matters to me what he does. What is important is that he lives from labor, that he is a working man.[57]

In 1953, as leader of the young State, he distanced himself still further from ideological class doctrines and asserted that 'man must serve the commands of history – fulfill the mission that his destiny prescribed for him, otherwise there is no reason to live. Any role which man fulfills without his serving an historical idea and an ethical value is of dubious importance.'[58] Either way, in many of his expressions there runs, like a scarlet thread, that insight which may be found in words and phrases such as 'redemption', 'the days of the Messiah', and 'the realization of the vision of the prophets of Israel'. In his eyes, these were the dimensions of his arena of action during the period in which Jewish sovereignty in Palestine was being renewed after almost two-thousand years.

In accordance with this historical perspective – and to the displeasure of many – he also tried to create a direct connection between the renewed sovereignty and its ancient ancestor, and even to cast aside the lengthy interim period (the greater part of which the Jewish people were in exile). In those speeches which dealt with daily life-experiences of the people in Israel, Ben-Gurion tied the life undertakings, which were growing by leaps and bounds in the re-emerging Israel, to the biblical kingship-period of David and Solomon. He never grew tired of reminding his audience that these were the glorious days of the

Kingdom of Israel – a time when it knew how to triumph over its enemies, to unite the house of Israel and to create a renowned and exemplary political, economic and social culture. In 1949 he wrote:

> We are an ancient people – in the process of rejuvenation. To the extent that we are rooted in our native soil, we are also rooted in the soil of our past. Whatever we are we cannot be without continuously feeding on resources from our ancient past and without fastening on to the roots of our past.[59]

Ben-Gurion, like the entire State, was in the midst of coping with waves of massive immigration which consisted, for the most part, of people in distress. The Zionist movement had committed itself to these people as part of its obligation to save whole communities residing in exile. Confronted with this new situation, the Prime Minister felt that many of his old conceptions were collapsing in the face of reality. The arrivals were a mixture of communities and tribes, each possessing a different culture, and without a common language. Some lacked a Jewish education and a Jewish cultural upbringing. Many were illiterate. Among them were survivors of the Holocaust in Europe, 'graduates' of the terrible chaos of the Second World War, and alongside them immigrants from the Arab countries, uprooted from an existence and an environment which had nothing in common with the social utopias of the workers' movement. In addition to that, Israeli society was divided. 'The minimum of integrity and unity which exists in any orderly state, despite the universality of social and political contradictions', he wrote, 'is noticeable by its absence in the State of Israel.'[60]

'Are we a people?' he asked in a speech in the first Knesset, and replied:

> Without fearing that they will tell me that I have no faith in the people and that I lack a Zionist ideology, I answer: 'We are not a people yet.' And I do not mean in the ideological or socio-philosophical sense of the term. I mean a unified community, rooted in its homeland, in its culture, in a nation bound by solidarity, capable of fighting to the last man and literally until the last drop of blood. I am certain that, in due time, we shall become a nation like this, committed, solidified, united, forged in the heart of the homeland, using our own language, and managing our own economy. By having this feeling of independence and fulfillment we will become a people no less than any other people.[61]

A recurrent expression from the same period is Ben-Gurion's notion of Israel as a 'melting pot', a metaphor which he applied to the various Jewish communities standing in need of being refined and purified of the dross which stuck to them during the long period of exile. The metaphor expands to embrace the notion of the dissolution of communal walls and the crystallization of a renewed nation:

> Increased immigration will require great efforts from us in order to create a unified nation. This nation is being built from rent tribes and we must solidify the dust of the Jewish man which is scattered around the world, in order that he return to his country, to a crucible of independence, and to the framework of a state. We must create a character and style which is Hebraic, which has not existed before, that could not be formed in exile in a people bereft of its native land, independence, and national freedom.[62]

The IDF was slated to fill a central role in these processes primarily because the War of Independence, as a total war, placed security and the young army of the embryonic State at the centre of social and political experience. Service in the army during the war became a central factor in the formation of the educational myth for crystallizing a national consciousness and unity. The IDF, its officers and soldiers, became the focus of national identification and a symbol for the realization of pioneering Zionism. At one and the same time, the IDF stood above political and ideological disputes and beyond communal and sectoral divisions. Ben-Gurion, who possessed keen practical instincts, was surely aware of this. 'Only the army', he said, 'can and must serve as a unifying factor in formulating the new image of the people and its loyal integration into the new culture and society being created in the State of Israel.' And he emphasized: 'The army's educational role is not only an internal national need; it is also a necessary condition for our security.'[63]

THE IMAGE AND ROLE OF THE IDF IN THE EYES OF BEN-GURION

Ben-Gurion, who was impressed and influenced by the early accomplishments of the Soviet Revolution, paraded what Moshe Lissak has coined 'statist voluntarism'. His approach was to infuse people with the spirit found in a mass-movement, but then to establish parallel tools and frameworks possessing authority and power sufficient enough to mobilize economic and material resources. First and foremost among these were human resources, to be called upon for the fulfillment of collective goals associated with the society and the State. Here was the source of his constant preaching on behalf of democracy, combined with his unrelenting claims for centralism – beginning in the Histadrut and the workers' economy and ending with the leadership of the State.

It is plausible that from the beginning Ben-Gurion hoped that the pioneering movements would succeed in drawing Israeli society after them, carrying out the major task of immigrant absorption and shaping the contours of a new society. But this did not happen, leading him again to demonstrate his ability to translate and adapt political ideas to a changing world. According to Josef Gorni, this was the principal power and originality of the man. In view of the seriousness of the situation and the imminent problems – immigrant absorption, widespread settlement, setting up of security systems, education and health, and the scope required by the new needs – Ben-Gurion brandished the banner of 'statism' and placed activities implemented by centralized and sovereign State institutions at the centre of national consciousness. As mentioned above, his statism was now advanced as a clear 'anti-thesis' to the divisiveness and ineffectiveness which characterized movement and party activities. Statism symbolized for him the unity of the people and the common responsibility for its fate and the fate of the State, the common national interest, which stood above all party and sectoral interests.

In association with this orientation, Ben-Gurion thought it was desirable to expend the main effort on youth. 'Rapid dissolution of the exilic mentality', he maintained, 'can perhaps only be achieved among youth who have just emerged from childhood and have not yet reached maturity. We have the ability to mould and create their image in accordance with the needs of this critical period in which the State's foundations are being established.'[64] Drawing upon his analogy between the early years of the State and the Biblical period, the youth, in his assessment, were the generation following the 'desert generation' – and in any case much more precious material. He thus requested that youth education be transferred from the voluntary youth movements to State frameworks. In following this course, he fostered the pre-military system of the Gadna.

In the meantime, until the Gadna came into being, the 'desert generation' fulfilled its military obligations through the National

Service Law, which required army duty from every citizen in Israel. Two frameworks were instituted: the regular army and the reserves. The law allowed for the induction of every citizen, making him/her subject to the imposition of duties and national tasks according to need. It was in this context that the idea originated, in 1951, for the establishment of work brigades that would direct new immigrants to productive labour enabling them to acquire job skills, learn Hebrew and obtain limited military training. The length of service would be identical to the length of regular army service. A special committee, established on the orders of Ben-Gurion, was charged with 'inquiring into the possibilities and ways of implementing the hiring of workers in public works and housing construction. This would be undertaken for the public good in the form of work brigades and gangs in military or quasi-military regimes, and not as enterprise for profit.'[65] In the end this idea was not put into practice but it clearly reveals Ben-Gurion's perception of the nature of the new instruments placed at his disposal through the policy of 'statism'.

A no less clear expression of Ben-Gurion's outlook may be obtained in the following declaration:

> Until now, the single instrument for state education – and this is perhaps surprising to many – is the Israel Defence Force. From the perspective of the security needs of the State of Israel, which are subject to special kinds of external and internal conditions, the IDF is to serve not only as an instrument for military training but also as a state school, teaching youth Hebrew, Jewish history, local geography, the basics of a general education, cleanliness and proper grooming, and patriotism.[66]

In fact, already at the height of the War of Independence, he had stated in this regard:

> We are now inducting people involuntarily. Among our recruits are illiterates, people at poverty level, rag-tag and street children. We have sinned against Eastern Jews. Our army is a distillation of the Yishuv, and its spiritual character will mould the face of the Yishuv … Neither sons of prophets nor people of rank may be found among us, nor is there a superior race and an inferior race; every Yemenite youth and every Kurdish youth, every Ashkenazi youth or youth from any other community is capable of rising to the highest levels of heroism – if only he be given what the

children of the kibbutzim and the Palmach were given. If only we attend to them with love and trust and provide them with the values of our Movement and the vision of our enterprise ... The single place in which youth from all walks of life without exception can meet is the army. Here are joined together workers and farmers' sons from the collective and cooperative settlements, high school students and students from schools of higher learning with youth from poor neighborhoods, and from all the communities the common people who do not know how to read or write. They are provided with a rare opportunity, unique in its kind, to join the seams of this patchwork quilt, to eradicate the deep differences and unite our public under conditions of equality, conditions which will create unity and Jewish brotherhood.[67]

This was not only a functional outlook. At its core was embedded a conception of the new Jewish soldier – extending from the Jewish Brigades to the IDF – as an exemplary symbol of the 'new' Jew who has erased the image of the weak Jew, the cowardly Jew who is not capable of bearing arms and defending himself and his honour. More generally, Ben-Gurion viewed the establishment of the IDF as reflecting a revolution in the life of the Jewish people. It would bring about co-existence with all peoples and exhibit healthiness in body and spirit. These features would receive even more emphasis in light of the fact that the victories of the IDF in the War of Independence raised the stature of Jews throughout the world and engendered a sense of identification with the Zionist enterprise in Palestine. A clear echo of these expectations was expressed by Ben-Gurion in an address to the Zionist Executive Committee in August 1948:

It is difficult to say what uplifted and enthralled the hearts of the Jewish people more, regardless of whether they lived in the United States of America or in the Russian Soviet Union, in the refugee camps in Germany or in the poor and suffering quarters of Yemen, in the far reaches of northern Scandinavia or in the gold mines of South Africa – the good tidings of the Jewish State re-established in our day after thousands of years of slavery, alienation and dependence, or the heroism of the Israeli army which arose in all its ancient glamor and youthful glory over the highlands of Galilee and the dunes of the Negev, on the Philistinian plane and in the Ayalon Valley, within the heart of Jerusalem and in the fields of Lod and Ramle.[68]

The IDF as a state instrument – and of course the IDF after the Etzel and Lehi crisis and the Palmach crisis – was to remain completely subordinate to the elected civilian echelon. Ben-Gurion regarded this as a litmus test for Israeli democracy and he strove to incorporate the spirit of this relationship, as we have noted in this chapter, from the moment he obtained the Security portfolio on the Jewish Agency Executive in 1946. 'With the conversion of the Hagana into an army', he declared, in a speech in June 1948, 'we must not be satisfied with a fictive authority of the state. An army which is not completely subordinate to the democratic government of the people will in the final analysis dominate the people and bring about military anarchy.'[69] More than a year later, at the end of October 1949, he explained his position regarding civilian–military relations in a concise manner:

> The army determines neither policy, nor the regime, the laws, or governmental proceedings in the state. The army does not even determine its own structure, its procedures, or type of operations. And of course it does not decide on matters of war or peace. The army is nothing but the executive arm, the defence and security arm, of the Government of Israel.[70]

Ben-Gurion explained relentlessly that an operational arm which concentrates the main national instruments of war in its hands, thus possessing tremendous and dangerous power, must be kept under iron discipline (especially if this framework is based on mass mobilization and is not restricted to a 'closed club' of loyal, elite units of volunteers). In February 1948 he stated:

> People who bear arms and have power which others lack, always constitute a danger to the public at large and to themselves. People who have surplus power lacking to others – and this power is not made subordinate to a supreme authority – constitute a public danger. Those people who are armed – their duty is to kill and be killed, that is the duty of a soldier ... and this also should not be forgotten – man is not an angel. All flesh and blood under certain conditions is [sic] liable to abuse the surplus power in its possession, if it is not confined to a framework which is able to prevent this abuse ... We must establish and reinforce the friendship and pioneering values of the Hagana, but we must join to these values ... strict military discipline not only with regard to the use of weapons – but also

in regard to all behavior and manners [of the conscript], including how he dresses and his hours of sleeping and eating.[71]

At the conclusion of his book *When Israel Fought in Battle,* Ben-Gurion affirmed that 'with the establishment of the State we created instruments and new tools to realize the dream of our salvation, but these instrument and tools will only have a value if we know how to bring about and fortify the pioneering volunteerism which was the spirit of the Hagana.'[72] He wrote these lines in a chapter entitled 'In Place of a Conclusion', and it appears that this is also an appropriate title for them in the present context.

NOTES

1. A. Shapira, 'Ben-Gurion and Berl – two leadership types', in S. Avineri (ed.), *David Ben-Gurion – Portrait of a Leader in the Workers' Movement* (Tel Aviv: Am Oved, 1986), p.47.
2. N. Rotenstreich, 'Summation', in ibid., p.155.
3. S. Peres, 'David Ben-Gurion: Portrait of a Leader', *Skirat Hodsheet* (November 1974), pp.1–4.
4. S. Avineri (ed.), *Varieties of Zionist Thought* (Tel Aviv: Am Oved, 1980), p.228.
5. Z. Tzahor, *Vision and Reckoning: Ben-Gurion Between Ideology and Politics* (Tel Aviv: Sifriat Poalim, 1994).
6. D. Ben-Gurion, *Memoirs* (Tel Aviv: Am Oved, 1971), p.120.
7. Ben-Gurion refers to Lenin as 'a perfect tactical genius' not 'snared by dogmas'. Quoted in M. Bar-Zohar, *Ben-Gurion: A Biography* (New York: Delacorte Press, 1977), pp.51–2.
8. See Z. Tzahor, *Vision and Reckoning*, p.58.
9. See D. Ben-Gurion, *Memoirs*, p.130.
10. Y. Ilem, *The Hagana: The Zionist Path to Power* (Tel Aviv: Zmora, 1979), p.24.
11. S. Teveth, *Jealousy of David: The Burning Earth* (Tel Aviv: Shoken, 1977), pp.331–2.
12. See M. Bar-Zohar, *Ben-Gurion: A Biography*, p.103.
13. See Y. Ilem, *The Hagana*, p.202.
14. See B. Bar-Zohar, *Ben-Gurion: A Biography*, p.516.
15. D. Ben-Gurion, 'At the Political Committee of the 22nd Zionist Congress', 18 December 1946. In *BaMa'aracha* (Tel Aviv: Ministry of Defence, 1950), pp.135–7.
16. BGA, Ben-Gurion's Diary, 27 May 1947.
17. Ibid., 28 May 1947.
18. Ibid., 3 April 1947.
19. Ibid., 'Megilat Hahagana', 8 June 1947. This was published as 'Instructions for the General Staff' in D. Ben-Gurion, *When Israel Fought in Battle [B'Hilachem Israel]* (Tel Aviv: Mapai, 1969), pp.13–18.
20. Y. Avidar, *The Way to the IDF* (Tel Aviv: Ma'arachot, 1973), p.267.
21. Y. Dori, 'From the Organization of Defence to a Defence Army', *Ma'arachot*, vols 118–19, 1959, p.34.
22. Y. Rattner, *My Life and Myself* (Tel Aviv: Shocken, 1982), p.368. For a letter of Y. Rattner to D. Ben-Gurion, see *War Diary 1* (Tel Aviv: Am Oved, 1978), pp.328–9.
23. D. Ben-Gurion, 'Security Problems and Self-Defence', in *When Israel Fought in Battle*, p.50.
24. See D. Ben-Gurion, *War Diaries* I, p.129.
25. Ibid., p.5.
26. N. Lorch, *History of the War of Independence* (Tel Aviv: Massada, 1958), p.114.
27. BGA, Ben-Gurion's Diary, 31 March 1948.
28. A. Shapira, *The Army Controversy, 1948: Ben-Gurion's Struggle for Control* (Tel Aviv: Me'uchad, 1984).

29. BGA, Ben-Gurion's Diary, 14 May 1948.
30. Y. Levi, *Nine Measures: The Battles for Jerusalem in the War of Independence* (Tel Aviv: Ma'arachot, 1986).
31. See A. Shapira, *The Army Controversy, 1948*, p.109.
32. M. Bar Zohar, in an interview with Yigael Yadin for Israel radio, 10 April 1971 in Bar-Zohar, *Ben-Gurion*, p.770.
33. D. Ben-Gurion, 'Our Path to War', in *When Israel Fought in Battle*, p.72.
34. BGA, Ben-Gurion Diary, 6 October 1948.
35. N. Lorch, 'The British Ultimatum During Operation Horev', *Ma'arachot*, July 1984, pp.76–83.
36. BGA, Ben-Gurion Diary, 30 December 1948.
37. Ibid., 8 January 1949.
38. D. Ben-Gurion, 'Order of the Day for the Establishment of the IDF – 31 May1948', in *When Israel Fought in Battle*, p.114.
39. See M. Bar-Zohar, *Ben-Gurion*, p.305.
40. From the words of D. Ben-Gurion at the fifth session of the Provisional State Council 23 June 1948, *When Israel Fought in Battle*, p.165.
41. M. Begin, 'The Altalena Affair', in M. Begin, *The Revolt* (Tel Aviv: Ahiasaf, 1978), pp.242–51.
42. BGA, Ben-Gurion Diary, 7 September 1948.
43. D. Ben-Gurion to Dori, 29 September 1948. Protocol of the Executive Committee of the Histadrut, 14–15 October 1948.
44. D. Horowitz and M. Lissak, *From Settlement to State* (Tel Aviv: Am Oved, 1977), p.279.
45. N. Alterman, *The Seventh Column* (Tel Aviv: Dvar, 1954), p.252.
46. BGA, Ben-Gurion Diary, 31 January 1950.
47. Ibid., 23 September 1949.
48. See M. Bar-Zohar, *Ben-Gurion*, p.330.
49. D. Ben-Gurion, *War Diaries*, p.902. The central components of his security outlook appear in a discussion of the Defence Service Law, 15 August 1949, *Army and Security*, p.103.
50. The title 'Hannuka Reflections' does not appear in the original but is given in the index at the end of the booklet.
51. SA, 130.02/2447/3, Ministry of Foreign Affairs.
52. D. Ben-Gurion, lecture for an officer course, 15 May 1949, in D. Ben-Gurion, *Army and Security* (Tel Aviv: Ma'arachot, 1955), p.86.
53. D. Ben-Gurion, 'Changing of the Guard', in D. Ben-Gurion, *From Class to Nation* (Tel Aviv: Davar, 1932), p.203.
54. D. Ben-Gurion, 'The Laborer in Zionism', in ibid., p.308.
55. D. Ben-Gurion, 'The Laborer in Zionism', in *From Class to Nation* (Tel Aviv: Eyanat, 1955), p.308.
56. See D. Ben-Gurion, *From Class to Nation*, p.21.
57. D. Ben-Gurion, 'Zionist Factors and their Role for this Year', in *Mishmerot* (Tel Aviv: Dvar, 1930), p.315.
58. D. Ben-Gurion, 'On the Mountain Top', in *Vision and Path* IV (Tel Aviv: Am Oved, 1956), p.244.
59. D. Ben-Gurion, 'Spiritual Revolution', *Vision and Path* I (Tel Aviv: Am Oved, 1942), p.32.
60. D. Ben-Gurion, *Eternal Israel* (Tel Aviv: Eyanot, 1964), p.146.
61. D. Ben-Gurion, 'A Response', *Vision and Path* I, p.233.
62. D. Ben-Gurion, *Vision and Path* I, pp.83–4.
63. D. Ben-Gurion, 'For Young Officers', Company Officers' Course, 4 November 1948, *Yehud v'Ye'ud*, p.43.
64. D. Ben-Gurion, 'Melting Pot Joins the People', in *Mission and Path* III (Tel Aviv: Am Oved), p.258.
65. For an expanded discussion on the Settlement Workers' Brigades, see M. Lissak, 'Building Institutions According to Ben-Gurion', in S. Avineri (ed.), *Varieties of Zionist Thought*, p.108.
66. See D. Ben-Gurion, *Eternal Israel*, p.158.

67. D. Ben-Gurion, at the Workers' Council, Tel Aviv, 19 June 1948, in Ben-Gurion, *Army and Security*, p.57.
68. D. Ben-Gurion, at the opening of the Zionist Executive Council, 22 August 1948, in *When Israel Fought in Battle*, p.215.
69. D. Ben-Gurion, Debate at Mapai Council, 19 June 1948, in *When Israel Fought in Battle*, p.154.
70. D. Ben-Gurion, *Army and Security*, p.138.
71. The words of D. Ben-Gurion at the Council of the Workers' Party of Israel (Mapai), Tel Aviv, 2 July 1948, in *When Israel Fought in Battle*, p.64.
72. D. Ben-Gurion, *When Israel Fought in Battle*, p.356.

Chapter 2

The Israel Defence Force and Settlement

Following the State's establishment, the IDF became involved in settlement undertakings throughout the country. This development was anchored in a conception which linked settlement with defence and, by extension, with national security considerations. Traces of this type of linkage can be found as far back as the second wave of Jewish immigration to Palestine, before the First World War (1905–1914). Members of the HaShomer (the Watchman) spoke in these terms even before they became firmly organized as a guardian body in 1909, and continued to espouse this orientation throughout their 11 years of existence. However, it appears that the first significant expression of this outlook occurred midway through the First World War. In 1916 a group of HaShomer members, upon hearing that the British army was about to cross the Sinai desert on its way to Palestine, set out for Upper Galilee and founded the village of Bar-Giora (today, Kfar Giladi). This pioneering group operated on the basic assumption that their dedication to guarding the Yishuv obligated them to assist in establishing facts, in anticipation of political decisions that were likely to occur at the conclusion of the war – and establishing facts meant settlement as a demonstration of holding the land.

In 1919, the General Assembly of the HaShomer expressed its firm belief in

> the need to begin widespread settlement close to the existing boundary lines for the purpose of defending the country and laying the groundwork for revolutionary national education. On the basis of this declaration the Assembly has decided to

found a string of special cooperative settlements in the spirit of the ideas and principles of the HaShomer, which will serve as guard-posts along the frontiers of our country.[1]

This conception included an additional component associated with 'the ideals and principles of the HaShomer'. According to Mendel Portugali, a leading figure in the organization, 'there is a need to integrate guard duty with labor in order that we be healthy in body and spirit'.[2] Ben-Gurion would draw upon this source in addressing the Nahal soldiers in November 1948: 'The HaShomer did not want their members to live by arms alone – that kind of life was liable to enervate and impoverish a person – and on this account they sought to blend a life of labor and settlement with a life of guard duty and defence.'

This orientation can also be found in the remarks of Joseph Trumpeldor, a pioneer and soldier who was killed at the battle of Tel Hai in 1920. He referred to:

> special military cooperative settlements, inhabited by families of the soldiers, where the soldiers can also labor intermittently, several months during the year, in agricultural work. With a workers' corps like this it will be easy in the future to shift to popular military training, that is, to methods suitable for a general militia.[3]

He, too, thought that combining settlement and security was an important condition for optimal contribution towards the advancement of the Zionist endeavour.

With the intensification of the dispute over the future of Palestine during the second half of the 1930s, settlement and defence became central factors in the political struggle. The combination of 'stockade and tower' (that is, the establishment of new settlements designed from the very beginning as fortified strongholds) was during these years the principal operative instrument guaranteeing the expansion of a Jewish hold on land, water sources and other vital physical features. It is very doubtful whether there was any other way in which the Yishuv could have established the borders of the prospective State.

It was in this fashion that various types of settlement, and especially the kibbutzim, became a most important pillar in the development of an independent defence force. The human composition of the kibbutzim, their structure and socio-economic base, made possible internal recruitment of many of their best 'native sons' to the super-numeraries, the British army and the Palmach. Moreover, without the absorption of the Palmach companies by the kibbutzim, these military entities would not have been able to sustain themselves as a recruit-ment force for the Hagana. A way of life which combined agricultural labour and military training – financial support for training was attained through the agricultural labour of the military trainees – was the only available option for organizing and maintaining a meagrely-funded military force. At the same time, the soldiers' residency at the kibbutzim, the daily contact with kibbutz mentality and experience (and also the fact that the kibbutzim supplied the Palmach with a reasonable number of its commanding officers) imprinted on these forces values and concepts of the working agricultural settlement. Voluntarism and self-discipline, team work and mutual help – all this was an important part of the formation of an *esprit de corps* and motivating force among the Palmach companies. In addition, it inspired not a few of the Palmach members to found their own 'soldier villages' – additional settlements steeped in security consciousness. Thus, between 1944 and 1946, the Palmach established five 'security villages' in sensitive areas in the north of the country – Beit Keshet, Birya, Ramot-Naphtali, Ein-Zeitim and HaHoshalim (later Ammiyad).

General Yosef Avidar (Reserve), one of the leaders of the Hagana and a leading architect of the concept of 'conquering settlement', provided a good description of the connection between settlement and security, including the development of the Yishuv:

> The settlement strategy throughout the period before the estab-lishment of the State could not have been realized without the potential of the pioneer-driven settlers who were prepared to face the most difficult economic conditions and grave security dangers. This [the 'conquering settlement' strategy] was in fact the main combatant factor which won out in the struggle for obtaining control over the land throughout the country.[4]

Even Ben-Gurion asserted at the height of the critical stages of the War of Independence that:

> without the steadfastness of the settlements in the campaign – it is difficult to estimate how the State of Israel could have stood on its feet in its infancy. We would not have withstood this campaign between unequals, of one against forty, without our

settlements, and first of all the working agricultural settlements. Had it not been for the type of individuals who comprised these settlements, vitalized by a vision which informed their life, and which they, their offspring, and the pioneering youth alongside them defended, our military force would not have perhaps made a stand for us and we would not have held fast either in the Negev, the Jordan Valley, or Upper Galilee.[5]

In a speech to members of the Zionist Executive two months earlier, Ben-Gurion declared:

We must establish a string of settlements of a new type, different from the regular ones, that are not based on the sacred writ of the military academy but rather, constitute mixed battalions of settlers and warriors, farmers and fighters. The special conditions of geography, politics, and agriculture of the Negev force us to do this. Without war we would not have settlement, and without settlement we will not have a military victory in the Negev.[6]

Towards the end of the war Ben-Gurion reiterated this view when he said that the fortified heights in the Negev must continue to be military posts, but every location to which water could be piped or which had a natural spring must immediately become a soldiers' farming settlement. He added that in the Galilee, too, it would not be sufficient to rely solely upon military power to consolidate gains and that there was a need to establish a line of military/agricultural settlements along the Lebanese border.

Thus, the entry of the IDF into the extra-military tasks of settlement during the first years of the State appeared to follow a very natural course. This undertaking took place in a systematically planned and organized framework, which merits a detailed description.

THE SETTLEMENT INSTITUTIONS

Settlement policy, as part of the delineation of the borders and programmes for controlling the country, was a subject of discussion on the eve of the State's founding and continued in various forums during and following the War of Independence. Initially, these matters were debated in the Settlement Department of the Jewish Agency, The Jewish National Fund (JNF), the senior organs of Mapai, and the

People's Administration; at a later stage, various State institutions inherited the responsibility for its determination. In the following paragraphs we will briefly review the central factors in this policy.

The Committee for Settlement and Irrigation Problems in the State

This was established by the Mapai Central Committee. It held its first meeting on 14 December 1947, two weeks after the United Nations General Assembly Partition Resolution (UNGA Resolution 181). Members of this Committee came from senior settlement institutions of the Jewish Agency, the Jewish National Fund, and the Agricultural Centre of the Histadrut (Joseph Weitz, Abraham Hertzfeld, Zalman-Lief-Lifshitz, Haim Halperin, Yehuda Horin), from the Mapai Secretariat (Ze'ev On-Isserson, Yehiel Duvdevani) and from Hagana Headquarters (Levi Eshcol and Shimon Peres). Chaim Gvati from the Agricultural Centre was appointed as head of the committee.

This body was instructed to prepare three-year programmes for the construction of an agro-economic, social infrastructure. Part of this task – the preparation of a settlement programme for the years 1947–1951, dealing with security settlement along the northern border and development in the Negev and the Central Region – was completed by 17 February 1948. Although the committee initially assumed that it could base settlement planning on the Partition Resolution as well as on negotiations with Arab residents for the purchase of land slated for subsequent development, it quickly became apparent that it had to change its basic conception. 'The three-year program', according to Yehiel Duvdevani, 'must be undertaken in consultation with army headquarters. We cannot in today's circumstances proceed on the basis of individual settlements alone. There must be a [military] strategy input and the plan must be coordinated with its needs.'[7]

Up to the establishment of the State, the committee dealt with matters of co-ordination among the various relevant groups involved in settlement policy; later, with the elimination of partisan involvement, it became a Government body known as The Committee for the Co-ordination of Settlement Institutions. Representatives from Government ministries responsible for different areas of agricultural settlement-planning and implementation became a part of the committee and Levi Eshcol became its head. Eshcol's dual roles as head of the Jewish Agency Settlement Department and as Acting Deputy Minister of Defence for Logistical Matters gave him the authority and the capability to guide and co-ordinate most of the activities connected with settlement security.

The Settlement Department of the Jewish Agency

This department began its work with national settlement during the period of the third wave of immigration (1919–1923). Until the State's establishment, it was subordinate to the decisions, policy and resources of the Zionist Executive and the Jewish National Fund. Its staff attended to physical and professional planning for the settlements and provided them with minimal equipment during the settlement process until basic economic consolidation was attained. Following the establishment of the State, the department, in co-ordination with Government ministries responsible for security, the economy and agriculture continued to be responsible for planning and determination of settlement locations. Settlement Department planners and IDF officers in charge of different regions visited the designated settlement sites in order to assess aspects of their security, ground layout and architectural structure (including the diffusion and concentration of public structures). In addition, the Settlement Department was assigned responsibility for:

- the financial support of new settlements until they were firmly established
- establishing a physical infrastructure for new settlements (including building construction and the laying of water and electrical power lines)
- purchasing agricultural equipment and an infrastructure for livestock
- preparation of agricultural land and the planting of crops.

The department's activities were co-ordinated with the Jewish National Fund, the Agricultural Centre of the Histadrut, the Settlement Movement, the Regional Councils, the Trade Union Associations and others. Many of these activities were undertaken through the combined efforts of the Settlement Department and the Ministry of Agriculture, principally through two organs – the Joint Centre for Planning and the Joint Centre for Instruction.

During the first years of the State, the Settlement Department of the Jewish Agency occupied a pivotal place in settlement policy and was the dominant factor in all the aforementioned areas. An indication of this was given in August 1948, when Ben-Gurion asked the Justice Minster, Pinhas Rosen, to prepare an order (legislation of the Provisional State Council) which gave the Jewish Agency the right to purchase immovable property throughout the

State and beyond its borders. The Prime Minister's intention was to employ the Jewish Agency for the expropriation of uncultivated land and the compensation of landowners, and to exploit these purchases for the settlement of new immigrants. In addition, public works projects and housing construction, initiated to provide jobs for immigrants as well as structural security for their residential quarters, were also implemented through the Agency. This order expanded the Agency's areas of operation and brought it substantial independence in settlement enterprises.[8] These steps enabled the Government to circumvent possible difficulties stemming from direct Government activities in State-controlled territories not included in the Partition Resolution, as well as to raise funds from diaspora Jewry. In addition, as an eleemosynary institution, the Jewish Agency would be freed from paying state taxes while engaging in these activities. From then on, the Settlement Department of the Jewish Agency was in charge of establishing new settlements, while the Government ministries, and especially the Agriculture Ministry, would provide assistance for existing settlements.

The special status of the Settlement Department was largely influenced by the type of people who were appointed to its leading positions in the first months following the Declaration of Independence. On 22 August 1948, Levi Eshcol was chosen as a member of the Jewish Agency Executive and Chairman of the Settlement Department and became the central figure in settlement policy. He served in this position for 15 years (during this period he was also Minister of Agriculture and Minister of Finance), until June 1963, when he became Prime Minister of Israel. Raanan Weitz was subordinate to him as director of the department. Eshcol, one of the founders of Kibbutz Deganya Bet, had dealt with settlement matters for many years in his position at the Histadrut's Agricultural Centre and as a founder of the Water Company 'Mekorot'. He served as Treasurer of the Hagana and after the establishment of the State he became the senior assistant to Ben-Gurion at the Defence Ministry. From October 1951 he was a member of the Government, and within less than a year he was appointed to the post of Finance Minister. At the end of 1953 Ben-Gurion wanted Eschol to succeed him in the office of Prime Minister. Thus, Eshcol's personal status clearly contributed to the centrality of the bodies which he headed, among them the Settlement Department of the Jewish Agency.

The Jewish National Fund

This fund was a senior partner with the Jewish Agency in settlement undertakings, with official responsibility from its inception for the purchase of land, its improvement and cultivation for settlement, and for the drainage of swamps. Following the State's establishment and the resultant change in the order of priorities and roles of the Zionist institutions, the Jewish National Fund received responsibility for the following objectives: afforestation and care of forests; and laying out and maintenance of roads throughout the State, mainly in the frontier areas.

At the close of the War of Independence and with the first large wave of immigration, the JNF purchased two million dunams (400 dunams = 1 hectare) of agricultural land from the State for the construction of new settlements. This step was in accord with the desire of the heads of the institution to continue in their role as facilitators in the transfer of territory in the Land of Israel to ownership by the Jewish people. In addition, these transfers energized fund-raising from world Jewry, injecting much-needed revenue into the State's coffers, and thus further advancing the settlement effort.[9]

Abraham Granot (Granovsky) headed the Jewish National Fund, but the 'strong man' in the organization was Josef Weitz, the director of its Lands and Afforestation Department. This industrious individual was appointed at the beginning of the War of Independence, on instruction from Ben-Gurion, as head of the Negev Committee which co-ordinated all the fortification and supply activities designed to help hold the Negev during the war. At the same time, Weitz co-ordinated activities of the northern Galilean settlements which found themselves outside State jurisdictional lines according to the Partition Plan.

Weitz, who for many years before the establishment of the State had championed 'conquest settlement' – establishing settlement strongholds at key security points – was overjoyed about the idea of linking the IDF to settlement enterprises, and was among the prominent leaders in bringing this about both during and after the War of Independence.[10]

The Agricultural Centre of the Histadrut

Headed by Abraham Hartzfeld, this was among the veteran settlement institutions. Its influence in settlement affairs was substantial. This body was in charge of the following tasks:

- co-ordination of the initiatives and requests of the various settlement movements in all matters connected to the establishment of new settlements
- participation in settlement planning and the determination of future settlement plans (including water planning)
- budget preparation and assistance in its acquiescence by State and other institutions
- representation of the agricultural settlement movements before State institutions
- provision of manpower for settlement through canvassing of families and youth, and the recruiting of agricultural instructors for the kibbutzim and new moshavim (co-operative villages)
- assistance and agricultural and economic training for fledgling settlements
- co-ordination of settlement training which entailed instruction and training activity for core groups of soldiers who wanted to go to agricultural settlements

The Agricultural Centre handled the consignment of soldiers without families to agronomic training programmes at co-operative settlements; this was done in co-ordination with the Co-operative Settlement Movement and the IDF. Immediately following the cessation of military hostilities, the Centre pressured army commanders for the release of agricultural instructors so that they could accompany settlement activity at close hand. At this time, the Centre inaugurated the Emek Hepher Agricultural Seminary in memory of Dr Rupin; the Seminary was to provide academic courses in the field of agriculture, for veteran and new farmers, and to base its practical activities on scientific grounds.

The Office of the Prime Minister

The Office of the Prime Minister entered the settlement-effort picture in the initial years of the State through the initiative of the Prime Minister who, of course, assigned strategic importance to this matter. A planning branch was added to the office and Aryeh Sharon, an architect by profession, was appointed to head it. The Planning Branch contained two main units: co-ordination and economic planning, and engineer planning. The former was responsible for co-ordinating all Government ministries involved in economic matters, and that clearly included settlement. It also dealt with population distribution and, together with the Jewish Agency, with matters relating to settlement, housing and several other relevant areas.[11]

The Ministry of Defence

This ministry attended to settlement matters as part of its security and military activities. Ben-Gurion, as Prime Minister and Minister of Defence, proceeded on three principal levels in his efforts to put into practice his settlement conceptions.

First he conducted discussions on settlement matters with central actors of the settlement institutions, security personnel and IDF officers. By acting as chairman of these discussions, and by holding them in his office, Ben-Gurion speeded up decision making and removed bureaucratic and establishment-related obstacles.

Secondly, he undertook organizational initiatives designed to advance planning and implementation of settlement: in the Defence Ministry, the Division for the Settlement and Rehabilitation of Soldiers; in the IDF, a staff officer for settlement, with responsibility for the Settlement Branch at General Headquarters Directorate.

Lastly, he assumed personal responsibility for the appointment of individuals to relevant posts, including central figures in the defence and settlement system. Many of these individuals had direct connections with Ben-Gurion and with the directors of the country's economy. For example, on 2 June 1948, Ben-Gurion appointed Joshua Eshel to head the army's Settlement Branch. Eshel was one of the senior commanders in the Hagana, one of the founders of the Hagana Air Force, in November 1947, and its head until it became the Air Force of the IDF. By virtue of his personality, his direct connections with Ben-Gurion and many of the Yishuv leaders and his organizational ability, he overcame a series of stumbling-blocks and disputes, shortened processes and assisted in problem solving and the by-passing of difficulties.

Another appointment of the same type was made in November 1948 when Ben-Gurion urgently recruited Josef Gurion, a member of Kibbutz Geva who had come to Israel in the second immigration wave and had served in the Jewish Legion. Josef Gurion received responsibility for the settlement of soldiers demobilized from the British army immediately after the Second World War and was now appointed head of the new Settlement and Rehabilitation Division in the Defence Ministry.

The Division for the Settlement and Rehabilitation of Soldiers

This division, created on 23 November 1948, handled all the absorption and rehabilitation problems of demobilized soldiers on their return to civilian life, as well as the rehabilitation of thousands of injured soldiers and families of the fallen. The Agricultural Settlement Branch was the first to operate within the division's framework. It was headed by Chaim Krishfein, a member of the Kfar Hittim co-operative settlement. Its first challenge was to direct thousands of demobilized soldiers to agricultural settlements, a move designed to solve their employment problem as well as contributing to solve the emergency situation in the agricultural sector of the economy. The economy was experiencing difficulty in providing an adequate food supply for the burgeoning State. Apart from these pragmatic considerations, this policy was informed by dictates of ideology associated with Zionism and the working movement's return to the land.

The roles of The Division for the Settlement and Rehabilitation of Soldiers were:

- to help the demobilized soldier who has chosen a vocation in agriculture
- to prepare new settlement programmes for demobilized soldiers
- to examine the capacities of the various types of existent agricultural settlements to take in new members and to direct soldiers to those locations
- to operate information services among the soldiers, both written and oral, (through pamphlets, brochures, lectures and meetings)
- to maintain connections with authorities in the army and with all the national institutions and organizations who wished to co-operate (dissemination of information, organization, programming, financing)
- to supervise the activities of national institutions and organizations and assist them in their activities of information dissemination and organization among the soldiers
- to approve soldiers who were candidates for isolated settlements in the various agricultural collectives
- to link the settlement bodies and settlement core-groups established among the soldiers and to determine their settlement locations
- to prepare programmes and the required budgets for settlement in co-operation with settlement institutions of the Zionist Movement and the State

- to organize and supervise agricultural training within the activity
framework of the Division for the Settlement and Rehabilitation
of Soldiers.[12]

In fact, the Branch for Agricultural Settlement, which operated in the
framework of the Defence Ministry, was intended as the civilian stay
of the Agricultural Branch at General Headquarters. It was to assist
this branch in matters of co-ordination and dialogue with national
institutions and Government ministries involved in settlement activities, and to support it in struggles and disputes which arose within
the IDF system.

The Ministry of Agriculture

In accord with the definition of its duties, this ministry was
entrusted with agricultural development throughout the State, and
the raising of standards in all its modalities: technical, scientific,
economic and social. The path to attaining these goals was based on
regional agricultural planning, on the assumption that in the long
run regional developmental plans would be combined with an
overall national development plan. This Governmental ministry, in
fact, carried the burden of building an agricultural infrastructure for
the State of Israel, in the wake of the complete destruction of the
Arab agricultural economy in the War of Independence and the
infliction of severe damage to the kibbutzim and moshavim. The
Jewish agricultural sector had suffered both from direct shelling and
lack of manpower following mobilization of farmers to the battlefield. Moreover, agricultural tasks became more expansive and
burdensome in light of the rapid growth in population brought
about by the waves of immigration.

Given these circumstances, the Ministry of Agriculture was unable
to carry the burden of preparing and establishing new settlements
and, consequently, these tasks were forwarded to the Settlement
Department of the Jewish Agency. The Agricultural Ministry,
however, had its hand in many ongoing activities of these settlements
– through, for example, the joint mechanisms of instruction and co-
ordination with the Agency's Settlement Department.

Israel's first Minister of Agriculture in the Provisional Government
was Aaron Syzling, a Mapam representative and member of Ein
Harod. Chaim Halperin served as director of the ministry. In the
Government formed in March 1949, after the elections for the first

Knesset, Dov Yosef received the Agriculture portfolio. He was also Minister of Supply and Rationing. At the end of October 1950, Pinhas Lavon became Minister of Agriculture and within a year he was replaced by Levi Eshcol, who continued to occupy the post of chairman of the Settlement Department of the Jewish Agency.

Settlement Bodies in the IDF

In the early spring of 1948, a Palmach platoon occupied a parcel of land belonging to the Jewish National Fund in the vicinity of the village of Breer, on the road to the Negev. The platoon established a new settlement on the location called Bror Hayil. According to all opinions, the entire undertaking – called Operation Abraham – was the first settlement action of the Army (which was not yet the IDF) during the War of Independence. Responsibility for its execution was given to Palmach headquarters, which had already succeeded in proving its ability and involvement in settlement matters and the settling-in stage.

At the beginning of May, a little before the establishment of the State, the supreme command entered the picture. Michael Schechter (Shaham) was appointed Settlements Officer at General Headquarters and the army's representative responsible for all activities related to new settlements. On 11 May 1948, this officer presented 'a suggestion for consolidating our borders – and the establishment of conquest settlements'.[13] This was a purely military project known as the Azarya Plan (after the underground name of Shaham-Schechter) and it is easy to see it as a clear successor to Plan Daled. This latter plan was prepared at General Headquarters in March 1948, in order to respond to the new needs of the war and to create conditions for an adequate deployment in advance of the incursion of Arab armies into the country.

Plan Daled was written up in a vague and general manner. However, operational orders given to different brigades on the basis of this plan show a clear tendency of the Yishuv leadership to control broad expanses of territory, to overrun Arab towns and villages, to create territorial continuity between the different Jewish regions – in short, to expand the State's territory beyond the borders designated by the Partition Resolution.[14] When the plan was put into action during April–May 1948, a mass flight of Arabs from different regions began, eventually reaching an estimated figure of 200,000 to 300,000 refugees.

This reality invited the creation of facts in the evacuated territory. In the first place, the many abandoned villages created a special opportunity for bringing about territorial continuity of Jewish settlements and defensible lines of transport, in accord with Plan Daled. At the same time, there was a compelling need to prevent the penetration of irregular Arab forces into the abandoned Arab villages (in particular, the forces of Fawzi El-Kaukji in the north and the forces of Hasan Salame in the central area). Such a development would almost certainly result in the conversion of these villages into operational bases against the Jewish side. Furthermore, the first ceasefire was about to take place and this awakened anxiety, which was expressed on 16 June in a letter from the head of the IDF's Intelligence Department to Reuven Shiloah, a senior person in the Foreign Ministry:

> There is a substantial return movement of the villagers who had fled to neighboring countries during this cease-fire. There is a serious danger that these returnees will refortify their villages which lie deep behind our front lines, and with the renewal of military activities they will become a fifth column, if not effective nests of resistance.[15]

This perceived feeling deepened sometime later. Although a ceasefire brought an end to the War of Independence, daily skirmishes all along the border between the IDF and 'infiltrators' continued well into the early 1950. Many of these incursions were carried out by refugees who had settled in temporary encampments in the Gaza Strip and the West Bank and were now attempting to return to their homes in order to cultivate their land. The infiltration started as a spontaneous phenomenon of shepherds, refugees, smugglers and thieves, and soon began to take the form of sabotage and terrorist activity. The continuing hostilities changed the map as settlements were set up as a means of plugging gaps along the border, in order to block and deter further incursions.

Plan Azarya was designed to bring about this change and contained an outline for the establishment of 82 new settlements – control posts and security strongholds, a variant of the 'stockade and tower' model which had dominated settlement defence strategy during the Arab uprisings from 1936–39. Combat platoons received orders to inhabit these settlements. At this stage, there was no orientation towards the economic and agricultural aspects which occupied the settlement institutions, and later the newly formed settlement bodies ensconced in the IDF.[16]

On 2 June 1948, Joshua Eshel replaced Shaham (who was appointed as the commanding officer of the 'Golani' Brigade) as Settlement Officer and began to build the Settlement Section of the IDF, within the institutional framework of the Operations Branch. Eshel's appointment, made on the explicit instruction of Ben-Gurion, was a clear indication of the importance which the Prime Minister attributed to the office. A further indication of this, no less transparent, appears in a communiqué written by the Deputy Chief-of-Staff and sent to the Government Secretary, the Department for Economic Planning, the Technical Department of the Jewish Agency, the Agricultural Centre, the Planning Division in the Prime Minister's Office and to several units in the Ministry of Defence. This announcement stated that 'the Settlement Office in the General Headquarters, commanded by lieutenant-colonel Eshel, is the sole military unit authorized by the army to handle matters with your institutions relating to planning, location, and setting up of new settlements. In light of this, please see to it that your contacts with the army in these matters is done through the above office.'[17]

The main operational areas of the Settlement Section, whether in its initial designation or as it developed over time, were:

- building an overall settlement plan, uniform and agreed upon by all levels of the military, based upon needs, initiatives and programmes
- determination of priorities for setting up settlements in terms of timing and geographic area
- determination of the exact location of every settlement, taking into consideration agricultural–economic needs, but giving priority to security aspects
- involvement and participation in the architectural planning of the settlement, layout of the living quarters, public structures, roads and shrubbery
- responsibility for recruiting manpower into settlement from among IDF soldiers, in co-ordination with the Adjutant-General Branch at GHQ
- co-ordination of IDF headquarters at all echelons in everything connected with settlement planning

The Settlement Section represented the IDF on a joint committee, along with the JNF, the Settlement Department of the Jewish Agency, the Ministry of Agriculture, and the Agricultural Centre of the

Histadrut. The last organization followed in the wake of the fighting forces with the express purpose of designating critical sites for security settlement. The section would represent the IDF on the Settlement Committee, which had been created in November 1948, and was intended to select settlement points based upon security needs and the particular stage of progression in the war. This committee continued to function following the War of Independence and participated in many joint excursions with senior military officers. These field trips were often initiated by the IDF when it saw the need to establish settlements in various areas.

The first settlement programme, presented by Eshel on 4 June 1948,[18] was co-ordinated with the settlement institutions. It related not only to military posts but also to actual stronghold settlements and their economic and agricultural future. It rapidly became apparent that this programme was primarily, in common IDF parlance, 'designed for change'. The military achievements on the battlefield required almost daily adjustment of the plans. The settlement-allocation map, presented on 1 August 1948, emphasized the integration of settlement and security conceptions.[19] This map was anchored in the establishment of 37 planned settlements in the centre and north of the country. The Negev, which was still cut off from the rest of the State, was not mentioned. On 6 August, the Section presented a new plan recommending 61 locations for prospective settlement. This list showed allocated settlement sites according to where the various brigades were stationed and enlisted their commanders in the preparation of the plans. The list itself gave special emphasis to areas in Western Galilee, which the Partition Resolution had not included in the Jewish State. Here there was a marked predominance of areas designated for the establishment of settlements in the centre of the country, as an integral part of the need to preserve the gains from Operation Danny (an attack to remove the threat of the Palestinian Arabs from the coastal areas near Tel Aviv) and to safeguard the route to Jerusalem.

At the beginning of October 1948, Eshel forwarded an operative report to Levi Eshcol for the establishment of 12 settlements during the second ceasefire (21 July–15 October 1948). The contents of the report were consonant with the August programmes: three in Upper Western Galilee, two in northern Upper Galilee, three in the valleys and two in the coastal plain. In February 1949, Eshel reported on the founding of 34 settlements: 20 in the area of the northern front; 5 in the area of the 'gimmel' front, which was the corridor to Jerusalem; and 9 on the dalet front – on the coastal plain and in the south.[20]

At the end of the same month, the commander of the 'bet' front, General Shlomo Shamir, explained in a letter to the Defence Minister and the Chief-of-Staff, the delays in establishing settlements during the battles, due to instability along the battlefront lines. In the same letter, he raised the request for the urgent establishment of 14 sites. 'We were quite aware', wrote Shamir, 'of the very grave danger to the extensive and most important areas which might be wrested from us if we didn't hold them by means of a controlling presence.'[21]

Again, in February 1949, district commanders were ordered to participate personally in the determination of settlement sites and to approve each and every site plan. The path of approval led from these commanders to a committee composed of representatives from the settlement institutions (the Settlement Department of the Jewish Agency, the Technical Department of the Agency, the Agriculture Centre, and settlement representation by way of proxy through the Planning Branch in the Ministry of Labour and Construction). Only afterwards were the programmes forwarded to the Settlement Section in the Operations Department of the Chief-of-Staff and presented to the Deputy Chief-of-Staff for final IDF approval.

On 18 April 1949 the Settlement Section presented a plan for the rapid establishment of 72 settlements: 26 along the northern front facing the Lebanese border, along the Jordan river and the Gilboa foothills; 13 on the 'Bet' front with a stress on closing the eastern border line; 8 on the 'gimmel' front in order to thicken the Jerusalem corridor; 25 on the southern front, the 'dalet' front in the Negev. This was the first plan presented by the section since the beginning of the war and the section's establishment (and of course, it became opportune with the removal of the blockade of the Negev). This plan emphasized the following military aspects:

- a continuous and dense line of settlements along the border
- settlements on the second line (of defence), creating a zone of settlement for frontier sites and ensuring a solid line of communication with larger regional centres (for example, the line Sufsaf –Gush Halav, Ras El-Ahmad, Delta, which was parallel and interior to the Sasa–Malkiya line, and so forth)
- exhausting all the possibilities for coastal settlement
- full and complete control over all the principal transportation routes in the country, in particular, the intersections
- Jewish settlement of entire areas regarded as important (central Upper Galilee, for example)

• control, as far as possible, of distant expanses (the south-western Negev)[22]

In June 1949, the Planning Department of the General Staff Branch GHQ published an instruction booklet for commanders at the front, touching on settlement planning stages and the district command responsibility for this. According to the document 'all the activities connected to preparing an area and making it secure and operative are assigned to the relevant district command'. It also conferred final authority on the front commander for determining whether an abandoned village, or any other designated location, was under current security conditions, suitable for settlement and reception of immigrants. The district headquarters was in charge of planning and delineating the scope of the area available for settlement and had overall responsibility for the defence of the entire settlement and its fortifications.

Evidence concerning the activities and involvement of senior officers in these settlement matters may be found, for example, in a document written by the general of the Northern Command, Yosef Avidar, on 31 October 1949:

> Wadi Ara is densely populated with Arab settlements. Because of the great importance of this territory, I concluded that there is an urgent need to strengthen our position in this area. Permanent habitation of three settlements south of the road will make our control over this area much easier. Consequently, I hereby request that the matter be handled with the greatest urgency by those institutions deemed relevant for purchasing land in Wadi Ara for the purpose of setting up settlement sites.[23]

Several months later, the Northern Command ordered that a settlement be established at Darbashiya, in the Hula region, in order to safeguard the territory from being ploughed by Arab farmers, and to prevent Arab refugees from taking control of the arable land. 'At present, it is not within our capability to superintend these territories without there being a serious settlement site in the vicinity', wrote a senior officer at headquarters. The demand was discussed in the Settlement Department and met with opposition from civilian representatives, but at the end of a long process the senior command attained its request and the site was established.[24]

One of the factors which greatly assisted the Settlement Section was the Operations Department in the General Staff Branch GHQ. In 1953, this body defined seven security principles for new settlement:

- self-defence capability of each settlement
- ability to provide mutual aid and assistance among settlements
- defence in depth
- construction of a complex of settlements which would occupy vital territory and block possible lines of incursion
- capability to hold out against an initial attack from the enemy
- capacity to provide a solid basis for regular armed forces which operate in the area
- ability to co-ordinate construction plans which could defend and enhance routine security measures during an era of peace[25]

The Engineering Corps was another important IDF body involved in new residential planning and construction for security needs. Its people, along with the Planning Department of the Jewish Agency, developed a number of new settlement models. This corps also published a manual entitled *Protected Settlements: Security Guidelines for Planning and Citing an Agricultural Settlement* which served as an important tool in new settlement planning during the first decade of the State. This publication also dealt with the defence of settlements against tank attacks.[26]

The daily contact between agricultural-settlement planners and the Engineering Corps led to the formulation of master plans for the establishment of new settlements. Its vocabulary contained military concepts such as 'depth', 'mutual assistance' and 'flanking fire'. Planners no longer deemed the 'ring' form of organization for a settlement an appropriate approach because it prevented mutual assistance between the different sectors and exposed the settlement to flanking fire. The publication noted that 'we can no longer build our defence on the basis of the faulty ring method. We must overturn the concepts associated with settlement planning in order to build defence on the basis of a zonal approach.'[27]

The new plans created a settlement structure based on neighbourhood housing clusters, each one comprising 20 to 30 family dwellings. These neighbourhoods were arrayed for broad-based defence so that, for example, protection could be provided by flanking-fire from adjacent neighbourhoods. Settlement headquarters was located in the central neighbourhood, which also contained the health clinic, the communications room and the ammunition depot. Clear instructions were given with regard to the location of public structures, children's houses, the school, the central mess hall (dining room) and the kibbutz lounge. The planners also detailed many different matters concerning the fencing of settlements, including the placement of military obstacles around the border fence, defensive shrubbery and a tree belt to serve as camouflage. In addition, both the specific security aspects and the agricultural and topographical data of each and every site were taken into account. Chaim Laskov, who was at the time the head of the Instructional Department of the IDF (and in this capacity was responsible for the formation of operational doctrines), concluded that:

> the solid basis [of a settlement's defence] must be founded on a natural or artificial obstacle which will force the enemy to attack as a combat team composed only of army regulars and artillery. It will contain the capability of being defended passively from air attack and have a mobile reserve capable of engaging enemy paratroopers. In summation, each settlement must be a fortified base.[28]

Moreover, the Engineering Corps and the Settlement Department demanded that the settlements themselves be built group by group (in their terminology, area by area) in such a way that each settlement area could include three to six settlements which would then comprise a tactical unit under a single command. The distance from settlement to settlement within a given area would be approximately 2,500 metres. Area headquarters would be located at a central point, at the intersection of convenient access roads hidden from the settlements. The settlements would be dispersed in such a manner that firing upon an attacking enemy from one settlement would not endanger another.

THE INVOLVEMENT OF THE IDF IN PLANNING AND ESTABLISHING SETTLEMENTS

Despite the fact that the IDF was a central actor in settlement undertakings, enjoying the direct support and guidance of the most senior person in the national leadership, and despite the unremitting Zionist tradition of blending settlement and security matters, there were, nonetheless, more than a few confrontations between army personnel and civilian representatives of the settlement institutions.

These disagreements occurred both during the period of the War of Independence and afterwards.

A considerable number of discussions with the district commands pertaining to settlement, especially along the borders, dealt with population composition. The Generals time and again called for the moral and social strengthening of settlement institutions, and requested that allocation of land along the first line of defence go to the kibbutzim. The IDF considered the ability of these settlements to withstand military attack higher than that of the immigrant settlements, both on the grounds of their accumulated experience and understanding of Israeli reality, and on the basis of the military training received by many of their members as veterans of the Palmach.

The disputes around this problem became more intense with the gradual diminution of settlement groups emanating from the pioneering movements. An example of this occurred towards the end of 1949, during a debate on the renewal of settlement at Mishmar HaYarden. The Northern Command emphatically announced to the Agriculture Centre: 'Following our oral conversation [sic], by the power invested in me, I hereby declare that the Northern Command will not sanction the return of a non-kibbutz body to Mishmar HaYarden or its vicinity. We will accede to a non-kibbutz settlement group on the second line, deeper within the State.'[29]

The settlement of a kibbutz group on the front lines was also not always a simple matter. The army urged civilian institutions to look after all the needs of the residents on the frontier settlements, while at the same time expressing a joint concern in regard to income sources and basic services for these settlements. However, the army's outlook was primarily security-centred, which meant that its orientation in regard to the establishment of settlements was geo-topographical. Settlement Department personnel in the Jewish Agency countered the army's position; they made pronouncements about the optimal exploitation of arable land, water sources, the layout of water pipes from these sources, and the growth potential of these settlements. A characteristic example of this dispute appears in the discussions surrounding the location of kibbutz Sasa at the beginning of the 1950s. The army, for obvious reasons, wanted to establish the kibbutz at the top of the mountain, whereas civilian representatives preferred the fertile valley in the foothills of the mountain. After extensive debate, the episode concluded with a clear-cut decision: 'In principle, the army chose the location as the indispensable place for the site, and thus, agricultural factors were not taken into account.'[30]

Many other choices for settlement location along the northern border also followed this course. For example, in the middle of 1951, the Settlement Department objected to the establishment of a settlement at Darbashiya because of the absence of any water source nearby and the lack of an agricultural infrastructure. At the end of 1952, there was vigorous resistance along the same lines to the transference of kibbutz Baram to its permanent location. But these objections, all of an economic nature, were rejected and the settlements were erected solely on the basis of security considerations.

The same story repeated itself with regard to settlement options along the Israeli–Egyptian border. In June 1953, the Settlement Section presented a proposal to the head of the General Staff Branch–GHQ and the settlers' institutions for the establishment of a new settlement in this area. The proposal recognized that 'since it is initially necessary to locate the settlement (Givat Ruth) beside the demilitarized zone, a place where there is no water or suitable terrain (because of the salinity), it is desirable that only a small party be sent in ...'[31] According to all the experts, there was almost no chance for an agricultural settlement to survive on this site (and immediately after this, the same assessment applied to an additional stronghold at Ketsiy'ot), but the IDF did not concede. Its representatives held to their position – and this time as well the most senior State officials stood behind them – and the settlements were founded.

A similar atmosphere prevailed to an even greater extent with regard to proposed settlement along the second line of defence. In October 1949, a forceful request was put forward by the Planning Department of the IDF aimed at safeguarding its involvement from the earliest stages of settlement planning for the entire State. The ostensible motive was to ensure that plans were not at cross-purposes with security needs. In June 1951, when it appeared that Moshav Hadid, which was situated between Lod and Ben-Shemen (not exactly on the border), had been recently settled without IDF approval, the head of the Operations Branch, Yitzhak Rabin, wrote a sharply-worded letter to the head of the Jewish Agency's Settlement Department, Levi Eshcol, demanding that work on the settlement be halted. 'We see in this precedent', wrote Rabin, 'a very serious and completely incomprehensible occurrence ... I hereby re-emphasize the special gravity of what has transpired, which the army, as the principal security agency in the State, cannot entertain.'[32] A month earlier, the head of the Settlement Section at GHQ had written to Raanan Weitz, director of the Settlement Department, about the lack of communication between the Department and security agencies:

Sir, I hereby direct your attention to the fact that agricultural settlement today constitutes one of the most important security factors in the State. Any lack of co-ordination between settlement institutions and the Settlement Section, and all negligence which may result from this, is likely to damage badly the security situation and thereby place difficult stumbling-blocks in the way of founding new settlements.[33]

In the wake of this letter, an urgent meeting was convened to discuss a reassessment of the Jewish Agency's settlement programmes for 1951. At the meeting the Agency continued to insist upon water sources as a *sine qua non* for the establishment of new settlements, but it did accept the army's request to raise the level of co-operation. Representatives of the IDF, nevertheless, upheld their demand for planning a security settlement in accordance with IDF plans, despite the problems connected with water sources. Raanan Weitz summarized the meeting as follows: 'In the new, agreed-upon planning scheme, some progress has been made towards accommodating the army. Since a number of settlements have been designated, I request that the army not create any difficulties with reference to these places.'[34]

Other disputes between the IDF and civilian settlement institutions touched on the master plans for the new settlements. The commanders in the field insisted that their demands in matters such as the location of public buildings (and especially children's houses and school buildings) in a protected and hidden area at the centre of the settlement be met, whereas the agency people (and even more so the architects who were involved in settlement planning) did not always commend this course. More than once the disputes over the master plan got to such a state that district commanders delayed construction work and development until the security demands were met.

Another problem in this connection arose from the desire of agency planners to establish blocks of settlements containing an array of services and mutual assistance at the inter-settlement level. Not only was this approach out of step with the military conception of founding individual settlement sites which would be distant and isolated one from the other (every instance was contingent upon security considerations), but also the idea of settlement blocks in itself created additional sources of friction. This occurred, for example, in connection with settlement planning for the Imra areas, today called the Tse'elim region. During the month of February 1952 plans were put forward for the establishment of seven sites in this area and the architects who worked in the Settlement Department complained about the demands emanating from army personnel. They claimed that these demands badly damaged agricultural and architectural requirements and were not truly anchored in security needs. In the end, the intervention of the Chief-of-Staff was required to settle a dispute that seemed to go on and on.[35]

Defence of the new settlement also raised antagonism between the IDF and civilian settlement bodies. With the conclusion of the War of Independence, the IDF assumed responsibility for defining frontier settlements, and these locations received funds from the security budget for carrying out fortification work, fencing, laying mines and building shelters. Beyond this, there was a need to allocate manpower to guard these settlements. In retrospect, it would have been possible to place this burden on soldiers, but they were needed for other duties – military training and routine security measures.

On 27 September 1949 the Minister of Defence and the Chief-of-Staff decided that the IDF would fund 1,115 civilian 'reinforcements' (who would be employed in guard duty and security activities) in 205 type-'A' frontier settlements (that is, kibbutzim which were judged to have the most acute security problems). The settlements would receive 30 Israeli pounds per month for the work of each 'reinforcement'. This arrangement did not meet the demand of the settlements for 54 pounds for each 'reinforcement' (a monthly salary acceptable at this period). Moreover, Ben-Gurion also asked 'for an examination to determine which sites required "reinforcements" and how supervision over them would be established in the course of their duties. In general, we should lean towards the elimination of "reinforcements". And their functions should be carried out by the District Defence Command, the Frontier Corps, and the police.'[36]

In 1950, the IDF reduced the average number of 'reinforcements' for each settlement to approximately 10 persons. By 1953, the number had been further reduced to four or five. At those sites in which there was a need for greater security, armed forces of squad size (7–8 people), and even company size (20–22 people), were maintained for routine security tasks.

Within a short time, with the deterioration of the security situation, the settlements found it difficult to maintain the heavy burden of safeguarding workers in the field. Kibbutz Sde Boker, for example, where Ben-Gurion would soon settle, employed 24 members in this type of activity, but received a budget for only five 'reinforcements'.

The Kibbutz turned to the Ministry of Defence for assistance, claiming that security problems were causing economic havoc[37] – and other settlements followed suit. In response, the ministry transferred part of the burden to the police and the border guard.

SOLDIERS AS SETTLERS

At the beginning of September 1951, the Settlement Department of the Jewish Agency suggested organizing an agricultural instructors course in the framework of army service; its graduates would afterwards work in immigrant settlements. According to the plan presented to the IDF, 100 soldiers who had each completed 18 months of their compulsory army service would be enrolled in their newly chosen field, where they would receive the fundamentals of agricultural training for the remaining 6 months of their service. This period of training was to be supplemented by six additional months funded by the Jewish Agency. The designers of this plan did not see any other way in which to enlist instructors, who were so badly needed.

The Adjutant-General Branch at GHQ feared that if they went ahead and opened an instructors course, they would become 'an employment office'. They retorted that it was not the role of the army to obligate soldiers to learn a vocation against their will, and raised doubts that participants would see the course through after they finished their compulsory army service. Army personnel in the Adjutant-General Branch also had reservations regarding an alternative suggestion of the Chief-of-Staff, to employ Nahal soldiers (the units had been created during 1948) as agricultural instructors. This sort of suggestion, they said, meant lack of control over 'mobile' instructors and would harm the routine activities of the Nahal Command.

In the next stage the plan reached Ben-Gurion, who ruled in the meantime that the IDF release its agricultural instructors and have them sent to the immigrant settlements. The Chief-of-Staff followed up by issuing corresponding instructions to the effect that 'all the volunteers [for the agricultural instructors course] receive their assignments in co-ordination with the Settlement Department of the Jewish Agency and the Operations Branch of the Adjutant-General's office', [that is to say, within the expansive defence establishment of the IDF].[38]

Thus the Minister of Defence and the Chief-of-Staff gave their backing to this initiative, but its realization became quite tangled.

When the Agency set out to enlist instructors, they were met with a wall of bureaucracy and various incongruous obstacles thrown up by the lower command echelons. In the end, only ten soldiers were released for the instruction mission which was deemed so important by the senior echelons.

The issue of agricultural instructors was rooted in the central problem then occupying the settlement institutions – enlistment of manpower for settlement. The number of settlers now required, following the establishment of the State and the War of Independence, was much greater than the various institutions had been accustomed to in the past, and in any case was far beyond their mobilization capabilities. They had no choice but to cast an eye toward the IDF. In the latter's framework, as pointed out above, there were thousands of youths about to become civilians who were contending with the problem of employment. Moreover, the atmosphere reigning in the IDF and its grasp of settlement as an inseparable part of defence and routine security programmes, prepared the ground for harnessing the system to efforts in information dissemination, agricultural training and mobilization of settlement groups, even prior to the conclusion of the War of Independence.

Thoughts about this were already being aired in the Mapai Settlement Committee in January 1948. The IDF settlement officer, Lieutenant-Colonel Joshua Eshel, addressed this issue in a report presented in August 1948 to the Minister of Defence, the Chief-of-Staff and Levi Eshcol. At this point, questions arose as to whether the time had come to pose settlement ideas within the IDF, and whether debates about these ideas would weaken the soldiers and distract them from war concerns. These and other questions were raised for discussion in a meeting of cultural and welfare officers on 1 August 1948.[39] Either way, in the wake of this meeting, cultural officers received responsibility for broaching the idea of settlement to soldiers in their units, via information dissemination sessions. Soldiers learned about agricultural life, participated in tours of farming sites, met with veteran settlers and were assigned workdays – all this aimed at eventually bringing about the organization of settlement core groups.

Cultural officers, who were converted into settlement officers in their respective units, called upon interested individual soldiers to join the core groups that were being formed, attended to the social and ideological consolidation of the core groups and fostered connections between them and the settlement movements. The central idea in the explanatory material used by these officers stressed the interdependency of settlement and security. Settlement activity would determine the borders of the State. Settlements had fixed the borders of the State in the past and would do so in the future. Several slogans were coined to reinforce this ideological orientation: 'Dense settlement is the path to the realization of our political and military attainments'; 'Military conquest by the unit is complete and guaranteed by settlement on conquered territory. A mark of honor for the battalion – to settle the land that it conquered.'[40]

The same spirit rang out in the titles of pamphlets distributed to IDF units at the end of 1948, with regard to development problems in the Negev. Banner headlines emphasized that conquest of the Negev, and making the desert bloom, jointly constituted the pioneering mission, that only the army, by virtue of its praiseworthy human potential, was able to cope with this. The pamphlets also urged army brigades, many of whose soldiers had fallen in defence and conquest of the Negev, to see their upcoming role as widespread territorial settlement. 'Conquerors and defenders must turn into settlers ... Soldiers who shed their uniforms and put on work clothes will then set out to pave roads, erect electric power grids, lay irrigation lines, and the like.'[41]

Information dissemination during the last months of the war also included, according to the IDF Cultural Department, 'Settlement Day' on the festival of Succoth, 1948. The contents of an information circular on this matter, published on 15 September 1948, stated that 'Settlement Day' would stress the historical value of Jewish settlement achievements during the conquest of the country and the establishment of the State; point out the military importance assigned to the situating of settlements on the frontier to counter Arab infiltrators; and bring about the recognition among army personnel that actual settlement was a continuation and fulfillment of their soldiery duties. On the list of activities slated for 'Settlement Day' were lectures, gatherings of soldiers mobilized from abroad, field trips and visits to moshavim and kibbutzim situated close to army units, meetings with veteran settlers and, of course, exhibits, presentations and the screening of movies appropriate for the occasion.

The Cultural Department went as far as defining Settlement Day as 'Battle Day'. The order-of-the-day stated:

> Soldiers of Israel, while the war is still ahead of you, while the military mission still sits on your shoulders, you are called to the banner of settlement ... We wish that our soldiers, after they have

fought with their weapons on this land for its freedom, its integrity, – will continue to do so with their spades and their ploughs … Today, through our manning of the military strongholds, we uphold the security of the State of Israel. These defensive strongholds will support our future peace and security.[42]

Orders-of-the-day at brigade level were also promulgated at this same event. The commander of Brigade 7 saw to it that the order was translated into several languages in light of the large number of immigrant soldiers serving in it, and promised in the order itself: 'This Brigade will offer all the help and encouragement to those who wish to settle and strike roots on their native land.'[43]

The title of a proclamation given to every soldier read: 'Soldier – Future Settler'. Its content stated: 'Frontier sites – they are the defensive walls of the State. He who settles there must be a fighter, possessing a high level of training and a determined readiness to man the gate … National and personal considerations coincide here.'[44] In addition, special editions of the army publications, *B'Mahane* and *Hahoma*, and a compilation of songs and stories were edited; special programmes were broadcast over the army radio stations, 'Voice of the Defence Army' and 'the Defender's Voice'; and humorous compositions and articles appeared in the civilian press. An article entitled 'Settlers' Army', which appeared in the Mapam newspaper *Al HaMishmar*, exclaimed:

> The meaning of the Zionist enterprise is conquest of the wilderness in a peaceful manner and preparation of the land for massive immigration. The Israeli Defence Forces, which embraces the masses and youth – by the nature of its creation, is a settler army. Israeli soldiers have not completed their tasks with the liberation of the State's territory from enemy forces. They must undertake the active burden of settling territory even before the arrival of peace.[45]

The erection of new settlements constituted the central event of Settler Day. Representatives of the national institutions and the Histadrut, and commanders of army units who had helped prepare the allocated sites as settlements and had formed the settler core groups, participated in the relevant ceremonies. At the formal occasion marking the founding of the moshav Tal Shahar, the president of the Provisional State Council, Dr Chaim Weizman, stated:

We were forced to go to war, but one hand was on the ploughshare and the other hand grasped the sword. Would that our hands only hold the ploughshare and the book. I don't know when the war will end ... but I place my confidence and my hope in our soldiers, the emissaries of our people, who will always keep our singular task in mind.[46]

Levi Eshcol declared at the same event: 'From this place we call upon our comrades-in-arms wherever they are, that they will see and do. Every battalion, every company, must form settler groups from their midst.'[47]

Among the celebrants at Settlement Day were members of the Revisionist Movement. Its leaders demanded that they be partners in activities involving the dissemination of information, but the head of the army's Adjutant-General Branch rejected this and prohibited all bodies and political streams from carrying out any separate propaganda within the IDF framework. This prohibition was only partly honoured. The Revisionists conducted several information sessions amongst those soldiers who identified with their movement, and in addition they distributed written material. In *BaSa'ar* [In the Storm], a publication of the youth section of the Revisionist Movement, an article proclaimed that 'the time has come in which even the youth of the Herut National Military Organization (Lehi) must report for service duty as conquerors with ploughshare and spade ... they also are summoned to be part of the military settlement operations on the land'.[48]

Information dissemination activities and the enlistment of soldiers for settlement through the Cultural Department of the IDF were not sufficient to recruit people from the settlers' political movements. A clear indication of this is found in an emotionally laden letter of Ben-Tzion Yisraeli to David Ben-Gurion in which he demanded 'settlement conquest as a continuation of military conquest'. Yisraeli, a native of Kibbutz Kinneret, and one of the leading personalities in Mapai and the Kibbutz Movement, stated in his letter:

For the sake of agricultural settlement and the tilling of the soil – adjusted to the needs of the military conquest, security, and mass immigration – there is an urgent need for hundreds upon hundreds of able-bodied individuals and core groups which will occupy at least part of the strongholds and barren and abandoned places ... The majority of bodies and core groups must and can be formed from among soldiers. Thousands of the best Israeli youth, both native-born and immigrants are concentrated in the army.[49]

In order to reach this objective, Yisraeli forcefully suggested expanding the scope of information dissemination in the IDF, creating a suitable administrative apparatus in the Ministry of Defence, harnessing settlement people to the undertaking, and finalizing the future settlement map. All this was to be done while bestowing responsibility for the mobilization of settlement units on the movements, settlement institutions and the army. As an important condition for success, Yisraeli urged that commanders be involved in trying to convince and mobilize potential settlers.

Ben-Gurion responded to Yisraeli's letter by summoning a special session of the General Staff under his chairmanship. They met on 26 November to discuss the different ways of implementing the letter's suggestions. At this meeting, the idea emerged of 'building the country through military regiments' directed to national tasks. In the meantime, Ben-Gurion appointed Yisraeli as co-ordinator of the Centre for the Establishment of Settlement Cores in the IDF.

The Department for the Soldier's Future, which was subsequently founded in the framework of the Adjutant-General Branch, GHQ, was designed, according to its definition:

• to channel the bonding and energy of soldiers to horizons desirable for the state, to co-ordinate their programmes with the Government's development programme and to integrate them with the values of the State
• to organize and unite soldiers in settler groups, to form co-operatives, and to encourage soldiers to establish industrial enterprises
• to see to the agricultural and vocational training of soldiers while they were still in compulsory service[50]

This department created settlement cells within the battalion and the brigade on every front. Each cell numbered six soldiers (administration officer, welfare officer, cultural officer and three NCOs), and dealt with the following tasks:

• guidance for soldiers in determining their future
• dispatching soldiers for agricultural or vocational training
• forming settlement cores and attaching individual soldiers to settlement frameworks

- organizing settlement cores and making arrangements for touring nearby settlements
- establishing regular communication between the different headquarters and command echelons and designated settlement bodies, in order to solve problems and facilitate the departure of soldiers to a settlement[51]

As cited above, parallel to the Department for the Soldier's Future was the Division for the Rehabilitation and Settlement of Soldiers that included the Section for Agricultural Settlement, headed by Chaim Krishfein. This section focused on help to Palmach veterans who were organized in agricultural training core groups from the different settlement movements (and from the youth movements which were under their aegis). In addition, it assisted soldiers who did not serve in the Palmach but wished to join new or existing settlements. According to a report by Krishfein, the latter settlement framework numbered about 480 soldiers, organized in 16 settlement cores, spread among different IDF units (they formed 'the service corps', that is to say, professional corps – the navy and the district corps were included in this).[52]

In March 1950, the Rehabilitation Branch announced that 9,000 demobilized soldiers – out of 90,000 – went to agricultural settlements. Three-thousand five-hundred had already settled down in 58 new settlement sites. Existing settlements took in 450 soldiers. Immigrant settlements and abandoned villages absorbed 250 soldiers. Seven hundred candidates for settlement were received in 30 settlements for a period of training. Twenty core groups were in line for settlement.[53]

The movement core groups were for the most part Palmach veterans who had served with the fighting units. Some of them were already in the process of being demobilized during the second truce agreement, following Ben-Gurion's decision that their channeling to new settlements was preferred to continuation in combat service. After several months, Ben-Gurion wrote in his diary: 'The Agricultural Center is requesting 22 settlement groups which are currently in [Palmach Brigades] ... 750 of them in the Yiftah Brigade, 220 in the Harel Brigade, 200 in the Negev Brigade ... the question is what should be done?'[54] After a month, the question arose as to whether this (i.e. channelling them to settlements) would bring about the dismantlement of entire units, at company and regiment level. Concerning this matter Ben-Gurion wrote: 'I said that if we decide, after an inspection of settlement sites and the military situation, to send out core groups ... we will reduce three brigades into two.'[55]

As indicated by their designated function, Palmach forces were from the start formed as groups intended for eventual settlement. The first Palmach companies on the kibbutzim were called 'training groups', mixing work and military exercises. The term 'training group' was originally meant to supply a convenient cover in order to avoid Mandatory suspicions. However, from the moment that the youth movements began to send their 'graduates' to the Palmach in an organized manner, the companies became agricultural training bodies in every sense of the word (some of them had already formed their own settlements before the State was established). In sum, from 1943 until its dismantling at the end of 1948, the Palmach organized 111 training groups. Of the 2,500 combatants in its services at the outbreak of the War of Independence, the majority, if not all, had undergone this training.

During the course of the war, the Palmach expanded from one brigade to three. Its ranks were filled by many who had not been members of these agricultural training groups, as well as quite a few recruits from abroad. In actual fact, towards the end of the fighting, with many of the 'original' Palmach soldiers killed or wounded, the number of foreign recruits (Gahal = new immigrants) among the Palmach units grew to such an extent that they now constituted a majority of the soldiers in its ranks. Some of these decided to join agricultural training groups, which now sought to realize their earlier-formulated settlement plans. Moreover, many Palmach training groups wanted to settle in areas where the fighting took place, areas where their comrades had fought and fallen. Settlement prompted by these considerations appeared as a memorial to the fallen and as means of preserving the ethos of the Palmach, which seemed on the verge of disintegration with the transition to statehood and the disbanding of its autonomous framework of the Palmach.

Echoes of these thoughts and feelings are found in the charter documents of kibbutzim established by the agricultural training groups during the first days of the State. For example, in the 11 April 1949 charter document of Kibbutz Palmachim, located close to Nebi Rubin on the Mediterranean coast, it was written:

> In our midst are native-born Israelis, members of the scouting movement and refugees from the Jewish holocaust in the Diaspora. It is the Palmach framework which has united us. Together, in the throes of battle and in the overcoming of difficulties in our path we bore the Jewish State; together we

struggled and suffered the birth pangs of the State and together
we came to build and be built by her. We are all disciples of the
Palmach. Nurtured from youth, we were forged by its vigorous
spirit and lofty values. Let the spirit of the Palmach continue to
direct and strengthen us in our new path and let the Palmach
be a torchlight for us, a light of settlement and defence as
towards its light we march.[56]

Ethos and pathos were not enough to draw all the Palmach veterans
to settlement, and definitely not for the long term. The list of dropouts
grew quickly as the training-group participants decided upon a course
of studies or took up positions in the different frameworks of the
young State (including the IDF). The fact that the war did not allow
core groups to consolidate with ease or to obtain orderly agricultural
training also harmed them. In summing up accounts, it turned out
that with the dismantlement of the Palmach at the end of 1948, there
were about 11,000 inductees (including the wounded and disabled
who did not go to settlements). About 2,000 among them were
residents of existing settlements, or kibbutz members who returned to
their homes; an additional 5,000 Palmach members joined new settlements.[57] More than half of the Palmach recruits, therefore, ended up in
settlements after the war. A check of the Harel Brigade reveals the
following facts: the total number of inductees preceding its disbanding reached 3,2000 men. Of this number, 416 fell during the war
campaign. The number of wounded and incapacitated was close to
200. Eight hundred stayed in the IDF ranks. Of the 1,800 demobilized
supernumeraries, 650 returned home to their kibbutzim. Of the
remaining 1,150 soldiers, 700 chose settlement. Some founded 14 new
settlements, others joined six existing kibbutzim. About 75 per cent of
the settlers were soldiers from abroad.[58]

   Before and immediately after the War of Independence, Palmach
training groups returning to civilian status reinforced 21 existing
settlements (among them 6 founded by Palmach veterans). The
majority of these settlements were situated on the frontier or had
been weakened during the course of the war. At the end of 1948 and
in 1949, Palmach agricultural training groups established 24 new
settlements. These groups made a decisive contribution to the stabil-
ity of the northern border of the State and created solid facts in
problematic areas, such as the hillsides around Jerusalem and in the
Negev. During its five years of settlement activity (1944–49), the
Palmach established and completed 52 settlements: 13 in Upper

Galilee, 5 in Lower Galilee, 6 in the Beit Shean Valley and Jezreel Valley, 6 on the Coastal Plain, 10 in the Jerusalem Hills, and 12 throughout the Negev.[59]

On 30 January 1949 the head of the army's Adjutant-General Branch transmitted an order from headquarters to all IDF units – the commanders of the various fronts, the brigades, districts, corps and services – to select groups of soldiers for agricultural settlement. 'It is incumbent upon unit commanders', read the instructions, 'to do everything within their power to bring about the successful implementation of this enterprise.'[60] According to the agreement concluded with the Agricultural Centre and settlement institutions, the IDF was obligated to send 300 soldiers per month to agricultural training. The background to this development stemmed from complaints by civilian bodies that settlement groups were not being demobilized in their entirety, thus adversely affecting their consolidation and their ability to organize for the purposes of founding new settlements. On the face of it, the army began to address the problem, but it quickly became apparent that the headquarters' order was not obligatory. Commanders in the field heeded it in accordance with the workload assigned to their units. A letter of 10 April 1949, from the commander of the Seventh Brigade to the head of the Adjutant-General Branch, provides evidence of this: 'Currently, we have been assigned operative duties', the brigade commander explained, 'that we can fulfill only with great difficulty, given the reduction in brigade manpower following the demobilization of a great number of our forces.'[61] Three months earlier, the headquarters of this same brigade had written to Levi Eshcol about the efforts undertaken within his military unit to organize soldiers' settlement groups (including English-speaking soldiers who wished to build their home in the country) and on the need to release these soldiers for agricultural training.

In other words, it was a change in circumstances which partly took the wind out of the sails of this undertaking. For example, only a third of the soldiers who received permission to take the agricultural training course in May 1949 actually did so. Furthermore, a month later, Chaim Krishfein was still forced to write to the Settlement Department of the Jewish Agency in the following terms:

> Despite the widespread investment of work and requests from every direction for a swift and general release of groups whose settlement locations have been arranged, the release has been

delayed. On the other hand, groups numbering 15–20 members, who are prepared to act as a vanguard for the group which will take possession and hold the land, are being released. In these latter cases, we suggest encouraging this positive development and avoid bringing about a break off of relations between the demobilized soldier and his core group.[62]

Despite this, many core settlement groups duly took advantage of the month of agricultural training allocated to them as well as the programmes that the Cultural Service of the IDF organized for them during that month. A salient example of this may be found in a story of the Yair core group, constituted at this time by veteran Lehi soldiers (Stern Group). It was clear to members of this core group and its leaders, who in the meantime had formed the short-lived Combatants Party, that the period of agricultural training was a *sine qua non* for the continuation of their initiative. The Division for Settlement in the Defence Ministry saw to their agricultural training arrangements at kibbutz Afikim, and welfare officers in the various units in which the 32 core group members served saw to it that the required leave of absence was provided. Members of Afikim welcomed them with open arms despite the ideological differences between them. The kibbutz secretary even requested that the welfare service extend the group's period of training until the date of their departure for settlement at the designated site. He wrote:

> We must note that members of the group show a serious attitude and great interest in the task which they set for themselves – the acquisition of agricultural training. In addition to their work in the various economic branches of the kibbutz, they have formed study groups in the various areas of agriculture. There is no doubt that the successful training of the group in advance of settlement is predicated on a more extended period of training.[63]

The IDF responded positively to the request – knowing that the core group was to establish a stronghold-settlement in the western Negev – and the training continued for another two-and-a-half months, until they departed for their site in June 1949. One of the core group members wrote the following in the Combatant Party's newspaper, *HaMa'as*:

The impression we made at the Kibbutz [Afikim] was very strong and surpassed the other training groups both in the organization of cultural life and also in responsibility toward work. If we take into consideration that not many among us, because of the conditions of the Underground, knew more than five people before we left for training, then one can understand how great this role was in uniting our comrades.[64]

In March 1949, a new idea was put forward in the field of IDF settlement activity – the founding of a school for the teaching of settlement enterprises. Beit Sturman, at Ein Harod, was established with the co-operation of the Cultural Department of the IDF and the Jewish National Fund. The initiator of the idea was Shmuel Saborai, a member of Ein Harod, who belonged to the second immigration wave. He was appointed commander of the school within several weeks of its establishment and given the rank of captain. The school programme included lectures on the following subjects: forms of settlement, basic factors in settlement, branches in agricultural settlement, crafts and industry in the village, settlement and culture, and settlement and defence. The regular course was designed for 10–14 days depending upon the composition of the students. Two additional courses were also planned: knowledge of settlement, an 'academic' course of four to five days; and getting to know settlement, a two-day introductory course for soldiers from abroad.

With the establishment of the school, Saborai turned to Jewish Agency institutions for funding.

Since the national funding institutions, together with the Settlement Department of the Agency are interested in directing army personnel – the best young forces in the nation – towards the path of settlement, we call your attention to the aforementioned school, which to a certain extent carries out your mission in the army set-up.[65]

The assistance requested was apparently not given, and the school for the teaching of settlement enterprises did not survive for long. At the end of May, the Cultural Department, for obvious reasons, requested the issuance of an order closing the unit: 'Since no particular specification was provided for the unit, there is no possibility of our allocating to it the minimal manpower.'[66]

In any case, the desire to prepare soldiers for agricultural settlement continued to occupy the settlement agencies and Ben-Gurion.
In the autumn of 1949, the Government established a Committee for
the examination of establishing agricultural farms in the Negev; the
committee submitted a report at the end of the year. Among its
conclusions was a suggestion for building two farms in the Negev
for the study of agriculture. These farms would serve in the army
framework as part of a year's agricultural training. The committee
stated that this was:

> an attempt to combine the solution to the problem of expand-
> ing agricultural studies for future settlers with their period of
> army service. The farms, which will be erected in the frontier
> areas, will also serve as defence centers and provide agricultural
> education and cultural activities for settlements in the area.[67]

Each one of them was designed to accommodate units of battalion
strength.

The committee even recommended that one of the farms be
established at Imra (Omer) and the other in the vicinity of Iraq El-
Manshiya (Hevel Lachish). It quickly became apparent that the
suggested sites lacked water, a factor which was sufficient to bring
about cancellation of the plan. At the same time, Chaim Gvati
claimed that the most efficient way to train inductees in agriculture
was through working in the kibbutzim, and on this matter he
succeeded in convincing everyone who was involved.

THE DEFENCE SERVICE LAW – 1949

Towards the end of March 1949, Ben-Gurion received a report
concerning 5,000 soldiers who were candidates for settlement
(excepting several, small, co-operative core groups). In his diary, the
Prime Minister noted that by July 1949, 7,500 soldiers had been
organized in 100 settlement groups, and that 3,000 from among them
had already been released for settlement. With regard to the remaining soldiers, he determined that:

> A joint committee of settlement bodies and the army will
> examine the situation of the army's settlement organizations,
> and enable the groups to depart for settlement, even if they

cannot release all group members. Regarding the release of individual soldiers the regulations will be different ... The Senior Committee for Discharging Soldiers will not decide ... but rather an army committee will decide in this matter. And military considerations will take preference over any other.[68]

Now, with the conclusion of the war, the IDF entered into a process of examination and re-organization. Its senior officers wanted to limit as much as possible the cuts in budget and allocation of manpower, and were not inclined to demobilize thousands of fit and experienced soldiers from the combat units to settlement objectives. Yigael Yadin, the number two man in the IDF and certainly slated to be appointed as Chief-of-Staff, was of the opinion that as long as the relations between Israel and the Arab states remained unclear, the State's security needs and the danger hovering over it required a large regular army on constant alert. Because he was aware of the high cost of maintaining such an army, Yadin suggested busying the soldiers in civilian tasks. 'Inasmuch as I see that funds cannot be found to maintain an army of 40,000 men and not even of 30,000 men, I say: place the burden of the problem of construction in the coming period on the army.[69]

Ben-Gurion, who related to the subject of national security from a wider perspective, devoted much time during this period to learning about the needs of the army and its organization. This stood him in good stead when he began to guide the passage of the Defence Service Law. This law, which received final approval on 15 August 1949, during the 68th sitting of the First Knesset, determined that the length of service for every young man and woman in Israel (including new immigrants up to age 26) would be two years. At the start, inductees would undergo basic military training for a period ranging from six weeks to three months; then they would be sent for a year of pioneer-agricultural training, accompanied by educational and cultural activity; the remainder of their time would be entirely devoted to military training and operational activities. All enlisted soldiers serving in the navy or air force were exempt from agricultural training. The Defence Service Law, therefore, regarded the IDF as an army which allots a considerable part of its time and activities to agricultural training, both for groups and for non-affiliated soldiers.

Ben-Gurion made the following remarks in his speech during the Knesset debate on the Defence Service Law:

The Defence Service Law which is before you is intended to impart to our army two basic characteristics required for our security: a military capability and a pioneering capability. The first year of service will be devoted principally to pioneering education in the army framework; after a few weeks of preliminary military training ... the age 18 and above cohorts, native born and immigrants, young men and women, will be sent for agricultural training. This will be accompanied by intensive cultural activity designed to inculcate the Hebrew language among youth who did not attend school or were deprived of it because of poverty, and to cultivate in the entire youth generation a sense of service, cooperative work, mutual help, responsibility, order and discipline, familiarity with the country, life in nature, and combatant and productive service. The agricultural training that will be given to all youth, including immigrants to age 26, has two objectives: military and settlement. According to the opinion of military experts with whom I consulted, including important experts from abroad, an efficient army will not arise in this country, a country of immigrants, if youth, and especially the immigrants among them, do not receive first of all agricultural education which will root them to the life of the homeland and accustom them to physical labor, teach them the language, overcome cultural gaps, induce order and discipline before they enter the regular army. Agricultural training will make the establishment of frontier settlements possible, for without them state security will not be firm. These border settlements will serve as the first defensive wall of the State of Israel. Not a wall of stones, but a living wall.[70]

Behind these words are hidden three worrisome facts: Israeli farmers were at this time cultivating only 10 per cent of the State's area; they were extracting only 15 per cent of the population's food from this cultivation (and thus there was no way of avoiding importing the remaining 85 per cent); beyond this there was an urgent need for diffusion of the population and the formation of a defensive belt of settlements in areas possessing strategic importance.

Of course, there was also the educational objective, which was mentioned in Ben-Gurion's remarks and repeatedly felt in his responses to those who disagreed with him:

The year of agricultural training is aimed first and foremost at the building of the people, of the blending of dust and man, that are gathering from the four corners of the world, into one national unit. To unite the fragments of the diaspora and the rent tribes and tie them together by bonds of language, culture, labour, settlement, knowledge of the country, love of homeland, mutual recognition, knowledge of the past, and a vision of our future.[71]

In practice, the content of the dual-character Defence Service Law quickly narrowed in its application to Nahal, but in the beginning the law served to accelerate the application of none too few soldiers to agricultural labour.

NOTES

1. Y. Slutzki (ed.), *The History of the Hagana*, Vol. 1, Part 2 (Tel Aviv: Am Oved, 1972), p.901. In the spring and summer of 1919, France and England were engaged in heated discussions regarding their respective areas of occupation in the Levant, and the King–Crane Commission was examining the narrower, but contentious, issue of territorial partition in Syria/Palestine. See Howard M. Sachar, *The Emergence of the Middle East: 1914–1924* (London: Allen Lane, 1970), especially ch.9, 'The Partition of the Levant', pp.252–90. The HaShomer were undoubtedly encouraged by ideological developments associated with the formation of the League of Nations, which gave a post-war voice in international political affairs to burgeoning communities seeking autonomy. Initially, the Shomer placed their trust in the British for carrying out the Wilsonian ideals in Palestine. For communal independence see Article 22.4 of the League's Covenant.
2. H. Givati, *One Hundred Years of Settlement* (Tel Aviv: HaKibbutz HaMeuchad, 1981), p.146.
3. G. Rivlin (ed.), *The Tel Hai Heritage* (Tel Aviv: Yad Tabenkin, 1992).
4. Y. Avidar, 'The Strategy of Settlement Before the Founding of the State', *Dapei Elazar* 3, Tel Aviv, 1981.
5. From a speech of Ben-Gurion before the Tel Aviv Workers' Council, 19 June 1948. In *When Israel Fought in Battle*, p.147.
6. D. Ben-Gurion, 'The Four Month Campaign and its Lessons', discussion at a session of the Zionist Executive on 6 April 1948, in *When Israel Fought in Battle*, p.91.
7. HALP 739/47, Protocol from one of the earliest meetings of the Committee for Settlement and Irrigation Problems in the State, p. 5.
8. SA, gimmel/5563/984, The Jewish Agency 1948–1951.
9. SA, gimmel/5493/2577, Sale of Government Lands to the JNF 1949–1950. Because of restrictions imposed by United States law prohibiting the transfer of philanthropic contributions to Palestine, the Government granted National Institutions permission to purchase land and responsibility for settlement. In this manner, American legal restrictions were by-passed, thereby allowing for the flow of philanthropic funds to national needs.
10. Weitz raised the idea of 'frontier guards' at a meeting with Y. Rochel (Avidar) on 23 October 1947 with the intention of winning him over to the idea. Weitz' position as head of the Negev Committee expresses the acceptance of the security conception that the process of settlement and the settlements themselves are part of the defence arrangements.
11. On the role of the Planning Branch in the Office of the Prime Minister, see *The Government Annual* for 1949.

12. CZA, File S15/9583 Ministry of Defence, Settlement and Soldier Rehabilitation, a document from 23 November 1948.
13. IDFA 1242/52–1, document of GHQ, Adjutant General Branch, to Yadin, 11 May 1948.
14. For a wide-ranging discussion concerning the position of the IDF with regard to the return of refugees, the destruction of Arab villages and the continuation of stronghold settlements, see B. Morris, *Birth of the Palestinian Refugee Problem, 1947–1949* (Tel Aviv: Am Oved, 1986), pp.184–265.
15. SA, 2426 9/48. Director of the IDF Intelligence Department to Shiloah, 16 June 1947. See also B. Morris, *Birth of Palestinian Refugee Problem*, p.193.
16. S. Shteptel, *Security Settlement and its Linkage to the War of Independence*, November 1947 – July 1948 (Tel Aviv: Ministry of Defence, 1992), pp.8–10.
17. IDFA 1166/57, Chief-of-Staff/Operations Branch/Settlement, June 1948, signed by the Deputy Chief-of-Staff.
18. IDFA 1186/782/65, in a letter directed to 'Amitai' [Ben-Gurion's code name], Eshel put forward the names of 13 sites which could be settled immediately. The plan was prepared with the co-operation of the settlement institutions and was ready for implementation irrespective of the ceasefire.
19. IDFA 1864/50, File no. 11, Chief-of-Staff/Operations Branch/Settlement Officer, 'Trends in Settlement', 1 August 1948.
20. Ibid., Report of September 1948, sent to L. Skolnik, Ministry of Defence, 3 October 1948.
21. IDFA 239/72, file 2156, 'Settlement Problems on the Bet Front', 28 February 1949.
22. See S. Shteptel, *Security Settlement*, p.17.
23. IDFA 1408/52, Document signed by the general of the Northern Command, Y. Avidar, 31 October 1949.
24. Ibid., 1408/52, Document from officer of General Staff Branch, GHQ, 3rd Brigade, Northern Command, 30 May 1950; ZA 389/1546, at Tserifin, summary of the department meeting with the army, 11 May 1951.
25. IDFA 108/52/106, File 31, General Staff Branch, GHQ, Operations Branch, February 1953 'Security Guidelines for Planning'. See a copy of the document at CZA S15/9786.
26. Ibid., 108/52/106, 'Protected Settlements – Conclusions', January 1950.
27. Ibid., p.1.
28. IDFA, 1166/51, GHQ/General Staff Branch – 8, 'The Agricultural Settlement and its Location', Document of the General Staff Branch/Department for Military Training, 'Sketches of Protected Moshavim', 30 March 1950.
29. IDFA 1408/52/9, Document from the northern General Staff Branch to A. Hertzfeld, The Agricultural Centre, 28 October 1949.
30. Ibid., Northern Command Settlement file. Exchange of letters between District 3 and Northern Command Headquarters concerning the exact location of Sasa on terrain of a destroyed Arab village, 13 March 1950.
31. IDFA 14-7/56, File 31, the office of the Head of General Staff Branch/Operations, general report, 6 June 1953.
32. IDFA 1166/51, General Staff Branch GHQ, document from head of General Staff/Operations Branch, Y. Rabin, to L. Eshcol, 18 June 1951.
33. CZA S15/9786, Letter from Lieutenant-Colonel D. Reshef to R. Weitz, 6 May 1951.
34. ZA 389/546 at Tserifin 'Debate About Settlement Matters 1951'. Summation of departmental meeting with IDF representatives, 11 May 1951.
35. IDFA 1166/52, GHQ/General Staff Branch – 8. See the document forwarded to the Chief-of-Staff on 15 March 1950, an accumulation of material touching on settlement in the Imra area. Report of the Engineering Corps, 14 March 1950; protocol from Review Committee 20 February 1950.
36. BGA, Ben-Gurion Diary, 27 September 1949.
37. IDFA 580/56, File 392, 14-7/56.31, Office of General Staff/Operations Branch, letter from Secretary of Kibbutz Sde Boker, 15 February 1953.
38. IDFA 79/54/27. The file contains much correspondence for the months March to May 1952. Included are lists of soldiers allocated for this teaching task. These letters also contain an order from the General Staff Branch and replies from the Manpower Branch which place a priority on every effort to seek out soldiers and free them for agricultural instruction.

39. IDFA 12/6/18mem, Circular from Cultural Service 316, 23 August 1948; *HaMagen*, nos 3–4, 15 October 1948, Jerusalem.
40. IDFA 794/50, Cultural Department, Section Titles for Information Dissemination, Weekly Review, 14 September 1948.
41. Ibid., 794/50, Development Problems in the Negev, 22 December 1948.
42. IDFA 1794/50/1, Settlement Day, promulgation of Order-of-the-Day (n.d.).
43. Ibid., Report of the Cultural Officer, Battalion 7, 22 October 1948.
44. IDFA 794/50, Cultural Department, Dissemination of Information in Newspapers File, 'The Soldier Settles', 14 October 1948.
45. 'An Army of Settlers – Towards Settlement Day in the Army', *Al Hamishmar*, 22 October 1948.
46. In *Davar, Ha'aretz* and *Al Hamishmar*, 28 October 1948.
47. Ibid.
48. *BaSa'ar*, Issue 5, Tishri 26, 1948.
49. IDFA 782/65/1186, Letter from Ben Tzion Israeli, 10 November 1949.
50. IDFA 67/51/228, 'The Department for the Soldier's Future – Structural Objective and Functions'.
51. IDFA 1551/51/223, Instructions from the Head of Manpower on order of the Chief-of-Staff in a circular signed by Lieutenant-Colonel Kit, 28 March 1949.
52. IDFA S15/9583, Document from C. Krishfein from the Section for Settlement and Soldier Rehabilitation, 17 December 1948.
53. CZA S15/9583, Document of the Ministry of Defence/Section for Soldier Settlement and Rehabilitation. Review of the activities of the Rehabilitation Section from 1 March 1949 to 1 March 1950, 12 March 1950.
54. BGA, Ben-Gurion Diary, 5 November 1948.
55. Ibid., 5 December 1948.
56. Charter document, Kibbutz Palmachim, 'Pages from the Palmach: 30 Years of the Palmach', 11 April 1949.
57. A. Tsizling, 'From the Palmach to Settlement', in Z. Gilad (ed.), *The Palmach Book II* (Tel Aviv: HaKibbutz HeMe'uched, 1956), p.712.
58. Ibid.
59. A. Brenner, *The Recruited Groups of the Palmach 1942–1948* (Ramat Eyfal: Yad Tabenkin, 1983).
60. IDFA 1368/50/25, Letter of Lieutenant-Colonel Kit, Manpower Branch, GHQ, 30 January 1949.
61. IDFA, 155/51/225, Letter from commander of the 7th Brigade to the head of the Adjutant General Branch, GHQ, 10 April 1949.
62. CZA S15/9583, Letter from the Ministry of Defence to the Settlement Department of the Jewish Agency, 29 June 1949.
63. H. Shalem, *To the Negev: Neve Yair – A Story of Settlement* (Tel Aviv: Yair, 1988:), p.13.
64. Ibid., p.25.
65. CZA S15/9583, letter of S. Saborai, 10 May 1949. School communications with institutions.
66. Ibid, Letter of Cultural Headquarters, 29 May 1949.
67. CZA S15/9602, Conclusions of the Committee for the Establishment of an Agricultural Farm and Agricultural Studies, December 1949; SA 2179 ג /5441, Letter from Halperin at the Agricultural Ministry regarding the aim of the committee, according to the suggestion of the Prime Minister, 10 October 1949; in the same file, 'The Committee's Conclusions'.
68. BGA, Ben-Gurion Diary, 20 July 1949.
69. Y. Greenberg, 'National Security and Military Power – Between Statesman and Military Commander', in *Studies in Zionism, the Yishuv and the State of Israel*, 1 (1991), pp.170–90. From the account of General Y. Yadin at a GHQ meeting, 16 April 1949.
70. National Service Law, 1949. In D. Ben-Gurion, *Army and Security*, p.107.
71. D. Ben-Gurion at the 76th session of the First Knesset, 5 September 1949, in Ibid., p.125.

Chapter 3
The Nahal

From its inception, the Nahal Corps – 'Nahal' is the Hebrew acronym for Pioneering Fighting Youth (Noar Halutzi Lohem)– was designated as an army unit that would combine military service with preparation for agricultural settlement and train its draftees for a life marked by volunteer activity. In retrospect, its birth was riveted in hard reality, in the dire shortage of combatant manpower during the first weeks of the State. In a diary notation dated 16 May 1948, Ben-Gurion wrote: 'People must be taken from the agricultural settlements.' Within a week, with the clear knowledge that this could severely harm morale, the productive capacity of the economy and the population's food supply (the very reasons that people from these sectors had not been not mobilized up to this time), he ordered the army to induct new immigrants and industrial workers.[1] When that proved insufficient, a Government session of 6 June 1948 decided to turn to an additional source: it ordered the mobilization of 17-year-olds, those born in 1931, with instructions to give them army training for two months and prepare them as reserve forces. At this same session, the Government decided that enlisting them for the military campaign would only be done on the basis of a special Government decision.[2]

The first contingent of recruits numbered 1,500 youth. They were sent for training at Camp 80, located beside the town of Pardes Hanna. Implementation of the programme was assigned to Gadna headquarters. Contrary to scheduled plans, instead of the youth being released after two months of basic military training, they were transferred, by Government decision, to various army units for vocational training. The decision was accompanied by an explicit instruction not to engage the new soldiers in battle actions unless so ordered by the Government.

Among the thousands of 17-year-old draftees were several hundred comrades belonging to the settlement core groups of the pioneering youth movements. They were linked to the kibbutz movement. The heads of the youth movements, already accustomed to a constant struggle with Palmach leadership on the issue of keeping the core groups intact, saw the Government decision as an explicit threat to the future of these groups. From their perspective, this also, by implication, had foreboding consequences for the future of settlement in general in the period following the War of Independence.[3] To cope with this threat, they relied upon the full weight and public standing of the youth movements. The comments of Dan Horowitz and Moshe Lissak are apposite in this regard:

> With the establishment of the State, the pioneering youth movements emerged as bodies possessing ideological con- scious-ness, social cohesion, and linkages to political institutions. These movements regarded pioneering Zionist ideology as the basis for their existence. Thus, they saddled themselves with a defined role in the national effort to build the country, namely, the realization of pioneering through settlement in the framework of the kibbutz and the kvutza [a diminutive for 'kibbutz' suggesting stronger communalism]. The educational system and the behavioral norms that developed within the movements relied upon a future-oriented, collectivist ideology which perceives member-ship in the youth movements as education for tomorrow in a context which builds and prepares the individual for realizing the goals of society.[4]

With this ideological underpinning, pioneering youth movements were able to gain the appreciation and support of the contemporary political leadership and some of the political parties. Moreover, they had an influential role not only in the very establishment of Nahal but also in the formation of Nahal's structure, the determination of its goals, the ways in which it was organized, its activities and all the remaining characteristics which marked its path over time.

Following extensive Defence Ministry debates focussing on the failure of the core groups formed from the 1931 age-cohort to bring about any practical integration between the army's needs and movement and settlement needs, the heads of the youth movements decided to turn directly to the Prime Minister. On 10 August 1948, representatives of the Akiva, Bnei Akiva, Ezra, Young Maccabees,

Scouting, United, Working Youth, Young Guard and Immigrant Camp movements wrote to him as follows:

> In connection with the discussion being conducted in the army concerning the future of members of these agricultural core groups and in the wake of the memorandums sent by us, Movement Secretaries met today. The meeting reaffirmed the position of the movements in favor of the establishment of a special framework for these core groups, which does not tie them to any army brigade, except for purposes of military training if this is warranted. In regard to the immediate future, it was decided to summon the core groups, including the girls, to agricultural settlements. If there is to be a continuation of military training, the integrity of the core groups must be preserved rather than be broken up into special army groups spread among the different brigades. We are following with trepidation the developments of the debate and fear the breaking-up of the core groups. We urgently request our presence at the debate and during any act of intervention.[5]

Following this letter Ben-Gurion held consultations with the Chief-of-Staff, Yaakov Dori, representatives of the Youth Branch at the Defence Ministry and personnel from Gadna Headquarters. Initial discussion revolved around the army's request for the mobilization of all manpower resources to combat brigades. An exception was made for high-school graduates who were to be assigned to the professional units – the airforce, navy, signal corps and artillery corps. Later in the discussion agricultural training and settlement needs were raised. The question arose whether there was room, from the vantage point of service conditions, for discriminating in favour of core group members of the youth movements, in comparison with their peers who were to be sent to regular brigades.

At the end of the exchange of views, Ben-Gurion agreed in principle to the demand of the youth movements, as is evidenced by his letter of response to them on 16 August 1948:

> Your desire to preserve the integrity of settlement core groups for the needs of settlement in the near future is basically correct and the Minister of Defence will give instructions to army headquarters in regard to this matter. It is blatantly obvious that as long as the War is not over, war needs and victory precede all other

considerations. Settlement core groups must not be allowed to unnecessarily disintegrate, and the Ministry of Defence willingly accepts your united stand of forming a special framework for the core groups, which will not be connected to any army brigade. After granting a week's leave, settlement core groups will have to continue their training in the fighting pioneer youth framework, and all measures for preserving the integrity of the core groups will be taken to the extent possible under war conditions.[6]

This is the first mention of the participation of a unit called Pioneering Fighting Youth, an idea that Ben-Gurion conceived during the course of the discussion, and which would soon be known by its acronym, Nahal.

The founding of Nahal took place at the same time that the Palmach was being disbanded. Moreover, at the very time that the establishment of Nahal was publicized, the Chief-of-Staff promulgated an order putting an end to the Palmach's taking in new groups of trainees who had just been inducted into the IDF. According to some researchers, the youth movements' request served as a pretext for Ben-Gurion to create a new military–state framework that would inherit the Palmach's crucial integration of security and settlement, while disassociating itself from the clear-cut political linkage to the upper echelons of the Palmach and from the influence of the Mapam Party. Shlomit Keren wrote:

> Abrogation of the historical relationship between the pioneering youth movements and the Palmach contributed somewhat to Ben-Gurion's objective of eliminating the influence of Mapam upon youth in the army and of grounding the security and pioneering heritage of the Palmach in a statist framework. According to this conception, Nahal was founded as an instrument for the realization of political objectives.[7]

Eyal Kafkafi adds:

> The connection between the establishment of Nahal and the disbanding of the Palmach was completely transparent to Mapam members at the time. It was clear to them that Ben-Gurion's aim was the disbanding of the Palmach and not simply the Palmach headquarters, as Ben-Gurion and Mapai party members claimed at the time. Preparations for disbanding the Palmach were

lengthy and planned; they involved, among other things, personal changes in the Gadna command and the insertion of Ben-Gurion loyalists into this framework. These steps played a key role in distancing the pioneering movements from the Palmach and bringing about their transference to Nahal.[8]

Anita Shapira held a similar view of these developments:

> It appears that Ben-Gurion sought to replace one military elite with another, an avant-guard of one type with an avant-guard of another type. He truly believed, and naively at that, that there was no longer any need for voluntary organizations, and that through the assistance of the state and its power, the same preparedness, the same enthusiasm, the same self-sacrifice in which people excelled, could be attained ... The state will establish a more praiseworthy 'Palmach', wider in scope, through the Party [Mapai].

In her conclusion Shapira adds that even if it were possible to understand the thoughts and considerations of Ben-Gurion, the timing and the way in which the Palmach was disbanded and Nahal established leave a bitter taste.[9]

Yoav Gelber, in contrast, praised Ben-Gurion as a person ahead of his generation for his grasping the State as an expression of Jewish sovereignty and as someone who fought for a pioneering statist path under clearly changing circumstances. Nonetheless, he too noted the connection between the two developments and claimed that:

> Before Ben-Gurion attempted to disband Palmach headquarters, he had to satisfy the Party and the settlement movements associated with it on an additional matter: the finding of a voluntary service niche for graduates of the youth movement which would permit them to preserve, especially while on active duty, the movement's character and the special social framework of the training group which was preparing itself for independent status.[10]

In any case, it is clear that ideological and party dissensions caused Mapai people and the youth movements connected to the party (their representatives were among the signers of the letter to Ben-

Gurion) strongly to oppose the new initiative. It was also clear that they were not strong enough to nip this in the bud. Thus, the Palmach was disbanded and the Nahal corps was formed as part of the IDF without any extra-statist label.

On 12 September 1948, the Chief-of-Staff published an order relating to Gadna's structure and aims. A special section in the order dealt with the creation of Nahal. It read:

> In order to preserve the pioneering element of the settlement enterprise the entity will comprise a special framework within the Gadna. This framework will include all the settlement core groups organized in the youth movements and in immigrant youth who are affected by mobilization order no. 31 or any other mobilization order and it will be called: Pioneering Fighting Youth (NAHAL). These core groups will also include young women. Nahal is subject to the same call-up orders and arrangements as Gadna except for those matters which touch on their organizational, educational, and social needs as groups destined for agricultural settlement.[11]

In addition, the same order determined that a special office in the Youth Branch of the Defence Ministry (which soon became the Department of Youth and Nahal) would be responsible for the integrity of the core groups and their preparation for settlement as a social pioneering body. The head of this office was, in effect, put in charge of Nahal unit commanders and the carrying out of Nahal goals – as long as his decisions did not interfere with the regular training and army exercises. If from a time perspective one wonders about the initial linkage between (pre-army) Gadna and Nahal (which was to occupy a conspicuous place within the military structure), it should be recalled that behind the initials of the acronyms stand the words 'youth battalions' and 'pioneer fighting youth'. 'Youth' encompassed simultaneously the combatant and pioneering functions.

The first head of the Department of Youth and Nahal was Eliahu (Elik) Shomroni, a member of Kibbutz Afikim, and a staunch Ben-Gurion supporter. He was among the conceptual formulators of Nahal, played a central role in the establishment of the corps, and left his imprint on its way of life. The objectives and principles of Nahal according to Shomroni were:

- forming an army which devotes part of its time to nation-building
- educating citizens for combat and settlement – a sort of synthesis between a pioneer who is prepared to settle the wasteland and build the homeland and a soldier who possesses the quintessential martial characteristics and is prepared under emergency conditions to sacrifice himself for his country
- cultivating pioneering values and a defender-tradition joined to loyal citizenship and combining them in the military service framework
- devising a full, seamless integration of Nahal's military mission into the general IDF framework in accord with instructions determined by the Supreme Command
- serving as a melting pot for the masses of young immigrants throughout the diaspora, thereby accelerating the process of their being rooted in the homeland as a merged national entity
- encouraging every sign of social cohesion among those core groups whose aim is pioneering settlement and expansion of the productive agricultural foundation, while at the same time exhausting all capacities and possibilities in the military sphere
- cultivating the settlement instinct among 'unaffiliated' soldiers, especially those who are new immigrants
- assigning priority to the frontier and the Negev and making these barren areas bloom to the enhancement of the Nahal missions
- providing Jewish, Zionist and pioneering education and cultivating an authentic Israeli experience, with the intention of creating a pedagogical environment within the army framework capable of elevating the soldier's spirit and culture
- achieving Nahal's objectives through living conditions, frameworks and real instruments such as: the blending of work and military training exercises, agricultural instruction, vocational training, contact with nature, the fortifying of body and spirit through work and field conditions, marches and field trips, familiarity with the country, acquaintance with the Hebrew village and its economic, social and cultural accomplishments, the bequeathing of the Hebrew language to new immigrants, a complete system of military training and preparation and finally, commanders-instructors who set a personal example for those under their command.[12]

These purposes and principles constituted the basis and the platform for the activities of Nahal during the first years of the State.

THE FIRST STEPS

Nahal headquarters, it should be recalled, was initially a secondary element in Gadna. The first commander of the comprehensive framework was a person from the kibbutz movement, Elhanan Yishai, a staunch supporter of Ben-Gurion. Much later, Yishai testified that the most important operation by far in those days was 'the establishment of preliminary frameworks for Nahal leading to its military and civil integration, namely, the creation of the first settlement core groups, the agreements with the kibbutzim, and the first patterns.'[13]

The first Nahal soldiers consisted of five settlement core groups from Working Youth, the United Movement, Bnei Akiva, the Scouts and Young Maccabees. Prior to the recruitment stage, two additional core groups were at the training base – the Immigration Camp Movement and the Young Guard. These latter groups, under the inspirational direction of their political patron, the Mapam party, opposed the establishment of Nahal. Practical expression of this opposition occurred when members of these core groups were mobilized hurriedly and by stealth into the Palmach and were sent – 'smuggled' according to Ben-Gurion's diary – to the kibbutzim of Menara (United Kibbutz movement) and Ayalon (National Kibbutz movement).[14]

The circumstances and background controversy, including its association with the not-so-military Gadna, created great difficulties during Nahal's foundation. Many of Nahal's problems were connected with the mobilization of manpower for command duties and military instruction, while other problems clustered around logistics. Many years later, Tzvi Levanon, one of the first Nahal soldiers and its commander for a lengthy period, wrote of 'the shortage of blankets, boots and food in the camp; sometimes we walked barefoot – the situation was disgraceful'.[15] Obstacles of the first type gave birth to unauthorized actions by Nahal commanders, such as the partisan recruiting of commanders from kibbutz members and other brigades. The second type brought about the establishment of the Nahal Fund. This fund may never have been founded had it not been for the establishment of a 'parents committee' operating in tandem with Nahal. This phenomenon was unprecedented in military tradition. The 'parents committee' organized a protest demonstration opposite the office of the Prime Minister. Only afterwards, with the direct intervention of the Prime Minister, was the full complement of basic equipment supplied to the first contingent of Nahal recruits.

Even so, they were still compelled to do the preliminary stage of military training at the former British army camp – Camp 80 – which, at this time, was abandoned and in ruins. After completion of this stage of their training, the Nahal contingents were transferred to the military airbase at Ramat David, where they received instruction in routine airforce activities such as loading bombs on aircraft and rendered assistance in guarding the base's installations. They continued with these duties even after the first agreement between the Defence Ministry and the kibbutzim was signed and the period of agricultural training at neighbouring kibbutzim had begun.

On 19 October 1948 the second contingent of Nahal recruits began their army service. This comprised 15 youth groups belonging to the Youth Aliya movement. It was mobilized following the agreement among branches of the settlement movement, the Jewish Agency, and the Executive Committee of the Federation of Labour (Histadrut). In the actual agreement, induction was confined to those youths who had resided at least nine months in the country. In addition, it was determined that after three months of concentrated military training each youth group would return to its own kibbutz to complete the compulsory education phase of their studies, provided that the security situation did not require continuation of military service. The mobilization of these youth groups, whose members were for the most part new immigrants without a home or family in the country, contained a special significance for the social and educational activity of Nahal. It provided an opportunity to reinforce their integration into the army and, following that, into Israeli society as a whole. This was certainly an entirely different initiative from that marking the mobilization and induction phase of the native-born Nahal recruits.

One of the innovatory elements associated with this second contingent of recruits was a get-together of the settlement core groups, a social gathering of young men and women from all the groups with members of the kibbutz to which they were assigned. Representatives of the movements were also present and their main role was to clarify social and organizational problems. Another innovation was connected to the Nahal long march 'following the path of the IDF's conquest of the Galilee'. At the conclusion of the first march in 1948, Nahal held its inaugural convention. Seventeen companies, in the presence of the Prime Minister, participated in this event. Ben-Gurion lectured the young soldiers on the topic 'An Army for Defence and for Construction' and brought to their attention the essence and purpose of Nahal. He gave an historical survey of the intertwined problems of settlement and security, from the period of the first encampments through the 'HaShomer' organization, the Hagana, the Jewish Legion and the Palmach and then placed Nahal in the line of descendants of these earlier undertakings:

> The security of the state will not be founded on the army's defensive strength alone. The ways in which we undertake settlement will determine state security no less than the building up of the army. Only dense agricultural settlement along the borders can serve as the most reliable shield for the country's defence against external attack. Our security settlements in the Negev must remain military security settlements. We will have to defend all this with the might of our weapons for a very long time. But security settlements alone are not enough – every location where we can guarantee a constant flow of water must be turned immediately into an agricultural settlement manned by soldiers. This is the special mission of the settlement core groups inducted into Nahal – a mixture of military training and physical prowess with agricultural and settlement training.[16]

A month after this convention, the Security Committee of the settlement movements received the design for new framework. This body examined Nahal in the context of the security system and on 11 February 1949 recommended that the Nahal framework be extended to all Israeli youth. The Committee stated that control over the country following the War of Independence meant the addition of hundreds of agricultural settlements and this entailed the establishment of a special type of framework to ensure that people got to these rural areas. In the meantime, however, despite these general agreements, and despite the backing of Ben-Gurion for the establishment and upkeep of Nahal, the confrontations and opposition to the military status of Nahal soldiers did not cease. Indeed, these confrontations lasted for a very long time.

In the 14 months between the promulgation of the order of the Chief-of-Staff with regard to Gadna and Nahal (12 September 1948) and the issuance of instructions from the Supreme Command on the establishment of Nahal as an independent body (24 November 1949), the Nahal forces were the object of suspicions and criticism on the part of military echelons to which they were subordinate. Indeed, there was a forthright lack of co-operation. An outstanding example of this occurred in a debate on the 1931 cohort and Nahal held on 24 March

1949 at the Ministry of Defence and headed by Ben-Gurion. Many security system chiefs and senior officers alike demanded that Nahal soldiers and prospective recruits be directed to the professional corps (navy, airforce, engineering, etc.). Shomroni, who presented an overview of Nahal's situation after seven months raised a central question: 'Was the founding of Nahal a temporary injunction to be discontinued after a particular time of need or was it a permanent order?'[17] Ben-Gurion asked him in return: 'If we take not the enthusiasm of the Palmach but rather the pioneering value of settlement which was unique to it, is Nahal a continuation of this?' Shomroni's response was brief: 'Yes, there is a division of this sort which continues that which was once the Palmach.'[18]

Consequently, Shomroni requested that the framework be expanded in such a way that it would not only embrace graduate recruits from the youth movements but all youth – at least during their first year of service – in order to train them and bring them closer to agricultural labour and settlement. This request was made against the background of security and economic constraints. Nahal, according to this proposal, was to serve as a melting pot for thousands of new immigrants and native-born Israelis, forging an Israeli experience before their dispersal, because of military requirements, throughout the IDF. Shomroni did not forget to emphasize that the soldiers' salary for agricultural labour would be transferred to the defence system and would add to budgetary savings. Likewise, he sought to establish battalion headquarters throughout the country to control Nahal platoons scattered among the kibbutzim, and stated that these platoons were to be integrated into the broader defence programmes when operational exercises were carried out.

Lieutenant-Colonel Israel Bar, the head of the Planning Department at General Staff Branch, GHQ, was quick to voice his reservations (which were, in effect, the reservations of the IDF's senior command). 'What does this give the army?' he asked Shomroni. 'Let us suppose that through this you achieve mobilization for the purposes of settlement, what does the army, whose function is to guarantee the security of the state, get out of it?'[19] Chief-of-Staff, Yaakov Dori expressed similar views: 'The narrow interests of the army', he said, 'do not justify the existence of Nahal.' In response to a question of Ben-Gurion, he pointed out that the IDF had need of quality manpower – especially in the airforce, the navy and the standing army – and he added that the length of service required to prepare professional corps is at least two years.

Now we must clarify to ourselves how we can exploit these two years [of compulsory army service] in the most efficient manner. If this is a standing army that requires high specialization, we must utilize it only for military training. In my opinion, there is a loss to the military as well; indeed, we want to employ youth of this age for very special things: armored corps, communications, artillery, and so forth – those areas for which training requires an extended amount of time. If we only have two years available and if ten months of this time is allocated to these youths working on kibbutzim – the conclusion is that only 50 per cent of the time will remain for purely military matters. This is a serious matter which cannot be ignored.[20]

At the end of this long debate, Shomroni's proposal was accepted with limitations, but the Chief-of-Staff continued to stick to his position:

I am ready to accept this proposal on condition that conscription begin at age 17, but army service will begin at age 18. In this instance, I want this program to guarantee the time required for training and army maintenance, so that it will be a standing army ... I am returning to my proposal, namely that conscription of 17-year-olds be not into the army but into the national service; army service begins at age 18.[21]

However, Ben-Gurion was also obstinate. He concluded the discussion with the decision that the Nahal framework would be inserted into the IDF structure. Following these discussions, the Defence Service Law was formulated, the very law which constituted the legal basis for the establishment of Nahal.

THE FIRST BATTALION

In the meantime, the first Nahal battalion was formed within the organizational structure of the Gadna. Following the first and second contingents (the latter finished its training in December 1948 and its recruits were scattered among frontier kibbutzim, where they underwent agricultural training), a third contingent was formed (this group finished its training in April 1949 and its members were similarly scattered among frontier kibbutzim). Nahal now comprised

24 platoons – one platoon per kibbutz – which were organized into three companies: Company 'A' in the Jezreel Valley, Company 'B' in the south of the country, and Company 'C' in the Jordan Valley. The Company functioned as a general organizational framework for Nahal units in given settlement areas, and the battalion served as an organizational unit for the Companies.

It should be pointed out that the first Nahal platoons were sent to those kibbutzim which had been badly damaged in the fighting and resultant siege. Two platoons reinforced the kibutzim of Ein Gev and Masada which had been almost totally destroyed by the Syrian army. These kibbutzim, which had also suffered from extensive desertion, faced the critical question as to whether they had the power to continue to exist. There is no doubt that Nahal reinforcements enabled them to respond positively to this question. The integration of Nahal soldiers into the kibbutz economy enabled them to recuperate from their difficult situation and provided hope for the future.

In January 1949 an additional settlement challenge faced the first battalion under the command of Mordecai Tamir (Lipsky). The settlement institutions demanded that Nahal send soldiers out to settle two new locations: Tse'elim in the Negev and Rosh Hanikra on the northern border. Tse'elim, in fact, entailed resettlement of a place which had its beginnings on 7 February 1947, became a military base during the War of Independence and was destroyed and abandoned in the course of the fighting. Rosh Hanikra was the first security settlement formed after the War of Independence; it was situated in an isolated area and was settled under the most difficult of conditions. Nahal carried out its mission in each of these cases (at Rosh Hanikra they shared the assignment with a core group of veteran Palmach soldiers).

In the next stage, soldiers of the first Nahal battalion were called upon to strengthen the security of settlements along the eastern shores of the Sea of Galilee. They were situated directly below the line of Syrian fortifications on the Golan Heights. From the historical-Zionist perspective, this step was also undertaken in order to relieve kibbutz Ein Gev from the isolation it had suffered since its founding in 1937. From a political perspective, this was an initiative designed to create de facto Israeli sovereignty over an area that was a subject of contention with Syria, and which had been declared a demilitarized zone in the ceasefire arrangements.

On 29 August 1949 the Tel Hai core group, composed of graduates from the Youth Aliya educational programme associated with the

kibbutz movement, founded Kibbutz Ha'On on land belonging to
the abandoned village of Samara. The launching of the settlement
was carried out in a military framework – Operation Kinneret Wall –
which caused a public stir. Members of the core group underwent
their final preparations at Ein-Gev. In the departure ceremony held
for them, Kibbutz member Zeev Ritter stated:

> We have reached a great moment, a moment in which a group
> of youth departs from us for settlement in this very area.
> During the time of the State's existence there have been many
> settlement launchings, all of which have had one thing in
> common – settlement in the wake of military conquest. Here we
> have launching of a different type, rare in the State of Israel, but
> widespread in the history of our settlement, namely that it is
> necessary to pre-empt through facts and deeds in order to
> acquire rights for immigration and settlement. And this
> morning, as our boats approached the shore we were about to
> conquer, I recalled how the clandestine Jewish immigrants
> ventured to the trackless shore, how we conquered parts of our
> homeland. And similarly with tonight's launching. In this
> manner, we succeeded in breaking the resistance of a great and
> alienating power. This path also lies before us tonight. We must
> cling to the shores which others threaten to cut off, thereby
> undermining our Jewish control.[22]

Members of the core group set sail from Ein Gev and within an hour
harboured at the Ha'On shore where they began foundation work.
Until early dawn they dug trenches and defence positions, set up
fences and the first huts. In the meantime, lorries brought manpower
reinforcements and heavy equipment from Ein Gev, thus speeding up
the work. At the end of the first day Elik Shimroni stated:

> The joy of settling on this patch of land, the link which connects
> the eastern shore of the Sea of Galilee with the settlements in
> the Jordan Valley and its western shore, is in effect a triple joy:
> it is the joy of Ein Gev which has emerged from siege after 12
> years of isolation and the nature of whose suffering only a few
> from the 'stockade and tower' locations of 1938–1939 have lived
> through; the joy of the core group which took part in all the
> pioneering efforts of our generation – the illegal immigration
> and detention in Cyprus, the agricultural training and military

defence, the induction into the army and military training – until we reached this moment of launching at this precious spot filled with magic and possibilities; and it is a joy of the youngest brigade in the Israel Defence Forces – the Nahal brigade – which today, for the first time, is contributing one of its core groups to permanent settlement.[23]

On 6 November 1949, Kibbutz Tel Katzir, situated close to Kibbutz Ha'On, was founded. Members of the Scouting Movement, core group 7, who were inducted into the IDF in June 1948, arrived at the fortified heights of Tel El-Kaser, which during the battles served as a Syrian artillery position and rained havoc on settlements in the Jordan Valley. Establishing a hold on this height had special importance in light of the fact that IDF forces did not succeed in conquering it, and its inclusion in the demilitarized zone was reached only in the negotiations which culminated in the ceasefire agreement. This time, as well, swift military action was undertaken in which Nahal soldiers invested a great deal of physical effort. But the story did not end there. In the first place, because of the great sensitivity of the place, shooting incidents took place almost on a daily basis. Secondly, because of a lack of water sources, the founders of Tel Katzir had to rely upon water supplied in containers, and the delay in setting up a power line did not make the conditions of life any easier. Thirdly, most of the area initially allocated for settlement was not suitable for agricultural cultivation, and thus economic difficulties could be expected. Nevertheless, Nahal soldiers were regarded as enthusiastic adherents of the idea. Perseverance in their mission allowed the settlement to survive and led to land being cultivated right up to the very border with Syria.

On 29 August 1949, the day on which Kibbutz Ha'On was founded, a core group from Noar Ha'Oved set out to restore the collective settlement of Abuka in the Beit Shean Valley. The former inhabitants had all scattered. Nearly three months later, on 20 November, a core group from HaPoel HaMizrahi composed of veteran Youth Aliya, founded Tsur Maon in the Negev. At the same time, core groups of the first Nahal battalion who had finished their period of training joined the young kibbutzim of Hatzerim, Mishmar David, Rosh Hanikra, Revadim, Sa'ar and Beit Ha'Emek and the moshavim of Kfar Yavetz, Shavey Tsion and Ramot Meir.

The broad settlement activities of Nahal during its first year helped it to overcome initial, obstructive conditions, including those caused by high echelons in the IDF; it also managed to establish firmly its standing in public opinion, and to increase the number of supporters advocating expansion of its ranks. In addition to all this, Nahal became involved in two pioneering ventures, Operation Solel and Operation Arava. Both operations were consonant with its basic principles and won widespread public approval.

Operation Solel arose out of ramifications stemming from Operation Uvda, the last of the operations during the War of Independence, which had brought IDF soldiers to Ein Gedi. As a result of this action, IDF forces controlled the entire western side of the Dead Sea, from Ein Gedi south to Sodom, but the connection between the two points was by sea only and created obvious security difficulties. Thus it was decided to pave a land route as quickly as possible from Sodom to Ein Gedi, a distance of 50 miles marked by rocky and rugged terrain. Building the road was assigned to Nahal. The order for Operation Solel proclaimed:

> On Sunday, the fourth of Nissan [Hebrew month], 1949, ten days before the Passover holiday, which celebrates our freedom, Nahal units stationed on their frontier settlements will rise to the occasion, and depart for the vast desert expanses in order to pave a road. This paved road will connect different settlement points. It will be an additional stage in bringing about an attachment of the young generation to places that shaped and were the courageous and powerful source of the ancient heroism of the State of Israel.[24]

Management of the operation was given to the Engineering Corps whose personnel laid out the plans. But it was the 550 Nahal soldiers who carried out the burdensome work, with their own hands and without any engineering tools. They topped off their four days of road-building by ascending to the top of the legendary stronghold of Massada, located beside the main road they had constructed.

Two months later, in June 1949, Nahal undertook Operation Arava, also an extension of Operation Uvda. Operation Arava was intended to fortify the Eilat area (whose conquest was the peak achievement of Uvda). In an order promulgated on 19 June 1949, the Operation's objectives were described in the following words:

1. The carrying out of construction work on the shores of the Gulf of Eilat according to the plans and methods determined by the rear area staff responsible for the Operation.

2. The forging of body and spirit in pioneering tasks and additional conquests during the course of the construction.
3. Prominent exhibition of the pioneering spirit embedded in Nahal.
4. Familiarity with the surrounding environment and its conditions of existence.[25]

Three companies took part in the seven-week long Operation Arava. The sweltering heat, supply difficulties, a shortage of water and the remoteness of the location created difficult working conditions for the soldiers but did not weaken their efforts. A member of the Engineering Corps in charge of the working plans had this to say at the conclusion of the Operation:

> The Nahal contingent exuded a spirit of pioneering labor in the Arava, and in particular at Eilat. It is noteworthy that this spirit continued to exist in Eilat long after the Nahal soldiers had departed. Clearly this was a personal and important educational experience to each and every one of the participants in the Operation.[26]

The newspaper daily, *Haaretz*, which was not prone to lavish excessive praise on the Nahal Corps, wrote:

> Their productive work supercedes that of the skilled laborer working in incomparably more comfortable conditions. Only unshakable faith and devotion to the mission could infuse the heart of these youths with the perseverance, with the magic of joy which unconsciously overcomes all the difficult things in life.[27]

The pioneering spirit created around the activities undertaken by the Nahal at Sodom and the Arava and the public enthusiasm which it stimulated were of greater import than the deeds themselves. Many of those who opposed the formation of Nahal, on the grounds that there was no vital need for creating this special framework within the army's ranks, changed their opinion following Nahal's role in the building of security settlements and the execution of pioneering operations in the south of the country.

At the Nahal dress parade which took place at the termination of Operation Arava, the Chief-of-Staff, Ya'akov Dori, praised the work undertaken. His concluding remarks contained more than hints concerning the future of Nahal:

This operation is reliable evidence that the pioneering ethos among Jewish youth has not faded and that there are organizational ways in which it can be integrated into the structure and military functions of the army. I offer you my congratulations and esteem for the wonderful work you have done. You have the right to be proud of it and perhaps the principle reward for your extensive efforts will be the great host of Jewish youth in the country who will shortly join your ranks. You will not remain few for long. Security needs together with settlement needs demand that Nahal's path be converted into a channel which others will follow.[28]

The Defence Service Law, passed by the first Knesset in the summer of 1949, specified, among other things, that the Minister of Defence would institute regulations guaranteeing the safeguarding of the integrity of the settlement core groups until their departure to the settlements. These regulations, which defined the membership of the settlement core groups as well as membership obligations and privileges, were published in due course in regulation booklet no. 54, on 12 December 1949. In addition, they stipulated the preliminary course of Nahal, namely mobilization of all members of the core group on the same date; the inductees would undergo basic training together at one base and then be assigned immediately to agricultural training in a central instruction location.

In February 1950, the Knesset passed an amendment to the Defence Service Law. The amendment was proposed in response to pressure from the Supreme Command, who insisted that patterns of obligatory service, as outlined in the original formulation of the law, constituted a decree that the IDF could not uphold. (An inscription in Ben-Gurion's diary of 8 February 1950 reads as follows: 'Shaul [Avigur] pressured as well and I agreed with great reluctance.')[29]

The revised law read as follows: 'The Minister of Defence has the right to order a deferral of regular service in agricultural training with regard to those 18 years or older who enlisted in the army or, despite the above clause (1), to order, in whole or in part, regular service which is not associated with agricultural training.'[30] In other words, the amendment to the law authorized the Minister of Defence to release soldiers, with no limit on their numbers, from obligatory agricultural training, except for members of the settlement core groups. Consequently, the scope of Nahal inductees was considerably reduced. In the service framework combining military

and agricultural training, only members of the core group, 'unaffiliated' soldiers, and new immigrants who required special absorption
conditions and pre-army preparation, remained. However, the
intention and the goals which created the basis for Nahal's establishment were not uprooted.

Ben-Gurion himself understood that army needs required these
changes and he implemented them in a practical way. Nevertheless,
he made sure that the above amendment in the Defence Service
Law would be a temporary measure, subject to renewal, only as
long as there was a need for it. Elhanan Yishai, the first commander
of the Gadna (including Nahal), recalled this matter at a much later
time.

> Ben-Gurion knew that the Law in its present form was not one
> hundred percent realistic. He knew that there were male and
> female soldiers who, in light of the security situation, could not
> abide by the Law's requirements, but he thought that in the
> future, when there would be peace or when the army would be
> large enough, the State would be able to apply the Law in its
> literal sense.[31]

In the meantime, despite all the reservations, on 24 November
1949, the IDF Supreme Command promulgated an order for the
establishment of the Nahal Corps as an independent unit,
completely separate from Gadna. Ben-Gurion personally
appointed Yitzhak Pundak as commander of the new corps and
told him:

> This is the future image of the Jewish soldier. I know that the
> army objects; some of their objections are based on valid claims,
> but this is the image of the future soldier. We have no money. To
> a certain extent, labor and military training will make it easier to
> budget the army. However, the main concern is not the core
> groups, but rather the 'unaffiliated' soldiers. They must learn to
> know and love the country.[32]

Between the lines of the order-of-the-day, promulgated by Pundak
immediately upon assuming his military duties, can be detected the
struggle waged by him and his colleagues against an army 'up in
arms' over the recognition of Nahal as a corps with rights on a par
with the other IDF corps. Pundak wrote:

On this day on which the order of the Supreme Command has been published, Nahal has departed from its narrow, unfamiliar framework, from a framework sparsely filled with soldiers, to a broad-based entity prepared to take in thousands of new recruits, instigate regular military training and military discipline, undertake agricultural labor and attachment to the kibbutz, and protect the borders of the country through the establishment of a continuous chain of frontier settlements defended by the best of Jewish youth ... Today we are few, without an adequate number of commanders and sergeants, without a framework, without training camps. We lack vehicles and equipment. But in one thing we are rich. In our hearts, there stirs the recognition that we have been summoned to a great undertaking, that we are creating something from nothing, that slowly, slowly the corps will rise.[33]

The Chief-of-Staff's order establishing Nahal defined its structure and organization, the conditions of service and the plans governing military and agricultural training. Among its stipulations was the directive that:

Nahal is an organizational framework for the absorption of enlisted soldiers during the first year of their regular service and for all practical purposes will be considered an indivisible part of the Israel Defence Forces ... The terms of service for headquarters, instructional and administrative staff of the Nahal Corps will be identical to the service conditions in units of the regular army. Service in Nahal will be considered for all practical purposes as full-fledged army service. The status of a Nahal commander will be identical to the standing of a first officer of a corps ... The training program will be determined by the head of the General Staff Branch GHQ Instructional Department in coordination with the commander of Nahal, with attention to values specific to Nahal such as education for security settlement and consolidation of settlement core groups.[34]

According to the order, Nahal units were organized in platoons of 50 male and female soldiers. Four platoons constituted a company and were set up alongside nearby settlement locations. The battalion framework comprised five companies, which constituted an organizational and administrative area headquarters. With regard to Nahal military objectives, each battalion was placed under the appropriate area command authority for regular security measures, and was available as an IDF reinforcement unit subject to operational needs. The military settlements were integrated into the defence layout of the area and were subordinate, in all matters connected to tactical operations, to the appropriate echelon in the area command. A special clause in the Nahal Establishment Order instructed each and every core group to set aside 15 per cent of its members for command duties outside the core group framework. An additional 5 per cent was selected for command duties following the completion of the first year of service. These instructions were intended to provide a solution to the problem of natural growth of reserve commanders in Nahal.

However, the Defence Service Law and the order for its establishment did not solve many of the difficult problems confronting Nahal commanders during its first years. Nahal continued to be a 'stepson' within the IDF framework, and most, if not all, IDF commanders continued to oppose its very existence. Echoes of the bitterness and frustration which engendered this orientation may be found in the following remarks by Pundak:

> Within the IDF, people did not know at all what Nahal was, and there was a tendency to drag out the matter of its establishment. All army personnel opposed the formation of Nahal, especially veterans of the Jewish Brigade, who viewed Nahal as a continuation of the Palmach with all its problems of discipline and politicization. Moshe Dayan was opposed to the formation of Nahal because he feared that the settlement core framework would take away the best of the youth, and instead of assuming command duties, they would 'grow potatoes'. Another problem, raised by Chaim Laskov, was the joint service of men and women. His opposition was expressed in the question: 'How many children will be born following the formation of the first joint contingent of Nahal?' Ben-Artzi, who was head of Quartermaster-General Branch, GHQ, opposed Nahal, and did not assist in the allocation of camps and requested equipment. It would have been possible to establish a Nahal framework if the army had not been opposed to it. But the opposition was carried on over a length of time, disrupting Nahal development and the realization of its basic objectives.[35]

Moshe Netzer, who was a second to Pundak and succeeded him as commander of Nahal (1950–54), was also witness to the difficult problems connected with the founding of the Corps. In his memoirs, he related, among other things, that the IDF abdicated its responsibility for establishing Nahal encampments and demanded that this burden be placed on the kibbutzim. In the end, the Defence Ministry allocated funds for this.[36]

Despite the difficulties, Nahal formed eight battalions within the first 30 months of its existence. These units were dispersed throughout the entire country (including boot-camps for new recruits in Pardess Hanna, Kfar Yona and the Allenby Camp in Jerusalem). These battalions reinforced the line of settlements along the borders, renovated settlements abandoned during the War, and were involved in absorbing immigrants both within the IDF and in the transit camps and immigrant towns.

Three mobilization dates were set during the course of the year 1950 – the months of June, August and November. Each mobilized contingent numbered 1,500 soldiers, and by the end of 1950 Nahal had inducted 6,000 soldiers into its ranks.[37] Enlistment remained constant for the next two years. The soldiers were mobilized from seven principle sources.

1. Members of settlement core groups from the youth movements

These were Israeli youths who had been counselled in the urban branches of the pioneering youth movements in preparation for settlement. In accordance with accepted practice, at the end of grade 11, members for the settlement core group were organized in a single cohort group, formed from a number of branches. A few core groups were slated to become independent and establish new kibbutzim, but most of them were assigned as complements to existing kibbutzim (the designated kibbutzim were decided upon before or immediately after induction). These core groups began their army service with a three-to-five-month period of basic training, all of which took place within a clear military framework entirely detached from their designated kibbutz. This was followed by 6 months of agricultural training, usually at a veteran kibbutz. This latter training was intended to expose the core group to the kibbutz way of life and to permit them to experience it at first hand, as well as to provide them with some practical training in the various productive sectors of the kibbutz. During this period they were in uniform and subject to a certain amount of military discipline, but in reality they were only part-time soldiers. For many of them, this was the first real encounter with the social, cultural and economic life of the kibbutz, and it was this encounter which determined their attitude towards the kibbutz in general and their prospective future on the kibbutz in particular. A term of service without pay followed the period of agricultural training and at its conclusion the soldiers were demobilized from the IDF. During this period of agricultural service, members of the core groups settled on their designated kibbutzim. They were not required to be in uniform nor were they subjected to army discipline; their sole obligation was to live and work on the kibbutz, the same as every member. They associated with kibbutz members at close quarters and became integrated into the social and working life of this collective community. The settlement movements hoped that members of the core groups, when they returned to civilian status, would decide to join the designated kibbutz. In fact, it soon became very clear that very few responded positively to these hopes. For example, between 1951 and 1953 only 31 per cent of the Nahal contingents – about one quarter of the total number of soldiers – joined the kibbutzim after completing their army service. In other words, even the very hard core groups which were at the heart of the first Nahal recruits, in which the settlement movements placed their trust and for whose sake they insistently demanded the establishment of Nahal, did not stay in the kibbutzim.[38]

2. Youth associations comprising groups of teenage boys and girls

These groups included both native-born and new immigrants, who had arrived at the kibbutzim through the framework of Youth Aliya, an organ under the auspices of the Jewish Agency. Beginning at age 13 to 14, they received their education in special frameworks detached from the regular kibbutz study programme. These associations were organized at the conclusion of the period of their schooling on the kibbutz as a Nahal core group, and in general the intention was that they would join the kibbutz in which they were reared. Naturally, the core group members of the youth associations had kibbutz and farming experience which was far greater than that of the urban core groups of the youth movements. Furthermore, the majority of members of the youth associations came to the kibbutzim because of family problems. The kibbutz became a home for them, so that their resultant integration into the working settlement following army demobilization appeared to be a natural course for them to take. However, this core group, too, was quickly exposed to the temptations of the period and the surrounding society, and their civilian future was not that much different from those of the urban core groups.

3. Core Group Immigrants

These included alumni of pioneering-Zionist youth movements from different countries who had organized in their country of origin after completing their compulsory education (and of course also after intensive education within the movements themselves). They were a unified entity when they immigrated to Israel, and began their Nahal career at service without pay at one of the kibbutzim. This period, generally lasting for a year, was devoted to social and agricultural preparation. These contingents were not in uniform and were distinguished from the regular groups, who were working without pay only in the timing of their assignment to this phase. When their term of kibbutz service was completed, members of the immigrant core groups underwent basic training. Afterwards, they continued to progress along the course laid out for Nahal training (except that the period of work without pay at the end of their service was shortened by the amount of time which they had accumulated by being assigned to it in advance of the regular schedule). Of course, these core groups contained a very high percentage of members with strong convictions, who had already made up their minds to live on a kibbutz, and this was reflected in their great success from the vantage point of the settlement movements.

4. Graduates of agricultural schools

Some graduates were members of regular core groups of the youth movements and reached Nahal units through their frameworks. But there were also those among them who organized as independent core groups without any connection to the youth movements. The Department of Youth and Nahal devoted efforts to encourage this tendency as a natural continuation of their studies in agricultural education, and extended its patronage to these independent core groups.

5. Kibbutz youth

Such youth were inducted into the Nahal as individuals only, and not in a core group framework, and were assigned to perform their military service within the command trajectory. With the completion of their basic training, they went to squad-commander courses and the best among them continued on to officer training courses. The reasoning behind having them join Nahal was based on the assumption that they would naturally return to their kibbutzim, and would thus project onto their soldiers not only a commanding authority but also devotion to the course of settlement. Indirectly, it was also a means of lessening the need to mobilize commanders from members of the core groups.

6. Volunteers from abroad

These were young Jewish men and women who came to Israel as individuals and volunteered to serve in the IDF. The duration of their service was set at 15 months and Nahal seemed to be the most suitable IDF framework for their absorption. During the period of their service they received educational instruction in a special programmatic framework, and in the remaining time they were affiliated with core groups either as individuals or in small groups.

7. 'Unaffiliated soldiers'

'Unaffiliated soldiers' in the Nahal lexicon embraces those thousands of inductees lacking any educational or pioneering preparation who arrived at the Corps in compliance with the obligations of the Defence Service Law. Many of them were new immigrants whom the IDF initially refrained from assigning to professional units. Their first year of service included three months of basic training and nine months of agricultural preparation. More than 7,500 'unaffiliated soldiers' were enlisted between 1950 and 1953; this comprised nearly 43 per cent of the total number of inductees in Nahal. In 1954 and 1955, the figures declined to 15 per cent of the total number of inductees.[39] Many 'unaffiliated soldiers' were regarded as disadvantaged children. The heads of the Department of Youth and Nahal, as well as Nahal commanders, saw to the channeling of youth from the eastern diaspora – Morocco, Turkey, Iran, Yemen and Egypt – to pioneering settlement activity, a Zionist-State challenge of the utmost importance. The task was extremely difficult. Among native-born Israelis there was a clearly marked decline in pioneering motivation and an equally clear increase in the desire for personal advancement. These pioneering enterprises were also the subject of cynicism and criticism from the public at large. Nahal even tried to harness the idea and the endeavour of pioneering settlement to those recruits who joined Nahal's ranks by chance rather than by choice, including those who were weak in Hebrew language skills and basic education. If that was not enough, many came from a background which looked down on physical labour connected with agriculture and valued several-times-over employment in trade and services. Notions such as the equal worth of all work, work for no direct financial recompense, and voluntary work beyond accepted working hours engendered ridicule and opposition. Pundak testified:

> They did not know how to use a toothbrush. They wanted to save the shoes they received for the Sabbath. We had to teach them the basic rules of sanitation. We had to devote time to teaching the Hebrew language and basic reading ... some refused to go to work and in one of the platoons in the south there was a strike and they didn't go to work. 'We came to serve in the army, not to work' they claimed before their commanders.[40]

It is not surprising that the combination of a strict military framework, with social and cultural integration into the surrounding civilian society of the kibbutz, created many disciplinary problems among the soldiers. However, a great effort of the command staff and instructors – which included broad-based educational and learning activities – brought about the formation of a system of effective norms and the attainment of a number of objectives. The 'unaffiliated' Nahal soldiers who lived and worked on the kibbutzim became acquainted with the basic values and experiences of kibbutz society and internalized something from them. Even if the majority did not become permanent settlers, their Nahal service contributed substantially to their successful integration into Israeli society. Summing up the first two years of Nahal, Shimroni wrote in his diary:

> The percentage of dodgers and deserters from work was zero. We definitely cannot say that the difficulties of the majority of Nahal soldiers in adjusting to work were greater than any other form of civilian work adjustment undergone by new immigrants.

More than once I have heard kibbutz members say that in their experience the work adjustment of the new immigrant in the Nahal framework is faster.[41]

Elhanan Yishai pointed out how Ben-Gurion saw Nahal's contribution:

He attributed tremendous importance to the pioneering corps and regarded settlement army service as a response to the gap in Israeli society. With the arrival of the massive wave of immigration comprising people who were quite different from those who were living here ... difficulties arose in coping with the problems of absorption and pioneering settlement. Nahal in particular was Ben-Gurion's response.[42]

THE MILITARY SETTLEMENTS OF NAHAL

From its formation until the end of 1956, Nahal soldiers founded 37 new kibbutzim and supplemented dozens of kibbutzim and moshavim, but its contribution to settlement in those years was fastened in public consciousness and in the ethos of the corps itself through the establishment of military settlements. In many respects, these latter undertakings have remained the hallmark of Nahal up to the present day.

The initiative for creating these security settlements arose against the background of increasing infiltration incidents and sabotage during the early years of the 1950s. This development, which threatened to harm new immigrant moshavim in the more remote areas of the country, forced the IDF to expand and deepen its routine security activities and augment its presence along the borders. From the very nature of Nahal's defined functions, its soldiers appeared to be natural candidates to shoulder the burden and fulfil these demands. In accord with this, the Deputy Chief-of-Staff, General Mordecai Macleff, sent the following order to the commander of Nahal in March 1951:

1. both security and settlement needs require an intensified effort in the field of pioneering settlement and the development of ways for directing the flow of individual volunteers to settlement at vital frontier points;

2. this effort will open up broad areas which up till now have been closed to immigrant settlement;

3. Nahal soldiers must make special efforts in order to ensure the success of this new effort.[43]

This order also explicitly mentioned the setting up of four settlement points manned by 'unaffiliated' soldiers during the course of 1951. The first two settlements were to be set up by 1 June and the other two settlements by 1 October. Each settlement was to be manned by a Nahal Company numbering 100–110 male and female soldiers (at a gender ratio of 2:1). In addition, the Company was to be part of the area's Nahal battalion and, when needed for routine security activity, it would be subordinated to the territorial defence in the relevant area. At the beginning, it had been decided that 'unaffiliated' Nahal soldiers would be stationed at these security settlements, and that they would volunteer for these duties in their second year of service. In the course of this undertaking, plans were also contrived to send 'unaffiliated' soldiers who were in their first year of service to these settlements.

The above order of the Deputy Chief-of-Staff emerged from a series of discussions in the defence establishment in which Elik Shomroni, the head of the Department of Youth and Nahal, played a central role. Shomroni regarded the innovatory step of deploying 'unaffiliated' soldiers at security settlements as an important contribution to the pioneering and pedagogic undertakings of Nahal among new immigrants. Discussions at Nahal headquarters envisioned the security settlements as 'pedagogical melting pots and schools for language acquisition, cultivating a particular way of life, inculcating work norms and values, and providing military training.'[44] They also provided a response to the manpower shortage in Nahal. The settlement movements, however, adamantly demanded that they receive consolidated complements of core groups for their existing settlements, some of which constituted part of the security belt along the borders. In effect, this meant that the border security settlements would be short-changed since there were not enough Nahal contingents to satisfy the manpower needs of both the settlement movement and border security locations. On the other hand, from the beginning it was clear that these same fortified locations – the security settlements – would be planned as permanent emplacements populated in due course by settlement movement core groups. Thus, plans were devised which assigned 'unaffiliated' soldiers as the first settlers in these locations. Initially, they would busy themselves in clearing the ground and preparing the initial infrastructure; afterwards they would join the core group of a permanent settlement as full members.

Plans for the founding of security settlements were formulated jointly by the Department of Youth and Nahal, and the Settlement Department of the Jewish Agency. From the latter's viewpoint, and in light of obligations on the part of the military that these locations would be manned until permanent settlers were found for each one of them, they were considered as new settlements in all respects. An official agreement between the two bodies determined that:

> The intention of this effort is to bring soldiers who have completed two years of service to permanent settlements on their own volition. Nahal will be responsible for manning these settlements until they are placed under the permanent jurisdiction of settlers. Given this objective, it is imperative that these settlements be built in areas which are vital for security, as well as permit an immediate start to developing an agricultural entity upon arrival of the soldiers.[45]

These two objectives were often not compatible since sites selected on security criteria were not necessarily viable agriculturally.

Levi Eshcol and Elik Shomroni agreed from the beginning that economic and administrative responsibility for the security settlements, as well as agricultural and cultural instruction, would be invested in a team of eight to ten civilians, emissaries of the settlement movement. This team would comprise the following offices: 'representative of the settlement [to external institutions and agencies], treasurer, economic coordinator, accountant, manager of food supplies, coordinator of construction work to whom were attached 3 to 4 agricultural instructors, teaching and cultural instructors.'[46] Several months later, important resolutions were added in relation to the Nahal contingents that were now residents of the security settlements. Again, it was made clear that they were to be soldiers stationed at strong points and subordinate to military discipline. But:

> in order to accustom them to management of an independent social and economic life, they will elect committees for the management of work and social life. If an organized group of soldiers wishes to remain at this location on a permanent basis and it obtains the approval of the Defence Ministry, the kibbutz and all its property will be turned over to it. If such a group does

not wish to stay, the security settlements will continue to serve as a transitional economic base for the training of other soldiers.[47]

A special committee was given responsibility for co-ordination among the different organizations involved in the founding and setting up of the security settlements. Its members included a representative from the Ministry of Defence, the director of the Economic Bureau of the Department of Youth and Nahal, and an agricultural training officer from Nahal Command. They were asked to conduct closed sessions in their examination of the problems of the different security settlements; this entailed visits to locations where they were to offer solutions touching on matters pertaining to manpower, equipment, finances and the like. The committee was also required to function as a constant channel of communication with Nahal headquarters to find solutions for military/civilian conflicts.

The IDF decision to construct security settlements was also based on economic and economizing considerations. The in-fighting over the defence budget and IDF allocations in 1951 to 1952 was particularly intense (and ultimately led to the resignation of the Chief-of-Staff, Yigael Yadin). During the course of the debates regarding this matter Yadin asserted that the State was under an obligation to maintain a large standing army; financial support for this could come from civilian labour input which the IDF would carry out in addition to its military tasks. He spoke about 'the assignment of developmental works [mostly in the Negev] and agricultural activity to entire military units in order to "reduce" the cost of every soldier.'[48] Building security settlements blended well with this outlook and in addition received the explicit approval of the Defence Ministry and the Jewish Agency on the grounds that:

> these locations would be erected and maintained by the Settlement Department of the Jewish Agency. The Settlement Department would construct the sites and assume all responsibility for maintenance costs. The IDF would supply the site personnel with services and food supplies delivered by an army vehicle. The financial cost for this would be covered by the Jewish Agency.[49]

On 1 April 1951, Moshe Netzer was appointed Commander of Nahal. He immediately sent all his soldiers a circular containing an important paragraph, in a personal tone, directed to 'unaffiliated' soldiers.

Your first year of service is drawing to a close,' wrote Netzer in a personal tone, 'and you face a decision regarding your future in the IDF ... During this past year you fulfilled a security role of the highest order as a member of your unit on the kibbutz and through your activities against infiltrators, personally participating in a responsible manner in the defence of the State. In your capacity as a soldier you came to know the area in which your unit was stationed and ways of life with which you were not formerly acquainted. You learned how to work and very likely acquired vocational skills. Your labor helped increase the agricultural output of our State. Above all you saw with your own eyes the major security role which frontier settlement provides today, as it had done in the War of Independence, when every border settlement was a bastion of strength in the face of invasion and attack. If you are a new immigrant, you learned Hebrew; if you participated in the life of your platoon, you learned to sing and dance. And if you will be honest with yourself, you will admit that you learned a little about order and cleanliness.[50]

The letter presented the 'unaffiliated' Nahal soldier with three available options: to transfer to one of the IDF units during his second year of service; to join one of the Nahal groups preparing for settlement; or to remain in the Nahal settlement without any prior commitment to permanent settlement while maintaining an option to stay at the location an additional year and thereby benefit from all the rights awarded to new immigrants who choose permanent settlement. Those choosing the third option were promised ownership of land, possessions and all livestock and property, as well as the assistance of the Jewish Agency in establishing the farm, and independence in deciding its future course.

At the end of June 1951, a final agreement was reached for the establishment of the first two Nahal security settlements – or Nahal farms. Nahala'im 'A', or Nahal Oz, was designated for an area opposite the Gaza Strip situated between Kibbutz Sa'ad and the ruins of Kibbutz Be'er Yitzhak. Nahla'im 'B', or Gonen, was designated for the Gurieyva area situated south of Kibbutz Lahavot HaBashan. In addition, vigorous preparations were begun for the building of a third Nahal security settlement, Yotvata, at Ein Radian on the approach to Eilat.

On 23 July 1951, Yitzhak Rabin, head of the Operational Department of the General Staff Branch, signed an order instructing

Nahal Headquarters to found permanent security settlements which would be military units in every sense of the term. At the same time, the order emphasized that the 'mission of the security settlement is to establish a frontier settlement and to have Nahal soldiers strike roots there with the intention of turning them into permanent residents and builders. In terms of its objective, the security settlement is identical to every type "A" settlement in the State.'[51]

The Nahal 'A' security settlement opposite the north end of the Gaza Strip was settled by ordinary soldiers from Nahal two days after the publication of Rabin's order. The Gonen and Yotvata settlements followed on 13 August and 29 October respectively. In a closely connected development, dated from 1 August, Nahal was granted recognition as an IDF Command, thus reflecting its elevated status in the eyes of General Staff Headquarters. The first document issued by the new Command Headquarters was a standing order with regard to security settlements defining them as:

> fortified settlement locations established and maintained by the Jewish Agency and inhabited by soldiers on active duty under instructions from the Operations Branch of the General Staff [as stipulated] in the Order of July 23, 1951 … The commander of each security settlement is the direct commanding officer of the soldiers and of the locality in matters pertaining to security, training, discipline, and everything relating to the existence of the agricultural site as a military unit; he is privy to voice his opinion on all matters touching economic management.[52]

The martial regulation in the standing orders specified that the security settlement would follow regimental discipline and military procedures as in the battalions, that is, that soldiers would appear in military dress and military working apparel. Only on Sabbath eves and holidays were white shirts allowed. In the clause relating to the regime of organization and procedure, emphasis was directed towards encouraging soldiers to remain at the location as permanent settlers, hence their participation in the organization of daily work and culture (through various committees).

The most important reference was clause 7 of the standing orders relating to the building of a 'family' at the security settlement:

1. A soldier-family means a male and female soldier who have undergone a marriage ceremony, whereby the female soldier has relinquished her right to demobilization from IDF service as

defined by orders of the General Staff. Or a female civilian married
to a soldier who has assumed all the obligations deriving from her
presence on a security settlement site.

2. A soldier-family on a security settlement is entitled to receive
separate housing.
3. The family will not keep separate kitchen or bathroom facilities.
4. Work discipline associated with the security settlement will apply
under all conditions to the wife as well.[53]

This revolutionary breakthrough – offering the possibility of establishing a family within the military framework, together with the
obligations and rights entailed in this – was credited to Shomroni. Its
purpose was, of course, to give expression to the clearly civilian aspect
of settlement life in light of the ultimate aim of establishing a permanent settlement at the location. The first application of clause 7
occurred several months after the first wedding at Nahal Oz.

Although the standing orders were detailed, it appeared that the
actual problems were not only difficult and complicated, but also
could not have been foreseen. Some of them are presented in the
following pages through an extended description of the first security
settlement.

BEGINNING STAGES AT NAHAL OZ

The first Nahal security settlement, situated opposite the Gaza Strip,
commenced settlement activities on 25 July 1951. Several days
earlier, a solution had still not been found to such central problems
as manpower supply, Jewish Agency budgets for the upkeep of
100–120 soldiers (according to the original plan), and water provision. On 5 July 1951, the Department of Youth and Nahal sent a letter
of complaint to the Jewish Agency regarding the unsatisfactory pace
of the preparatory stage. This letter pointed to the problem that
threatened the entire initiative. The date for arriving at the new
security settlement had been set according to the designated date for
the dispersal of the Nahal stream of recruits completing their first
year of service. Any delay might result in the dispersal of the 'unaffiliated' soldiers among the regular military units.

Nahal personnel nevertheless completed their main preparations. Major Yaakov Naim, commander of Battalion 904, the Nahal
battalion in the area, promulgated a warning order called 'call-up for
the security settlements' and detailed all the relevant matters. An

advance party numbering 40 men, commanded by company-leader
Dan Matt, was supposed to have arrived at the location two days
before the date officially set for settlement, to undertake preparation
of the grounds.

The first settlers at Nahal 'A' were drawn from several different
sources which included 'unaffiliated' soldiers who had undertaken
agricultural training at Kibbutz Tel Yosef, a Romanian immigrant youth
group, who received agricultural training at Kibbutz Neve Yam, and a
supplement of soldiers from additional agricultural training courses.
They exhibited no special enthusiasm towards this assignment. Dani
Matt, who met with them at the battalion base at Bet Darass, reported
his initial encounter with the contingent many years later:

> I stood at the gates to Bet Darass awaiting the arrival of the lorries
> carrying the soldiers. Suddenly, I heard a feeble, plaintive voice,
> much like a Cossack song, which ever so slowly increased in
> volume as the lorries approached. And then I deciphered the
> song emanating with great gusto from their lips – 'We don't want
> security settlements! We don't want security settlements!'[54]

Matt recalled searching for suitable words to encourage the
soldiers and spark their motivation for carrying out the assignment,
but quickly concluded that he must first apply strictures of discipline
and order and only at a later stage continue with educational-Zionist
work. He was aware that the area in which the settlements were
based was rife with infiltrators from the refugee camps in the Gaza
Strip and would require extensive military activity. His behaviour and
command style followed from this knowledge. Thus, it was clear that
in the first stage security needs preceded all agricultural tasks.

The settler arrival ceremony symbolized the duality of Nahal life.
The security settlement soldiers lined up in two groups – one group in
blue work clothes carrying pickaxes, the other group in army uniform
carrying rifles. Among the honoured guests were the Commander of
the Southern Front, Moshe Dayan; Commander of Nahal, Moshe
Netzer; additional senior officers; and several representatives of the
Settlement Movement.

In his words of greeting, Moshe Netzer stated:

> I am very well acquainted with the troubles and difficulties
> which most of you underwent in deciding upon your future
> course. Many of you wished to finish your service in Nahal and

transfer to other units in the IDF; many others among you were inspired by the joint labor and production of the kibbutzim in which you lived. And as soldiers on frontier settlements, you imbibed the spirit of heroism and exemplary steadfastness which were exhibited by these settlements during the days of siege ... you are still soldiers, you still see this as your place of residence, the stationing of soldiers in a security settlement facing the enemy. But I am certain that the day will soon come when many of you will unite in one body, a society of soldiers/workers who will be tied to this fortified strongpoint – and will convert this into a bastion of work and creativity ... Your future will serve as an example to thousands of soldiers who will follow you in the ranks of Nahal.[55]

Hopes were high, and it soon became apparent that so were the difficulties. The first days were marked by adjustment problems to the hard physical work, the heat of the day, and to the guard duty and night patrols. Work itself centred upon the building of the encampment, the fencing of the security settlement, the digging of personal emplacements and defence trenches – in other words, the construction of a security settlement in every sense of the word. A report from the weekly newsletter of the settlement conveys something of this experience:

Thus we worked by day and guarded by night in military positions darkened from sunset to sunrise. We felt that we were defending the borders of our country, that we were protecting our State with our bodies. It was on guard duty that our comrade, Aharon Ben-Mor, fell, defending the State with his body.[56]

In another report in the same newsletter, the settlement experience is told with greater bitterness:

We would exert all our energies just to receive a mess kit with still so-called 'pioneer' water, boiled and filthy. Until we got used to this life, we felt quite embittered; there was no running water and we would shower approximately every two weeks. Work began at five in the morning and lasted until six in the evening, so that we had a 12-hour continuous workday. In the evening, we lined up for inspection in work clothes because there was nothing else to wear and there was no orderly laundry service.[57]

At the conclusion of the initial organization period of the security settlements, as security settlements, and following a decline in the number of infiltration incidents in the sector, work began on the digging of trenches for a water line. Alter Zass, one of the first agricultural instructors at Nahal Oz, regarded the trench digging as a means of creating personal attachment to the locale, whose importance went far beyond the technical objective of supplying water. He testified:

> I encouraged the select group to begin digging the trench with their own hands. The soldiers initially agreed because they assumed that a digging machine would arrive in a short time. And so we dug and dug. The soldiers repeatedly dug and cried miserably, from time to time begging to stop and thereby speed up the arrival of the digging machine. But I didn't give in. 'If you dig and by your own efforts bring the water, you will feel the connection, or feel what land and water really are, feel it in your very bones'. Thus we dug a channel four kilometers in length.[58]

The report of David Koren, Nahal's Education Officer, written a month after the soldiers arrived, indicates that 40 soldiers undertook the digging of the water channel, a handful of soldiers undertook cultivation of field crops and a great many were involved in the military activities of guard duty and area security. This report also pointed out the difficult physical conditions, including living conditions. Soldiers were quartered in tents, each with an occupancy of about 20, and without any possibility of rest after work hours and lengthy stints of guard duty. Koren reports that according to the settlement's deputy commander, 'morale was declining. They go off to work reluctantly, but half the soldiers are resigned to life on the security settlement and are prepared to work on its behalf.'[59] Nahal file reports from other commanders during the same period add that only strict and overbearing discipline from the command staff, together with close supervision and the personal example of the agricultural instructors, who were members of the kibbutz, permitted development of the site as an agricultural settlement during its first years.

Parallel to their work and military activities, efforts were undertaken to amplify somewhat the education of the 'unaffiliated' immigrant soldiers. The educational staff sergeant at the security settlement organized Hebrew lessons and other subjects for those who required it. The following letter from one of the soldiers was published in the settlement leaflet:

> When we got here we were given tests for Hebrew language abilities and we were told that we would learn Hebrew twice a week. In fact, we began to learn, but after a week, a month, we stopped learning. But now, we had two weeks of Hebrew lessons and I want to tell you that we learned quite a bit and we sweated over the Hebrew.[60]

As winter approached, there was an urgent need for a solution to the housing problem. In any case, it was necessary to reach a decision on a permanent location for the settlement. At the end of September 1951, the Nahal Command and the Settlement Department of the Jewish Agency decided that the location of the current security settlement would serve as the permanent site. Within a short time, in an unprecedented operation, a thousand dunams surrounding the security settlement were placed under cultivation. The entire achievement was carried out under the authorization and extensive assistance of the Southern Command and was intended to reinforce Israeli control over territory up to the border boundary-line.

On the Sabbath preceding the Jewish New Year (1952), the water pipeline to Nahal Oz was officially opened. It was now possible to develop new agricultural branches on the kibbutz, principally field-crop irrigation, and to receive the side benefits of a daily shower and potential laundry facilities. This improvement in living conditions brought about an elevation in the soldiers' morale. One of them wrote in the local newsletter:

> When I arrived at this Nahal outpost, I had a very uncomfortable feeling. I thought that I could never become accustomed to living here. But nevertheless, I got used to it and I feel good here. But the way of life here is not so good – it is even quite difficult because one gets time off once every month or two and it is difficult to be so far away from home. And guard duty is difficult here, since one has to guard every week. But when you get used to it, this is already not difficult.[61]

Six months after the first soldier/settlers arrived, the encampment numbered 70 Nahal soldiers and five civilian instructors. Five blocks of living quarters, a dining room and kitchen were in place. Work at the security settlement was carried out with the aid of three tractors, a truck, a combine harvester, and a thresher. The soldiers seeded 4,000 dunams of winter crops and 2,000 dunams of summer crops, cultivated a vegetable garden on 60 dunams of irrigated land, and a non-irrigated vegetable garden on 400 dunams. In addition, they constructed a hen roost for 1,000 birds. The civilian instructors estimated that the entire first-year income of the security settlement was 70,000 Israeli pounds, a sum which considerably exceeded the 60,000 Israeli pounds invested in the enterprise.

Flumin, a member of kibbutz Tel Yosef and one of the instructors, reached the following conclusion:

> This Nahal security settlement experiment is the first of its kind and it is now possible to say that it is a successful experiment ... When we first arrived at this site, we were confronted with the problem of how to combine the various army roles with those of building a kibbutz. A second problem was how to create a united society from the social mix that assembled here for agricultural work and state security. As a first-time project, basic experimental lines were set up from the start. And no one was certain whether they suited reality. Today, after the experiment has proved itself, it appears that the directives were useful and most were consonant with actual conditions. The roles referred to above blended quite well, and this savage place on the border with Gaza became quiet, quiet and secure, guarding the entire area. In addition, we created substantial kibbutz assets, a testimony to which are the numbers presented in the list we are presenting. The site area given over to our cultivation is about 8,000 dunams. We quickly acquired suitable agricultural equipment which was distributed with the utmost comprehension by the Jewish Agency. We made a great effort not to forfeit the fall and winter season. Time was short and water was about 4 kilometers distant. We worked in earnest to create a water pipe-line in time. We were allocated a small quantity of water, a factor which creates difficulties to this day. We hope the situation will improve ... It appears that the crops are of average yield and even above average. We hope the crops will bring in a high income. Lacking a finished plan for the location, we could not put in a request for the construction of permanent buildings. But we erected the wooden sheds. Today, the program has been completed and we are already building different structures on the permanent location, among them an American-style hen roost for 1,000 fowl, a produce warehouse, a hayloft, and a thatched covering for machinery. The blocks for the buildings we prepared ourselves. In the near future we will also begin building

a cowshed. We put forward a plan for intensified construction in a new area and when the planning is completed we will put forward a scheme for an orchard area. In conclusion, we hope that net income for the year 1953 will reach about 80,000 [Israeli] pounds. The lion's share comes from the garden, the remainder from the non-irrigated field crops and various other labors. There is no doubt that the economic future of this location is assured and the various crops are succeeding quite well. Nahal is the principal driving force building this site and my desire is that the permanent settlement groups will coalesce – this has not been fully realized. But without doubt, with the help of Nahal – this matter will also come to fruition. Settlement activities of this sort, of the army, settlement on the frontier, and agricultural training are some of the successful activities and the true way – the way for all.[62]

Concerning the military activities throughout this period, Danni Matt has this to say:

The sector for which we received responsibility stretched from Miflasim in the north to Tel-Re'im in the south. Our activities were carried out in vehicles and on foot. We set up ambushes and laid out mines. I can confidently say, although I am not proud of it, that this constituted the greatest part of our work. Until the end of my term of service at the security settlement, the number of infiltrators and others killed reached about 50 and we rounded up hundreds of sheep and cattle which constantly penetrated our area. Gradually, we imprinted our presence on the entire area. They got to know us quickly enough. And when the situation settled down, more or less, we could devote more of our time to economic concerns.[63]

Indeed, the patrols and ambushes carried out by the security settlement soldiers provided the basis for Israeli sovereignty over no man's land. Until the establishment of the security settlements, many Gaza inhabitants grazed their flocks in the territory of the Israeli State, reaching the edges of the kibbutzim Sa'ad and Be'eri. In addition, theft of agricultural equipment increased. In the coming days, border fences would be laid out and border guards entered the picture, but in the meantime it was the Nahal 'A' people who guaranteed that routine security was properly carried out in the area.

Nevertheless, it appears that most of the soldiers did not want to remain at Nahal Oz as permanent residents following their demobilization. A number of soldiers upon conclusion of their service even left the settlement during the summer, at the height of the agricultural season. As expected, this resulted in tensions between settlement commanders and civilian instructors. The former stood firm in regard to the execution of all military missions for which the settlement, a fortified position along the Gaza Strip, was responsible. The latter claimed that the shortage of working hands would irreparably harm reaping and the future agricultural potential of the security settlement. An accommodation was reached with the decision to place the settlement under the command of the Basadeh (literally, Field) settlement group, and to inaugurate civilian procedures – that is, the establishment of a permanent settlement.

Members of this settlement group, cadets from the Me'uhedet movement, completed their term of basic training and continued their agricultural training at Kibbutz Ma'ayan Baruch. They were known as a cohesive group, large enough to meet any of the demands which they might be called upon to fulfil, and possessing social vigour. The challenge presented them captured their imagination. Geisy, who to this day is a member of the Nahal Oz settlement group, related:

> We wanted to settle at Ein Gedi or Ein Radian but the army and the institutions determined that the Nahal posts opposite Gaza were to be converted to civilian standing. We took it as a great privilege to be the settlement group chosen to realize this and thus we went wherever they sent us. We knew that the considerations that led to the conversion of this location to civilian status were principally matters of security. To establish here [on the Gaza border] a civilian settlement which would cultivate the soil up to the border made the difference between potential and de facto sovereignty.[64]

The settlement group BaSadeh reached Nahal Oz on 7 July 1953, for a short agricultural training period before its conversion to civilian status. The group members were still in uniform and were under strict army discipline which had not been applicable to them when they were at Ma'ayan Baruch. This resulted at the start in a burdensome feeling, which became more severe because of the security activities and the great economic impositions. Immediately upon arrival they joined in the reaping of barley and the harvesting of

126 *The Israel Defence Force and the Foundation of Israel*

tomatoes, carrots and beets in the vegetable garden. In any case, after a short time, the core settlement group received responsibility for different operative areas; this, together with the anticipation of the award of civil status, created a better atmosphere. On 15 September 1953, they received a letter from the Department of Youth and Nahal:

> We are happy to announce that beginning from 16 September 1953 [the next day] your Nahal security settlement will become a permanent settlement and the IDF will cease to operate it as a security settlement. Nahal soldiers who remain at this settlement will be under conditions of training similar to those at a frontier kibbutz.[65]

In effect, all the Nahal soldiers who were members of the core settlement group BaSadeh then transferred to service without pay according to IDF and Nahal regulations. They handed in their uniforms and from this point they had to run Nahal Oz as a regular kibbutz.

The official ceremony converting the first security settlement to a civilian settlement was conducted on 29 September 1953, with the participation of 1,500 guests, parents and representatives of the institutions and movements. Almost all the newspapers published accounts on their front pages in banner headlines: 'NINETEEN-YEAR OLDS COALESCE ON BORDER'. Kibbutz Nahal Oz became a symbol and an example for thousands of Nahal soldiers, youth and Israeli society in general during the early 1950s.

The following Nahal security settlements were established before Operation Kadesh (popularly known as the 1956 Sinai Campaign or Suez War):

- Gonen (in the Huleh Valley, August 1951)
- Yotvata (in the Arava, October 1951)
- Dardara (or Ashmura, in the Huleh Valley, October 1952)
- Ein Gedi (on the shores of the Dead Sea, January 1953)
- Bachan (known also as Fortification '82, on the triangle border, April 1953)
- Shazor (in Central Galilee, August 1953)
- Segev (Central Galilee, August 1953)
- Arutz Hayarden (close to Ayelet Hashachar, September 1953)
- Ketsiy'ot (beside Nitzana, October 1953)

- Magal (on the triangle border, October 1953)
- Givat Ruth (in the Nitzana area, October 1953)
- Lachish (in the Beit Guvrin area, June 1955)
- Amatzia (in the Beit Guvrin area, June 1955)
- Nechusha (in the Beit Guvrin area, June 1955)
- Nir Oz (beside the southern border of the Gaza Strip, October 1955)
- Ezuz (or Be'erota'im, in the Niztana area, March 1956)
- Shelah (or Shdemot Shizaff, in the Nitzana area, June 1956)
- Shivta (in the Nitzana area, June 1956)
- Ashalim (or Pekuah, in the Nitzana area, June 1956)
- Kerem Shalom (opposite the Rafiah Corridor, June 1956)
- Dekel (opposite the Rafiah Corridor, June 1956)

Twelve of the security settlements became permanent settlements seven kibbutzim and five moshavim:

- Gonen (March 1953)
- Magal (June 1954)
- Bachan (July 1954)
- Nir Oz (January 1956)
- Ein Gedi (March 1956)
- Yotvata (January 1958)
- Kerem Shalom (May 1968)
- Lachish (May 1956)
- Shazur (in 1956)
- Segev (in 1956)
- Amatzia (May 1957)
- Nechusha (October 1957).

Nine additional security settlements were abandoned or became IDF bases without any links to the settlement movement.

Every one of these security settlements, of course, had its own human, military and settlement story, but each one arose on the basis of stopping security breaches and creating facts in areas encumbered with problems. In each one, from the beginning, there were agonizing deliberations which wavered between military constraints and undertakings, and efforts to build and develop an agricultural economy. (The security settlements in the Nitzana area were an exception since they were primarily intended to assist in solving territorial disputes with the Egyptians and to ensure Israeli sovereignty in the demilitarized zone, and therefore great efforts were not expended in the direction of agricultural development. It is not by chance that all these security settlements are included among the abandoned ones).

The varied time delays between the scheduling of the foundation of the security settlements and their conversion to civilian status emerged from a combination of considerations and circumstances. At least two security settlements – Yotvata and Ein Gedi (or Nahal Settlements 'C' and 'E') – extended their period of military status until solutions to the difficult problems of developing their economic structure were found; both were established in remote desert areas, and doubts were often raised concerning their future. On 18 February 1953, Nahal Command received the following Report:

> The most severe problem at Nahal 'C', Yotvata, concerns the water supply for the kibbutz. The Mekorot Company began laying down a water pipeline to the Israel copper mines (at Timna) and to Eilat, and perhaps in this manner they placed all the economic developments at Yotvata in question.[66]

Another report, which Keren Kayemet sent to the Jewish Agency's Agricultural Department on 5 May 1953, stated in the matter of Yotvata and settlement in the Arava in general:

> The soil conditions are largely saline and characterized by boulder formations, the climatic conditions exhibit an almost complete lack of rain and strong gusty winds; [there is] a lack of reliable data regarding the amount and quality of ground water – all this limits the ability for planned agricultural development until measured experiments suitable for the terrain are carried out ... The replication of agricultural settlement patterns drawn from other areas is likely to fail. In the programs aimed at local problems, a great deal has been done to assist failing settlement, at tremendous financial cost and with meagre outcomes ... Doubts arise regarding the integration of Nahal in the development of the settlement at Ein Gedi and Ein Radian. The carrying out of these programs involves enormous difficulties, demands a settler who clings to the place and who sees his future there as well. Our Nahal group is nothing like this. Its members see their being stationed in the Arava as solely a military service, and the shorter the time, the better. Their eyes are cast to the north, not even to the agriculture there, and this entails an additional difficulty to the natural difficulties which block the path of settlement development in the Arava.[67]

The fact that at both Yotvata and Ein Gedi the sceptics were proved wrong, and that strong settlements developed at both sites, is principally connected to the human component and to another aspect of the security settlements episode. In both sites, settlers were consolidated core groups composed of graduates from the youth movements who succeeded in carrying out the tasks involved in the change to civilian status. (Of course, this was accomplished with the assistance of the settlement institutions, and helped by the fact that the security problems turned out to be relatively light). At Yotvata and Ein Gedi and like the others that became civilian settlements, almost no 'unaffiliated' soldiers were left from those that carried the burden at the initial stage. In this respect Nahal did not succeed in forging its programmes, which raises doubts as to whether they had any basis to begin with. Looking back, it is hard to understand the grounds of faith from which the experience at the settlements was drawn (for example, the laying down of a water pipeline by manual labour); or what would convince more than a handful of soldiers to choose a way of life which did not especially appeal to them (not to mention a way of life that did not appeal to a majority of that generation). On the other hand, it appears that those who became addicted to this enterprise – for example, as volunteer instructors – and hoped that this would draw in the masses, were infused with faith. Who will judge them from such a distance in time and under the circumstances?

NAHAL'S ASSISTANCE IN THE FIELD OF AGRICULTURE

While the terms 'pioneer' and 'soldier', in the Nahal name, were the salient characteristics of the Corps, it is not possible to disconnect Nahal completely from an additional factor which contributed to its birth. The problem of a food shortage – insufficient supplies of local agricultural produce in relation to the growing population size – placed a big burden on the Israeli State in its initial years, and the IDF was called upon to help solve it, in particular through Nahal.

In 1949, at the end of the War of Independence, following the almost complete cessation of the Arab village's contribution to agricultural production, as well as the damage that the war had caused to the Jewish agricultural economy, the cultivation of crops was extended – both irrigated and non-irrigated – to an area of 524,000 dunams. Nearly seventy-thousand dunams were allocated to the growing of vegetables. According to official statistics, these areas increased by hundreds of percent over the following two years, to more than 3.5 million dunams of cultivated field crops and 150,000 dunams of vegetables. But this was not enough, especially since the cultivation of thousands of dunams in the Negev never got past the ploughing stage.[68] To make matters worse, 1951 was a year of drought. The development of the water system and the expansion of fields for cultivating crops did not advance at the required and planned rate. Thus, for example, the new settlements were given 3.5 dunams instead of 10 dunams of irrigated land per settler. The supply crisis led to a rationing of basic food supplies and, parallel to this, a black market developed, and this was naturally accompanied by widespread demoralization. These developments are reflected in an article by Shabtai Teveth, written in *Ha'aretz* on 21 September 1951, in which he wrote that:

> the lack of any Government control over supplies and food, and the pricing policy, not only prevented a just distribution of the same limited quantity of basic foods available to us, but also brought about a reduction in the area of cultivated summer and fall produce, in addition to the shortfall caused by the drought. Moreover, the lack of control over supplies to agricultural settlements and the unrealistic pricing policy has brought about lawlessness and the black market to the very portals of the Government's best friends – members of the laboring agricultural settlements.[69]

Against this background, Chaim Gvati, a senior official in the Agriculture Ministry (and from 1964 to 1974 Minister of Agriculture) initiated a country-wide programme for the growing of vegetables on 36,000 dunams of irrigated soil. Shortly thereafter, the idea was raised of calling upon the IDF to carry out this mission. This was in the spirit of Ben-Gurion's conception of placing the army at the centre of State undertakings. It was also in harmony with the tendency of the Chief-of-Staff, Yadin, to engage military forces in civilian projects in order to reduce the cost of maintaining them. In this connection, two possible options were posited: the growing of vegetables in each and every one of the permanent IDF barrack camps on a small scale and with no additional agricultural equipment; and the establishment of a unit engaged in farming activity on a wide and professional scale within the Nahal framework. Although the second option seemed more serious and realistic, after discussions among senior personnel in the Defence Ministry, the IDF and the Agricultural Ministry reached a decision to grow vegetables in each of the IDF's existing units.

On 20 November 1951, the Minister of Agriculture, Levi Eshcol, wrote to the Chief-of-Staff, Yadin:

> Following our meeting, I examined the problems you raised regarding the growing of vegetables by the IDF.
> 1. Mr. Chaim Gvati told me that he had informed and explained to army leadership that the IDF would receive seeds, manure and pesticides from the Agricultural Ministry for the areas under cultivation …
> 4. The Ministry of Agriculture will put Mr. Slomnitzky, one of its best experts in the field of vegetable cultivation, at the disposal of the IDF. Our Ministry will be prepared to the extent requested and required to continue in its advisory and guidance role.[70]

The IDF selected the Quartermaster General, GHQ, as the senior authorizing agency for vegetable growing. The responsibility for implementation was then delegated to the Agricultural Production Bureau of the Food Branch in the headquarters of the chief supply officer. This unit saw to the co-ordination between the army vegetable growers and all the civilian agencies connected with this branch of agriculture as well as to the acquisition and distribution of production equipment and marketing. The Defence Ministry looked after orders for the agricultural products, crating and marketing. Army orders granted units the use of 20 per cent of their product for their own consumption with the rest of the crop earmarked for delivery to the Supply Corps.

In September 1951, the Deputy Chief-of-Staff ordered Nahal Command to establish a unique battalion that would be engaged in the growing of vegetables while continuing its routine basic training. The battalion would number 800 commanders and soldiers and be accompanied by civilian instructors. The Nahal commander presented the initial programme on 21 September 1951, and his reservations with regard to the entire proposal can be clearly discerned between the lines. The very establishment of such a battalion, claimed the Nahal commander, would seriously harm the situation of the regular Nahal units, including the Nahal platoons stationed on the kibbutzim, and thus would have deleterious effects on agricultural production itself. Moreover, Nahal was already found to be lacking manpower in its rank and file and Headquarters was demanding about 2,000 soldiers from the General Staff to fill its depleted platoons. Given these circumstances, it was understandable that there was an unsettling concern over the implications which the removal of 800 soldiers would have upon the regular framework. Moshe Netzer, the commander of Nahal, wrote to the Deputy Chief-of-Staff Mordecai Macleff:

> Today, dozens of Nahal camps are empty. The removal of manpower from their work program on the kibbutzim will directly impair agricultural production and vegetable growing in particular. In addition, there is no serious possibility of building units and turning them into military units – infantry companies – without the minimum of required manpower: a supplement of 2,000 soldiers, men and women, will just barely solve the minimum request.[71]

In the meantime, there was no way of avoiding the fulfilment of the order and thus Battalion 906, consisting of two companies, was founded. One was sent to the Beit Dagon farm and the other to the Masmi'a farm. Each company initially numbered about 120 Nahal soldiers. The two companies were reinforced by 120 Gadna recruits and about 120 soldiers from other IDF units. Each farm was to cultivate 1000 dunams of tomatoes, potatoes, cabbage, beets and spring vegetables.

The enterprise of vegetable growing in the IDF caused quite a public stir. Almost all the newspapers carried the following statement from the IDF spokesman:

> The General Staff has promulgated an order to IDF units with regard to the matter of growing vegetables by members of the units within their camps. Taking into consideration the situation with regard to the supply of vegetables in the country, each IDF unit which has at least one dunam of land must use it for vegetable growing. This is on condition that the dunam is a single block, is not in use, is suitable for agricultural cultivation, and has enough water for agricultural cultivation. Those units in which the current means of irrigating the arable area are not suitable for the crops, will grow crops not requiring irrigation. Most of the work shall de done with suitable work implements already in the possession of the unit. To the extent possible, regular soldiers shall carry out the work itself during their free time.[72]

Throughout the year, newspaper reporters were invited to the IDF bases to observe the strange and unique spectacle of soldiers occupied in vegetable growing and to bring this to the attention of the readers. Thus, for example, there was a report about the Armoured Corps' commanders who expressed their 'appreciation' for the undertaking, after initially voicing doubts about its usefulness and rejecting the very idea and the possibility for its realization. Now they, too, had the opportunity to explain that this was mainly an educational enterprise drawing the soldier closer to working the land and to the sources of his nourishment – to which there was a secondary objective: assistance in increasing the agricultural produce and supply of food under difficult circumstances.

A characteristic headline, 'The Army Grows Vegetables' related on 26 May 1951:

> I think that the main utility in the army's vegetable growing program, without the army being caught up in considerations of 'it's worth it or not worth it', is that it proceeds according to orders. The situation in regard to our supply [of the State] is known. Much of the shortfall and obstacles stem from the 'not worth it' response, while the needs obligate undertaking it. The army's considerations are different. It is the consideration based on a command. The IDF was ordered to grow vegetables and it grows vegetables. It was ordered to prepare 'reserves' of vegetables for a seasonal shortfall. It prepares.[73]

Nahal's large agricultural farms created greater media excitement than the small plots of several isolated dunams in the IDF camps. However, the actual agricultural output was not impressive. Reports about the situation of the cultivation battalion during the course of 1952 point to faulty agricultural planning, problems of manpower utilization, the adjustment of its scope to seasonal oscillations and too few agricultural instructors. They also refer to soldiers, Nahal and others (sent to help with the farm work), who were not appropriately equipped.

On 10 October 1952, for example, the Co-ordination Committee for the Nahal Agricultural Enterprises toured the two farms and found that a fungus disease had attacked the tomato crop at Masmi'a. Most of the plants were wilting, and the crop was meagre. At Beit Dagon it was evident that only 20 out of 170 dunams allocated for tomatoes were yielding fruit. The potato-growing areas at the two farms were also in bad condition, without any hope of a serious yield. Noxious weeds had brought about complete disarray in the onion area, leaving no choice but to uproot and recultivate the plot. At their 7 November 1952 meeting, the managers concluded:

> It appears that a lack of light equipment such as rakes and hand-cultivating tools are impairing work. It is not clear who should receive credit for this failure; it is inconceivable that there should be a lack of hoes and trowels in a unit which is growing thousands of dunams of vegetables ... The fact is that the seeding is carried out by a sowing machine which should be towed by animals, and the soldiers are pulling it.[74]

At the same meeting, in response to concerns raised about economic criteria, the management voiced claims that there was a 'lack of vision' on the part of the project's critics, and that 'the area must be seeded in its entirety, and that even if the chances for success are one in nine, we must do something'.[75] Even Mr Slomnitzki, the chief agricultural instructor of the enterprise from the Ministry of Agriculture said:

> Two hundred dunams of tomatoes were planted. For lack of working hands, there was no possibility of weeding the plot. The plot was neglected and they were late in planting refills. The result – relatively empty fields ... In fact, what was required was a tilling of the entire area but for reasons of morale preservation, nothing was done. It is true that the tomato crop at Beit Dagon is a complete failure.[76]

The principal contribution of the effort and of the crop-cultivation battalion attached to it was, thus, not from the land yield but rather in terms of morale, myth and IDF folklore. The picture of a fighting soldier cultivating the land when there is a national need for it became a central component of the information dissemination system. The image of a female Nahal soldier proudly carrying a basket of oranges against an agricultural background was an obvious choice when imprinted on an Israeli half-pound coin (minted in 1958). There were also songs of the Nahal choir – for example, 'Twelve Tons' and 'Tomatoes on a Spear' – which were composed against this background and contributed to the raising of morale (not to mention the slang of the day, 'Nahal Tomatoes').

In any case, in February 1953, a decision was taken to close the agricultural farms and to disband the Crop Battalion. From then on, no one talked about the employment of the IDF – or of the Nahal within it – in assisting with the solution of economic problems. Afterwards, Nahal contingents were allocated within purely military frameworks – the next designated Nahal battalion was known as Nahal Paratroops and not as an agricultural unit, and therefore is outside the scope of this book.

NOTES

1. See D. Ben-Gurion, *War Diary*, 16 May 1948, p. 430; also, 24 May 1948, p. 454.
2. D. Ben-Gurion, *The State of Israel Renewed* (Tel Aviv: Am Oved, 1969), p. 157.
3. UKA, Series 23, Container 1, File 1. Lecture of S. Avi-Ad, on the topic of the mobilization of the 1931 cohort and the establishment of Nahal.
4. D. Horowitz and M. Lissak, 'The Yishuv as a Political Society', *Megamot* 17, 1970, p. 116.
5. UKA, Series 23, Container 1, File 1. Letter from the youth movements to the Minister of Defence on 10 August 1948.
6. UKA, Series 23, Container 1, File 1.
7. S. Keren, *Between Ears of Corn and the Sword* (Tel Aviv: Ministry of Defence, 1991), p. 9.
8. E. Kafkafi, 'Changes in United Kibbutz Movement Ideology During the Cold War, 1944–1954', Ph.D. diss., (University of Tel Aviv, 1989), p. 101.
9. A. Shapira, *The Army Controversy, 1948: Ben-Gurion's Struggle for Control* (Tel Aviv: Kibbutz Meuchad, 1984), p. 62.
10. Y. Gelber, *Why They Dismantled the Palmach* (Jerusalem: Shocken, 1986), pp. 217–19.
11. E. Shomroni, *Scythe and Sword* (Tel Aviv: Ma'arachot, 1955), Appendix 1, p. 159.
12. Ibid., p. 44.
13. M. Michaelson, 'Nahal', in A. Kfir and I. Erez (eds), *The IDF and Its Corps: Encyclopaedia of the Army and Defence* (Tel Aviv: Revivim, 1982), p. 13.
14. BGA, Ben Gurion Diary, 6 September 1948, report of E. Shomroni to Ben-Gurion.
15. UKA, Nahal file, Division 25, Series 23, deposition of T. Levanon, which appears in a special edition of the convocation for the first Nahal contingent, *In the Nahal Camp* (1984).
16. D. Ben-Gurion, 'Army for Defence and Construction', speech at a Nahal parade on 13 November 1948, in D. Ben-Gurion, *Army and Security*, p. 66.
17. UKA, Container 1, E. Shomroni, Protocol of the session on the mobilization of the 1931 cohort and the establishment of Nahal, *M'Bifnim*, April 1988, p. 2..
18. Ibid., p. 4.
19. Ibid., p. 5.
20. Protocol of the session on the mobilization of the 1931 cohort and the establishment of Nahal, *M'Bifrim*, April 1988, p. 92.
21. Ibid., p. 98.
22. 'Nahal Core Group Settles to East of the Sea of Galilee', *Davar*, 4 September 1949.
23. I. Doar, *Nahal Units Album* (Tel Aviv: Ministry of Defence, 1989), pp. 20–1.
24. See E. Shomroni, *Scythe and Sword*, p. 25.
25. Ibid., p. 30.
26. Ibid., p. 30
27. *Ha'aretz*, 19 August 1949.
28. UKA, Nahal, Division 25, Container 1, File A, E. Shomroni, remarks of the Chief-of-Staff, Y. Dori, to Nahal units which participated in Operation Arava, 13 September 1949.
29. BGA, Ben-Gurion Diary, 8 January 1950.
30. See E. Shomroni, *Scythe and Sword*, Appendix 4, p. 163.
31. BGA, Nahal file, 'The Elder and Nahal', interview with Elhanan Yishai in the newspaper *B'Mahane*.
32. Interview with I. Pundak, 15 March 1993.

33. See A. Shomroni, *Scythe and Sword*, Appendix 6, p. 165.
34. UKA, Nahal, Division 25, Series 23, Container 2, from Instructions of the Supreme Command, 8 November 1949.
35. Interview with I. Pundak, 15 March 1993.
36. Comment of M. Netzer, in the volume 'Nahal', on the non-co-operation of the IDF in the construction of base camps, which appears in A. Kfir and I. Erez (eds), *The IDF and Its Corps Encyclopedia of the Army and Defence* (Tel Aviv: Revivim, 1982), p. 24.
37. ZA 1166/51 (31 á – b), 'The Nahal Corps' – summary of a meeting held with the Deputy Chief-of-Staff, 21 March 1950.
38. For a comprehensive research report on the absorption of Nahal core groups in settlements, and a statistical and sociological analysis of the different factors, see D. Atid, A. Kahanovitz and S. Lifshitz, *Absorption of Nahal Groups in Settlements* (Rehovot: The Centre for Rural and Urban Settlement Research, 1975).
39. I. Doar, *Nahal Units Album* (Tel Aviv: Ministry of Defence, 1989), p. 221.
40. Interview with I. Pundak, 15 March 1993.
41. See A. Shomroni, *Scythe and Sword*, p. 48.
42. BGA, Nahal, File 1, interview with Elhanan Yishai, 'The Old Man and Nahal', in *B'Mahane*.
43. CZA S15/9602, Order of the Deputy Chief-of-Staff: 'Settlement of "Unaffiliated" Nahal Soldiers',18 March 1951.
44. UKA, Division 25, Series 23, Container 4, 'Fortified Strongholds', Information Sheet, 31 August 1953.
45. CZA S15/9602, 'Summation of Conversation between Levi Eshcol and Elik Shomroni', 5 February 1951, on Settlement of Nahal soldiers.
46. Ibid.
47. UKA, Strongholds – General, File 2, 'Regimen and Procedure Law for the Stronghold', committee proposal of 10 June 1951.
48. For a comprehensive article on the struggle about the defence budget during these years see: Y. Greenberg, 'National Security and Military Might – Between Statesmanship and Militarism', *Studies in Zionism, the Yishuv and the State of Israel* 1, 1991, pp. 170–90.
49. CZA S15/9602, 'Settlement of "Unaffiliated" Nahal Soldiers', 18 March 1951, p. 92.
50. UKA, Section 25, Strongholds – General, File 2, Letter from the Commander of Nahal, June 1951; see A. Shomroni, *Scythe and Sword*, Appendix 9, pp. 172–3.
51. CZA S15/9602, Order from General Staff Branch – Operations Division, 'Nahal Frontier Strongholds', 23 July 1951; IDFA, Nahal File, 1951.
52. IDFA 81/1687/85, Document from Nahal Command Headquarters, 'Standing Order for the Nahal Stronghold', (n.d.).
53. Ibid.
54. From a recorded interview with Dani Matt, 1 February 1990, edited by I. Leschinski.
55. See A. Shomroni, *Scythe and Sword*, Appendix 10, speech of M. Netzer on the day of settlement, 25 July 1951.
56. NOA, Container 7, Weekly Leaflet, Stronghold Newsletter, pamphlet no. 10.
57. Ibid.
58. Recorded interview with Altar Zass, edited by I. Leschinski, in 1982.
59. IDFA 80/1687/85, Report of Major Koren David on 22 August 1951.
60. NOA, Weekly Leaflet, Stronghold Newsletter, pamphlet no. 10, p. 9.
61. Ibid., p. 13.
62. Ibid., pp. 2–3.
63. From a recorded interview with Danni Matt.
64. In an interview with I. Leschinski.
65. NOA, document of the Defence Ministry, Youth and Nahal Branch, 15 September 1953.
66. IDFA 84/1687/85, Report from the meeting of the Committee for Factory Co-ordination, 11 February 1953. Also document from 18 February 1953.
67. Ibid., document of Keren Kayemet sent to the Agricultural Department of the Jewish Agency, 'Development of Agricultural Settlement in the Arava', 5 May 1953.
68. IDFA 219/8/71, Shabtai Teveth, 'What Happened in Agriculture?', Part I, *Ha'aretz*, 16 September 1951.
69. Ibid., Part II, 21 September 1951.
70. SA ℥/5436/1449, at Tzrifin, Letter of the Minister of Agriculture and Development, Levi Eshcol, to the Chief of Staff, Yigael Yadin, following their meeting on 20 November 1951.

71. IDFA 2/321/54, Nahal Labor Battalion (growing of vegetables), letter directed to the Deputy Chief of Staff from the Nahal Commander, M. Netzer, 16 September 1951.
72. IDFA 1317/8/7/1, Publication of the IDF spokesperson, in *HaBoker, Herut, Ha'aretz, Davar*, 3 January 1952.
73. N. Ben-Avraham: 'The Army Grows Vegetables', *HaBoker,* 26 May 1952.
74. UKA 25, Series 23, Nahal, File Battalion HaShalchin. 'Summary of the Meeting of Field Managers for Battalion 906, 7 November 1952', Document of the Committee for the Co-ordination of Agricultural Enterprises, 12 November 1952.
75. Ibid.
76. Ibid.

Chapter 4

Army Assistance for Transit Camp Residents

During the difficult years of the transit camp period – 1950 to 1954 – the IDF was called upon to help their inhabitants. Were these instances of rescue and technical assistance a type common to other mobilized armies when emergencies arise, or can they be character- ized as a more encompassing involvement, stemming from Ben- Gurion's outlook of state-guided pioneering with the army as its central agent? And if there was involvement of this nature, what constraints were placed upon it and what responses did it engender? These questions are explored in this chapter.

During the State's first three-and-a-half years, 700,000 immigrants passed through its gates: 102,000 in 1948; 240,000 in 1949; 170,000 in 1950 and 175,000 in 1951.[1] The combination of immigration and natural growth doubled the Israeli population during these years. By any criteria, this created tremendous challenges – social, economic and cultural – whose dimensions grew even more because of the high birth rate of the new immigrant population. They came from different countries, bringing with them a variety of cultures, customs and languages. What they had in common – their Jewishness – was by the nature of its origins an opaque mixture of religion and nationalism, providing a fertile ground for antagonism and friction. This was exacerbated by the fact that a portion of the newcomers maintained their traditional religious observances, while others were quite distanced from the very foundations of religion and Jewish tradition.

Approximately half of the immigrants during the first three years of State independence came from Asian and African countries: 35.3 per cent from the former and 15.4 per cent from the latter. Immigration from Europe comprised 48.6 per cent of the total arrivals and the remaining 0.7 per cent came from the Americas and Oceania. The relative weights of groups of origin changed with the waves of immigration. In 1948, the majority of immigrants (about 86 per cent) were of European origin. Commencing in September of that year, most of the immigrants from the displaced persons camps in Germany, Austria and Italy arrived in Israel, as well as immigrants who had been interned by the British in camps in Cyprus. In the following months they were joined by 37,000 Bulgarian Jews and 7,500 Yugoslavian Jews. After this date, the rate of immigration from Europe started to decline (although from 1948 to 1951, 106,000 Jews arrived from Poland and 118,000 from Romania). The Libyan Jewish community (31,000) and the Yemenite community (48,000) immigrated to Israel in 1949 through 'Operation Magic Carpet'. In 1950 and 1951, Operation Ezra and Nehemia brought 123,000 Iraqi Jews to the country. This shift raised immigration originating from countries in Asia and Africa to 71 per cent in 1951.

These numbers contain a special significance given the demographic structure of the population at the time of the State's establishment. In 1948, native-born children comprised more than 35 per cent of the population. With regard to foreign-born people living in the country at this time, 65 per cent had been in the country at least ten years. Of the foreign born, 85 per cent were born in Europe or America. This meant that there was a decisively homogeneous core population in terms of country of origin, whose shared life experiences and exposure to historical events strongly shaped its social and political culture.

By way of contrast, in 1953 only 29 per cent of the population was native-born (this percentage included many of the children of new immigrants). More than 70 per cent of the country's residents who were born abroad had been living in the country for only a short time. The percentage of African and Asian-born in this population stood at 38 per cent. Moreover, 3 per cent of this population were 15 years of age or younger. Only 2 per cent were 60 years of age or older. This age structure arose out of a selective immigration policy which preferred youths of working age, and attempted to prevent immigration of the elderly on the assumption that they would have trouble adjusting to manual labour (including agricultural work).[2]

The educational level of the 1948 – 1951 immigration cohort was considerably below that of the native-born population. For example, only 16 per cent of male immigrants of 15 years or older had four years of high school education (this was not, however, equivalent to a high school matriculation diploma), compared to 34 per cent of the native-born population. Among the combined Asian and African population, only 8.5 per cent had completed 12 years of education (without a matriculation certificate). Among the Moroccan male population, only 2 per cent had completed high school, from Libya only 3 per cent, and from Yemen less than 1 per cent.[3]

Many of the immigrants, principally from Asia and Africa, engaged in largely unskilled jobs in small-scale commerce and service occupations in their countries of origin. In Israel, they had to turn to other occupations. Many were integrated into unskilled jobs in industry and farming, characterized by low salaries and no opportunities for advancement. Moreover, the new arrivals had large families to support and this situation thrust them into the country's lower socio-economic strata. Thus, from the start, there was a deepening social and economic gap between this strata and the better off levels of society; this created centres of friction and bitterness.

Jewish Agency personnel assigned to the task of immigrant absorption were therefore confronted with difficult and complex problems of a social, economic, communal and religious nature – and the means they were given for the job were meagre and poor. Moreover, the economic resources allocated for mass immigrant absorption were very limited, having been taken from a budget that had to finance serious security needs, cover the damage costs incurred during the War of Independence, and contribute to State development in general. Against this background, there was a very marked lack of co-ordination between the various implementing bodies.

In the first stages, new immigrants were housed in residential quarters vacated by the flight of the Arab population – in the towns of Jaffa, Acre, Lod and Ramla, and in the neighbourhoods of mixed towns such as Jerusalem, Haifa, Tiberias and Safed. During this period, other immigrants were sent to camps previously occupied by the British army and not being utilized by the IDF. At the end of 1949, 89,000 immigrants had settled in these camps. At a later stage, immigrants were settled in the abandoned towns of Beersheva, Ashkelon, Beit Shean and Yavne; in addition, about 200 immigrant moshavim were set up throughout the country in the context of a large settlement programme.

In the meantime, because of the rising tide of immigration, hurried settlement of immigrants took place in camps and new immigrant-hostels throughout the country. These residential quarters lacked a suitable infrastructure and had negligible sanitation facilities. Many camps were without showers, and their inhabitants had to make do with a limited number of outdoor toilet facilities and a few water taps. Essentially, inhabitants lived in densely built living quarters comprised of shacks, overcrowded with beds and the immigrants' meagre belongings, and devoid of privacy. The dining rooms set up in these crowded conditions provided skimpy meals which were foreign to the accustomed tastes of the immigrants and were usually thrown into the garbage bin. Now and again, there were outbreaks of infectious diseases.

Dr Giora Yoseftal, who was at this time the head of the Absorption Department of the Jewish Agency, gave bitter testimony relating to some of the above distress.

> Approximately 50 men and women, including the elderly and children, inhabit a single sleeping quarter, a situation which unquestionably creates an intolerable atmosphere. These are degrading conditions and it is impermissible for us to keep people there. There are social crimes of every sort in these camps including murder, prostitution, theft, and violence. The number of 'good' people who come to these camps declines in a short time; they sink into a depression which leaves them with no strength to do anything but weep in silence.[4]

Another testimonial, which also recalls many of the reasons for the situation in the camps, appeared in a 1959 Jewish Agency publication entitled *Eleven Years of Absorption*:

> It should be emphatically pointed out that this operation of rapid lodging was carried out without any orderly financial resources. The means would arrive only after some time, and usually there was a need to operate without any means at all. A source of interim financing had to be sought in order to obtain loans on the account of funds that were scheduled to arrive. It was necessary under all conditions to set up kitchens even though it was not always possible to pay the food suppliers, who more than once announced to the kitchen directors that it was no longer possible to provide supplies on credit.[5]

Apart from all this, the immigrant population living in the camps was closed and withdrawn, cut off from the country's population.

Every camp was a territorial zone in itself, without any link to the outside environment, and the inhabitants were prohibited from finding work outside the camp. Depressed and frustrated, they had nothing to do but bide their time, powerless and dependent upon bureaucrats who managed their daily lives.

The Israeli public soon began to make its acquaintance with the difficult living conditions of the new immigrants in the camps, in part following a series of articles published in April 1949 by the *Ha'aretz* reporter, Arieh Gelblum.[6] A question of principle emerged from these articles: was it not desirable, for the benefit of the immigrants themselves and for the benefit of their absorption into the economy and society, to reduce the immigration rate and plan its handling in accord with the actual absorption capabilities of the Government and the Jewish Agency? In an alternative formulation, the question was put as to whether there was a place for introducing selection among those who requested to immigrate to Israel.

The first to call in a frank manner for a reduction in immigration was Meir Grossman, a member of the Jewish Agency Executive from the Revisionist movement. On 25 March 1949 he declared: 'Let's not make immigration a risky affair.' Within a short time, the Minister of Finance, Eliezer Kaplan, added his voice to this view, although not publicly. Giora Yoseftal, the head of the Jewish Agency's Absorption Department, Chaim Shiva, director of the Ministry of Health, and prominent members of the Zionist Executive in the United States added their reservations as well.[7] The Prime Minister, David Ben-Gurion, opposed this position with all his might. In his opinion, as long as the gates of the communist-bloc countries remained open and as long as it was still possible to bring large communities from the Arab countries, there should be no hesitation in taking full advantage of this historic opportunity for large-scale immigration. Indeed, the gates were not closed and the serious absorption problems continued.

At the beginning of 1950, the conditions of the immigrants in the camps worsened to the point that it created an explosive situation. Among those who recognized the full gravity of the situation was Levi Eshcol, treasurer of the Jewish Agency and head of the Settlement Department. At a meeting of the Jewish Agency Executive on 27 March 1950 he stated:

> One hundred thousand persons are living in these camps today, without work, without anything to do, eating bread charitably distributed by the Jewish Agency ... and we are about to add

more than two hundred thousand individuals … During this past month I have visited the camps numerous times and have absorbed the atmosphere of bitterness surrounding their lives … A solution must be found … The work must be taken out of the hands of dedicated officials … and placed on the entire Yishuv. On its towns, villages, moshavim and kibbutzim.[8]

Two weeks later, in the same forum, Eshcol detailed his proposal:

to close the camps [and] not to expand their capacity. To establish immigrant housing or immigrant neighborhoods through- out the country, even for a transition period only, ranging from Dan unto Beersheba … We can convert part of the basic provisions we give them into economic benefits that we offer to the immigrants for the purposes of productive investment.

In other words, Eshcol wanted to grant the immigrants responsibility for their lives and livelihood (and to that purpose to open the camps to their surroundings), and to spread the burden of absorption to broader elements in the nation. At the same time, he also wanted to transfer part of this responsibility to State and municipal institutions. The immigrants should seek out work and support their families through it, and even housing problems would be resolved by what was soon to be called *ma'abarot*, that is, 'transit camps'.

These transit camps were intended as temporary living quarters, on the assumption that immigrants would be there for a short period, until they were firmly established and could integrate into neighbouring settlements. The majority of transit camps were established within the jurisdiction of municipalities, a decision which took into consideration a number of factors such as the availability of suitable ground plots, the need to disperse the population, employment possibilities, transportation services, the supply of food and water, and the like.

The transit camp consisted of simple and moveable structures, both because it was necessary to erect it in the shortest time due to the 'impossible' constraints stemming from the unexpected waves of immigration, and also in order to economize on resources. It was comprised of tents, canvas-covered huts, tin shacks and, later, wooden huts, which were purchased mainly from leftover stock of the Allied armies and the displaced persons' camps in Europe. The dimensions of an average apartment unit was between 10m^2 and 15m^2, and the deficient infrastructure did not include, for example, a hookup of the units to the water system or the electrical grid. The sewage and drainage system and the dirt roads were of the lowest quality. At the end of 1950, the country numbered 62 transit camps inhabited by 93,000 persons (out of 133,000 who lived in temporary housing). During this period, the 'co-ordinating body' for the Interior Ministry and the Absorption Department of the Jewish Agency determined that immigrant families who still lived in these camps because they had not succeeded in managing on their own had to move into the transit camps. This directive brought about a substantial increase in the transit camp population. Now the country contained 123 transit camps, the number of inhabitants having risen from 132,919 in July 1951 to 220,517 by the end of the year.[9] The majority of transit camp inhabitants were immigrants from Romania and Iraq. A minority of inhabitants, those possessing skills or helpful connections, moved out of the camps quickly. As time passed, the concentration of weaker elements in the transit camp population increased.

The 1952 report of the Inter-Ministerial Committee for Transit Camp Affairs indicates, for example, that in the North Tira camp there was an average of 5.5 persons per room. In three other transit camps, the average room density was five persons. At Kurdaney Transit Camp 'B', 336 persons had to share one shower. At the Karkur Camp, there was one toilet for every 53 individuals, and at the Kastina Camp one for every 48 individuals. At the Zichron Yaakov Camp, 23 families had the use of one water tap. At the Rishon Le Tzion Camp, one garbage pail was allocated to 30 families. The Geivim-Dorot Camp (today the town of Sderot) had no link to any transportation routes and the closest telephone was 10 kilometres away, as was the nearest doctor. The Tel Yeruham Camp had no telephone either and here the closest doctor was 'only' 53 kilometres![10]

The desire of Eshcol to shift the responsibility for the plight of the transit camps to 'the entire Yishuv' gave birth to an excess of caretaker organizations, which further aggravated the difficult situation of the immigrants. In a retrospective calculation, it turned out that 27 institutions were intervening in transit camp caretaking. They included institutions of the Jewish Agency (primary among them the Absorption Department), the Interior Ministry, the Ministry of Labour, the Health Ministry, the Sick Fund, the local authorities, and many others. The Supreme Council for Planning, which managed the establishment of the transit camps, comprised representatives from seven Government ministries in addition to representatives from the Jewish

Agency and the Jewish National Fund (Keren Kayemet). What was lacking from the plethora of authorities was a body that could accept comprehensive responsibility for the complicated co-ordination problems of the immigrants. At a session of the Institution for Co-ordination among Absorption Organizations, chaired by Ben-Gurion on 7 February 1952, the Finance Minister, Kaplan, had this to say: 'The situation is as follows. There are seven nursemaids simultaneously attending to this child and there is a danger that that he will remain without a mother.'[11]

Faulty planning in the setting up of the transit camps sometimes stemmed from the inability of absorption bodies to cope with the strong municipal authorities, which did not want the camps located within their jurisdictions. The largest city, Tel Aviv, which contained 0.25 million inhabitants in 1948, took responsibility for only two transit camps. Ramat Gan objected to receiving a transit camp under its aegis, and other veteran and established towns followed suit. On the other hand, small and weak local authorities, such as Tel Mond and Kfar Yona, were forced to augment their population by hundreds of percent and were unable to bear the financial costs.

The Jewish Agency, which bore responsibility for managing the entire complex of immigrant problems before the transit camps were set up, retained not a little authority following their construction. Dr Yoseftal gives evidence for this in a letter to the director-general of the Interior Ministry dated 8 December 1950, following the transfer of some responsibility to the municipal authorities:

> The Jewish Agency remains the body in charge of the transit camp and its duties are: 1) to establish and maintain the transit camp buildings; 2) to establish and maintain the tents in the transit camp; 3) to establish the shops and their allocation; 4) to determine who will be the transit camp occupants and bring them to the camp; 5) to cover the costs of the initial arrangements for the inhabitants, to distribute equipment and to attend to constructive loans; 6) to attend to the operation of services which other ministries (such as Education, Welfare, Supply, Interior, Transportation, Health, and the Sick Fund) are obliged to provide for the transit camp.[12]

The Jewish Agency also appointed the manager for each transit camp and provided him with minimum resources, enough for supplying elementary services to the camp's inhabitants.

Education in the transit camps was, above all, confronted with the dimensions of the problem. The waves of immigration more than doubled the school population – from 91,000 pupils in 1949 to 185,000 in 1951. Within a very short time, it was necessary to more than double the number of classrooms, the scope of building and their furnishings, the number of textbooks and the other teaching equipment, and above all the number of teachers. A tenuous solution to this last issue was found through the hiring of many unqualified teachers, including volunteers and female soldiers (see below). As to be expected, they were directed to the transit camps and not to the educational institutions in the veteran Yishuv, with all the implications that this was to have on gaps in the level of education.

Beyond this, education in the transit camps served as a focus and a lever for political, religious and communal power-struggles. At this time, education was not controlled by the State but was in the hands of politically partisan 'streams', which had been formed during the pre-State years. Illustrative details in regard to this may be found in Zameret's *Days of the Melting Pot*, which deals, among other things, with the investigatory Committee regarding the education of immigrant children and the developments which led afterwards to the fall of the first elected Government. This committee, headed by Judge Gad Frumkin, was established by the Government on 17 January 1950, following numerous complaints of anti-religious coercion filed by the Religious Camp in regard to education in the immigrant camps, especially those inhabited by immigrants from Islamic countries. The committee harshly criticized the Unit for Hebrew Language Acquisition and the Unit for Spiritual Absorption of Immigrants, which operated within the framework of the Cultural Department of the Education and Culture Ministry, and the Cultural Department in general, for offering a uniform educational programme for children in the immigrant camps. In the opinion of the committee, the uniform programme sought to adapt immigrants quickly to the labour-pioneering values of Israeli society and to make them forget the values of religion and tradition.[13]

Three bodies looked after health matters in the transit camps: the general Sick Fund (which operated, almost naturally from its beginnings, as an organizational arm of the General Federation of Labour), the Ministry of Health and the Hadassah organization. Every transit camp had a clinic belonging to the Sick Fund. Medical teams took up residence in 93 transit camps, but only in 17 of these did the team include a doctor. As detailed in Sternberg's, *Absorbing a Nation*, the

1   IDF Commanders visit a transit camp, Photographer unknown

2   IDF Commanders visit a transit camp, Photographer unknown

3   Soldiers help erect tents in a transit camp, Photographer: Z. Kluger

4   Soldiers help erect tents in a transit camp, Photographer unknown

health and sanitation situation was most difficult, and the reasons for this were clear. In the first place, substantial elements of the transit camp population brought contagious diseases such as trachoma, ringworm, gastro-intestinal disorders and skin infections from their countries of origin. Secondly, the overcrowding and the defective infrastructure increased contamination and the danger of infection. Thirdly, the average level of sanitary awareness was low. Time and again it was necessary to issue general instructions regarding basic hygiene, and to enforce sanitation norms and the broad application of preventive medicine. In the meantime, health hazards greatly increased.

In the main, in the field of health, as in the case of education, no sufficient response was found to the difficult and manifold problems which massive immigration posed for the system at the beginning of the State's existence.

In the winter of 1950, in tandem with the establishment of the first transit camps, the Government initially called in the IDF to help ameliorate the situation. This winter was particularly harsh, with snowfall occurring even along the coastal plain. It was a foregone conclusion that climatic damage to the transit camps would be extensive, given the fact that the temporary construction was built on the most rickety of foundations and, what was worse, in low-lying areas. Many transit camps were flooded and turned into swollen mud holes; tents, canvas huts and wooden shacks collapsed or were washed away; access roads (most, if not all, unpaved) were cut off, thus preventing the supply of vital, elementary services. In a number of places matters reached life-threatening proportions. The IDF was also requested to assist in the emergency operations. Despite the gravity of the situation, the problematic focal points were never dealt with.

In addition to low morale, heavy damage caused by the harsh winter created resentment and violence among transit camp inhabitants, further heightening loss of control over daily life by public institutions. Giora Yoseftal wrote in his diary:

> At this very second I have received information via the telephone from Tel Aviv. They are informing me that residents in the Petah Tikva transit camp have burst into the small, roofless huts, removed the workers from them, and are carrying out roofing by themselves. They invaded the camp offices. At the Hiria camp, they burst into the camp offices and into the huts of the veteran residents; the staff fled. They burst into the

storerooms and stole their contents. At Kfar Ono, they broke into the offices, stole from the grocery store; the staff fled.[14]

There were many days like these.

In light of the above, the Jewish Agency asked the Government to grant the IDF authority for maintaining order in a group of transit camps located in the Jerusalem corridor, the Negev and the north of the State. These camps were deemed to be in the direst of straits. Giora Yoseftal demanded that the 'army's assistance for these locations concern itself with tents and tin huts, sewage, drainage and sanitation in the camp, access roads to the camp, medical aid, transportation of supplies, maintenance of children's institutions during emergency periods and organization of a camp guard'.[15] Minister of Labour, Golda Meir, who headed the Committee for Co-ordinating Immigration and Absorption, forwarded the request to the Chief-of-Staff, Yigael Yadin, and he in turn ordered the General Staff into session on the subject. Consequent to this, Yadin reported to Golda Meir: 'I arranged a discussion of the transit camp issues at General Staff Headquarters and we can rest assured that the army will take this up with enthusiasm.'[16] Immediately afterwards, a committee with representatives from the General Staff, Logistics and Manpower Branches were appointed to attend to transit camp issues. In addition, area commands were ordered to conduct a survey in areas under their security jurisdiction and identify the transit camps in which geographic conditions, the housing situation, and engineering, medical and morale problems were in a critical state.

All IDF commanders involved in the new operation, including the Chief-of-Staff, clearly knew that the transit camp problems had a strong impact upon national security. They sensed, from their prior schooling and on the basis of the general outlook inculcated into them by Ben-Gurion, that the military strength of the Israeli State was also measured by the social cohesion of its inhabitants. Medical problems, social problems and low morale among immigrant concentrations thus seemed to constitute a danger with which the IDF had to cope as part of its routine duties. Moreover, a good portion of these immigrants resided short distances from the State's borders, and social and economic difficulties occurring in the immigrant moshavim became difficult problems affecting routine security. The IDF could not ignore these adverse developments. Thus, the Jewish Agency and its senior personnel called upon the IDF to render assistance to the transit camps because of the emergency conditions within. Senior officers were assigned activities of a broader purview as part of their Zionist-pioneering outlook.

A despatch sent by the Chief-of-Staff to commanders of IDF units reads:

> With the first rains, there is an increasing fear for the fate of the immigrant inhabitants of the transit camps. Their state of health and the supply situation arouse concern and even cause their morale to plummet. All this requires immediate rectification. The Government has decided to deploy the IDF as a helping hand for this major mission; we are called upon once again, now that the battles are over, to show that our duties and missions have not ended. Nor will we refrain from extended participation in carrying out this pioneering duty of immigrant absorption, which is of the utmost importance and possesses great significance for the security situation confronting the State of Israel. We are also called upon to show the immigrants, who were used to seeing the army in their native country as the enemy and oppressor, that the army of the State of Israel is their protector and helper. The security importance of the mission is of the first order. The transit camps play an important role in guarding the State's borders. If each transit camp is not turned into a fortified position, and all its inhabitants into people that know how and are prepared to defend themselves, we will not have provided for our security ... I know that the burden is great, but being convinced, together with you, that there is no more lofty, important and educational duty for our army than this task, I believe we can live up to it as is proper and fit for the Israel Defence Forces.[17]

Documents from the General Staff Branch–GHQ, Operations Division reveal that the IDF planned to care for 25,000 transit camp inhabitants under its responsibility – in areas ranging from engineering assistance to complete medical and health care, from food supplies and its distribution to intensive activities in education, learning and culture. In order to emphasize the tremendous importance and urgency he attached to this mission, the Chief-of-Staff conducted a tour of the Adjour transit camp, accompanied by the heads of the General Staff Branches and their deputies, generals from the various commands, commanding officers from the various corps, and area commanders.

The Transit Camp Operation Order, published on 17 November 1950, following the despatch of the Chief-of-Staff (mentioned above), further informs us of the extent to which this matter headed the IDF agenda. The mission was described in a laconic manner: 'Transit Camp Assistance for the Days of Winter', but an examination of this order again reveals that the army dealt in depth with the problems, going beyond the requests for technical assistance emanating from Jewish Agency personnel. Following an examination of 138 transit camps, immigrant camps and labour villages, 37 (Class 'A' camps) were selected as targets for immediate assistance. Local conditions largely determined the eligibility criteria which included the sanitary situation, quality of manpower, level of the institutions and staff, length of time in existence, internal social organization and, most importantly, its capability to withstand the deteriorating conditions of winter.

The order spoke of the army receiving responsibility for Class 'A' transit camps and managing them through the existing camp organization. In order to bring this about, the IDF will receive command responsibilities over local agents of the Jewish Agency stationed in the camps.'[18] It was a foregone conclusion that such a formulation would create misunderstandings and conflicts with the Jewish Agency. The areas of 'designated responsibility' in the Order were as follows:

- Organization of the transit camp, while upholding order and State laws
- Sanitation and preventive medicine for the transit camp population, dissemination of information with regard to these matters, facility maintenance, dusting, hygiene inspection, and the like
- Medical care for the transit camp population. For routine cases, the erection of sick bays for local hospitalization in the camps; for more serious cases, hospitalization at permanent hospitals in co-ordination with Government bodies and the Sick Fund
- Handling of children's institutions, including medical care and inspection
- Maintenance of physical structures, tents and other public facilities;
- Drainage both within the camp and its immediate surroundings in advance of and during the winter season
- Guaranteeing a concentration of emergency supplies for all transit camp inhabitants
- Plans for emergency evacuation of the transit camp inhabitants and their absorption into neighbouring settlements and camps.

In addition, the IDF also assumed responsibility for about 100 transit camps (Class 'B') which had received a higher emergency ranking according to criteria of the General Staff. In these transit camps, the area commands were required to focus their activities on preparations for the winter season, concern themselves with sanitation, and assume responsibility for all the children's institutions.

IDF units entered the transit camps within a few days of the issuance of the orders. Companies began stabilizing tents and structures of various types, setting up additional shacks, digging drainage ditches, leveling problematic land areas and hooking up water and sewage systems. Female soldiers aided mothers in taking care of their babies, played with the younger children and undertook instructional and informational activities among teenagers. The army did not establish new frameworks for this operation but instead allocated transit camps to area commands, and to the navy, airforce, Nahal, Gadna and Israeli police. The professional corps (signal, quartermaster, supply, engineering and medical) were called in, each one in its area of expertise, to help headquarters deal with their respective tasks.

The Northern Command was given responsibility for six transit camps (this included one camp under the aegis of the navy). Central Command received responsibility for 12 transit camps (this included one camp under the charge of the police). The Eighth Command, which operated at this time as the General Staff Reserve in the area of the Central Command, took responsibility for four transit camps. The Southern Command was responsible for 15 transit camps (one of which was under the control of the Israeli Police). Regular soldiers comprised the manpower commissioned for the operation; an additional contingent of reserve soldiers was placed on stand-by service for use if needed. In principle, permission was granted to mobilize six reserve soldiers for every 100 transit camp families who needed comprehensive assistance and two reserve soldiers for every transit camp falling within the category of the army's higher ranking. In addition, two female reserve soldiers were mobilized for every transit camp belonging to this second category and an officer from the Women's Army Corps was assigned for every three to four transit camps to supervise these female soldiers.

A special instruction in the Transit Camp Operation Order related to the setting up of children's absorption centres, one in each area command and an additional two in the Navy and Airforce Corps. These centres were prepared to take in altogether 1,500 children between the ages of 5 and 14 years. The children were to receive a full complement of clothing (and clothing assistance to the extent possible for the rest of the camp inhabitants). From the arrival of the first group there were centralized feeding arrangements for all the children and the preparation of a week's stock of emergency supplies for all the centres.

The widespread activities of the Medical Corps actually began several months before the Transit Camp Operation. At the end of June 1949, Ben-Gurion wrote in his diary: 'Professor Adler visited the camps and was shocked by the mortality rate among children. The Health Ministry does not know how to relate to the health of a nation and tragedy will ensue if the matter is not immediately handed over to the army.'[19] Following this notation, a meeting was called to discuss the health situation in the immigrant camps, and Ben-Gurion then charged Dr Chaim Shiba, chief health officer of the IDF, with the task of examining mortality among camp children and investigating whether the army was able to handle this distressful situation.

Shiba commandeered Dr Avraham Atzmon for this undertaking. Atzmon was about to replace Shiba as IDF chief health officer (Shiba himself was soon to be appointed as director of the Health Ministry). Following his investigation, Atzmon made the following recommendations:

> The problem of hospitalizing immigrants can only be solved through the setting up of hospitalization facilities in the transit camps. What institution in the country can fulfill this task? The Ministry of Health is not organizationally equipped for this. In terms of organizational scope and geographical distribution, the Sick Fund of the Histadrut can assume this statist mission but so far the required steps have not been undertaken. The Medical Corps is the only body which today is capable of looking after new immigrants, on condition that the required material means are made available to it.[20]

Atzmon and Shiba were aware of the basic fact that the military apparatus, in contrast to the civilian systems, could operate throughout the country through orders and commands free from financial, political and organizational problems which plagued the Sick Fund and the Health Ministry. Whereas, for example, the civilian echelons found it difficult to send doctors and nurses to remote and isolated locations, the army could do this through its regular and reserve medical team, avoiding extended discussions of financial and other terms. The devotion, understanding and determination of senior personnel in the Medical Corps also contributed to the IDF's rapid entrance into the picture.

At the beginning of July, shortly after Shiba had presented Atzmon's report to Ben-Gurion, the green light was given to start operations within the guidelines of the report. The Medical Corps mobilized about 200 doctors, including reserve soldiers (who were called-up following consultations with civilian hospitals regarding their own medical needs). At the same time, it became apparent that the few registered nurses working in the civilian hospitals prevented any possibility of recruiting a group of them for reserve duty in the transit camps. Against this background, Ben-Gurion ordered a postponement in the demobilization of nurses in the regular army service and compensated them with improved economic conditions (including a civilian salary). In addition, a special investment effort was made in the IDF School for Registered Nursing, which had been established in April 1949, at the Tel Hashomer Hospital in Tel Aviv. In the first two classes – the second class began in October 1949 – 64 nurses were admitted.

The activities of the Medical Corps in Operation Transit Camps were divided into three categories:

1. Full medical treatment (to 6,500 patients) in 18 transit camps;
2. Medical inspection and full hygienic care in 20 transit camps;
3. Partial sanitary care (spraying, dusting and instruction) in all Class 'B' (about 100) transit camps.

Permanent clinics were set up or completed in all the above camps and from this stage forward every clinic had a medical team fitted out with proper equipment and an army doctor present throughout the day. In addition, eye, skin and children's doctors provided services akin to those received by the veteran population. The medical teams carried out intensive treatment of all transit camp inhabitants who had contracted infectious diseases, and also carried out comprehensive vaccinations for a host of diseases (first of all, chicken pox). In addition, regular medical surveillance was undertaken at every public school. The majority of people requiring hospitalization were admitted to seven central sick bays located at Central Command and Southern Command and three sick bays set up at the children's camps.

The report written by the Chief Medical Officer in March 1951 observed:

> It can be said that as a result of the Medical Corps' activities during the last three months, medical treatment in the transit camps can now be handed back to the civilian institutions ... There is an additional improvement with regard to the trachoma situation, there is no more scabies, and other skin diseases have almost completely disappeared.[21]

This report also dealt with the fear that many immigrants felt towards doctors. Many women, for example – including pregnant women – refused to be examined by male doctors. Some of them even preferred to give birth in their temporary residences and receive the assistance of elderly women who were residents of the transit camps. Noting this avoidance of male doctors, the report stated that the Medical Corps had begun to send women doctors to the camps. In many instances, however, immigrants of both sexes chose traditional medical treatment, which was familiar to them from their country of origin. This resulted in many cases of children's diseases receiving no treatment over a long period of time.

Despite that, more than 1,400 children who contracted ringworm and trachoma were treated at special camps. Consequently, these two epidemics were almost completely eliminated among this population. During 1951, the treatment camp set up in the Schneller compound in Jerusalem took in 176 children suffering from consumption, trachoma or ringworm from three transit camps in the Jerusalem corridor. All consumption patients were hospitalized; ringworm and trachoma patients were treated as ambulatory cases at the Hadassah Hospital. They were returned in good health to their homes within six to eight weeks of their stay at the camp. At the Rosh Ha'ayin camp, 145 children taken from the transit camps under the jurisdiction of the Southern Command, were treated for ringworm. At the Tel Nof camp, 154 children received treatment for trachoma during 1951.

The IDF continued to hold on to the children's camps for the purposes of medical treatment following the completion of the Transit Camp Operation of 1951. In anticipation of the 1952 winter, the treatment team's scope of operations was even increased, and accordingly it looked after 200 children with ringworm at the Schneller compound. The camps at Rosh Ha'ayin and Tel Nof were expanded.

Alongside the camps for medical treatment, IDF soldiers built children's camps for rehabilitation and recuperation; part of them were used for receiving children evacuated from transit camps during the winter months. One of the more prominent camps was Fadun, erected at Tel Nof under the aegis and responsibility of the Air Force, and intended to house 1,000 children aged 14 to 15 years. In fact, 420 children arrived at the camp and stayed there for four months.

The senior echelon of the Air Force had command responsibility for Fadun. The man in charge of instruction, co-ordination, manpower allocation and resources was Colonel Ezer Weizmann. A special order from the Air Force Chief, Personnel Branch, Colonel Shmuel Eyal, stated:

> Transit camp children brought to the camp are the guests of the Corps for the winter. We wish to make it as easy as possible for them during their stay away from their homes and families. Each soldier of the Corps will do his best to offer clothes, games, toys, musical instruments and other suitable items for children between the ages of 5 and 13.[22]

The direct commander of the children's camp was Lieutenant-Colonel Yaakov Frank, who was called up for special reserve duty precisely for this task. Accompanying him, in his capacity as representative of the Chief Rabbi of the IDF, was the rabbi of the air force, Major D. Cohen. This latter appointment was made when army officials became aware of the fact that very many children in the camps were religiously observant Jews. A detailed account in the Air Force newspaper reveals that arrivals at the camp were from Yemen, Iraq and North African countries. The Yemenites, adds the newspaper, were quiet and disciplined whereas the North African and Iraqi children constituted an educational challenge for the Air Force soldiers and the civilian caretaking teams, which included personnel from the Education Ministry and the Jewish Agency. All the children lacked basic values of order and discipline, proper hygiene, eating habits and norms of living together. The teachers and instructors invested most of their day engaging the children in studies, games and sport. The children, reports the newspaper, regarded the soldiers as good friends whose fellowship and social intercourse helped to pass away the difficult period of separation from home and adjustment to camp conditions.

The words of greeting from the Chief-of-Staff at the concluding ceremony held at the Tel Nof camp pointed towards the broad orientation of the IDF within the framework of assistance to residents of the transit camps: 'The mission did not begin at the beginning of winter and will not end with the last rains; it will continue as long as immigration continues and the IDF will continue to look after the frontier transit camps and the youth camps.'[23]

Other prominent camps established during the first year of the Transit Camp Operation included Tira (which took in 500 children in 1951 and was expanded to absorb 700 children in 1952); Damun (established by Gadna, destroyed during the winter of 1950 and rebuilt by Gadna before the winter of 1951/52 in order to receive 250 non-religious children); Kedoshim under the responsibility of the head of Manpower and Personnel Administration (also known as Ariel, and established at Base 780; it hosted 350 religious children for one month during the winter).

In the framework of the Transit Camp Operation in 1952, the IDF set up three camps for religious children: Camp David under the Northern Command, Camp Neve Sha'anan under the Navy, and Camp Ramat David under the Air Force (as a replacement for a camp set up at Tel Nof the year before). These three camps were run by the Military Rabbinate Corps following detailed instruction of the acting head of Adjutant-General Branch, GHQ: 'The religious children's camps will be run along religious lines ... The IDF Rabbinate will cultivate a religious way of life and supervise the carrying out of a religious life-style in the children's camps.'[24] The Chief Rabbi of the IDF had responsibility for appointing the commanders of these camps; the commander of Camp David was the army Rabbi for the Northern Command.

This approach raised difficulties both with regard to the level of teachers and instructors and in the matter of educational topics. Mounting criticism by children and their parents was followed by a mass exodus from the camp. The head of the Operations Department at headquarters, Yitzhak Rabin, was sent to inspect the phenomenon (an indication of the importance accorded it) and his conclusions were clear: the subordination to the army rabbinate brought about a low level of instruction and the use of corporal punishment towards children. He recommended removing instruction from the control of the army rabbinate and employing instructors from the religious youth movements.

Another report on this topic arrived at the Chief-of-Staff's headquarters from Lieutenant-Colonel Gidon Shoken, acting head of Adjutant General Branch, GHQ, who wrote:

> In many instances the level of the teachers was not high. There were not enough textbooks and notebooks and there was a high turnover of teachers. The level of child counsellors was low in a majority of cases and their approach to the children was tough, lacking understanding and love. They do not know how to have fun and play with the children nor to occupy them in the hours after school. They themselves are not very clean and they do not provide a good example for the children. Their approach draws from the Biblical dictum warning that 'he that spareth his rod hateth his son'.[25]

He added that a number of the children left the camp at their parents' initiative after rumours, initiated by political party organizers, spread throughout the transit camps, that children remaining there would prevent an improvement in the living conditions awarded to their parents. This was a clear-cut indication of processes revealed with greater force, some time later, when Gadna operated the camps, including the initiative of the 'Striking Roots' camps (discussed below).

All camps located in remote areas received communication equipment. The Signal Corps, in co-ordination with the Postal Service, was asked to link the camps to the civilian telephone lines. Moreover, since there was now an army unit in every transit camp, the Army Postal Service in the Signal Corps began to operate between the camps and supplied regular postal services to all its inhabitants.

Preparation of the ground in anticipation of winter, as well as preparation of the main routes and access roads, was assigned to area command engineering companies and area engineering units (including heavy equipment units). These units were also assigned responsibility for providing assistance in times of emergency, for keeping main roads open and for towing and rescuing when requested. For carrying out the engineering tasks alone, the commands were allocated 12,000 reserve duty days in addition to regular army manpower. Beyond this, a special order was issued to area command engineering officers to break up army roads which were no longer in use and to use the material for improving roads leading to the transit camps and within them.[26]

The Quartermaster-General Branch–GHQ, supplied 15,000 shirts; 9,000 pairs of trousers; 12,000 jackets; 10,000 coats; and large numbers of blankets, sheets and mattresses. In addition, the army organized a mobile shop for the sale of clothing through the auspices of Hamashbir and the Merchants' Association. This shop travelled through the various transit camps and supplied basic clothing needs on the basis of easy credit arrangements to all the immigrants.

The generals of the Commands and officers under them began this operation even before the detailed order, including its professional appendices, was issued from General Headquarters. Thus, for example, in the operational order of the Central Command published on 13 November and signed by its General, Tzvi Ayalon, it was stated:

> The settlements selected were those which the institutions regarded as the worst off. I have no assurance that this is an accurate picture. Thus, the Brigade (area) Commanders must tour all the locations under their jurisdiction in which there are immigrants who were transferred there from absorption camps of the Jewish Agency, such as transit camps, labor camps and moshavim, and check the main conditions of immigrant life in light of the winter conditions.[27]

In follow-up instructions from the General of this command, the mission itself was also expanded. Treatment of the settlements and the immigrants was to be carried out with the intention of activating the people who lived in the settlement so that they could improve their quality of life, and deal with the difficult conditions by themselves. To this effect the commanders were also asked to pay attention to creating social and cultural life to the fullest extent possible.

In every relevant settlement within the area of the Central Command, a command group was formed, which included the commander and a number of assistants, adjusted to the size of the settlement. Apart from the regular forces of the Engineering Corps and Medical Corps, this team was provided with a number of female soldiers. Their duties were to instruct the immigrant women with regard to the rearing of children, personal hygiene and household management.

Brigade commanders were to make arrangements for daily tours of the communication cars and to assure that these vehicles would visit each settlement three times a day. These visits were also

intended to respond to morale needs by reducing the feeling of isolation among the residents and strengthening their self-confidence.

At the conclusion of Ayalon's Order, he stated that: 'The teams are
not to operate according to a regular schedule but rather must
develop their own initiatives in finding solutions for overcoming
obstacles and the difficult life conditions.'[28]

Commanders in other units of the IDF instructed their units in
the same spirit. In almost every one of the operative orders and
instructions, there was a clear summons to field commanders to take
on extra responsibility. An examination of the orders also discloses
instructions touching education and information dissemination at
every stage of the operation; in addition, there were to be organized
visits of immigrants to IDF units, kibbutzim and veteran moshavim.
There were also references to establishing joint efforts between the
camp youth and youth from the surrounding area.

At the start, it was not clear who would bear the financial costs of
the operation and what the extent of these expenses would be. There
was little doubt that a considerable sum of the needed funds would
come from the operating budget of Government ministries, the Jewish
Agency and the Sick Fund, but there was equally no doubt that there
would be a need for substantial additional funds. The Defence
Minister and the Chief-of-Staff (Ben-Gurion and Yadin) issued instructions to solve all the problems, including those in the area of food and
clothing, without waiting for budget approval from any Government
ministry, except the defence establishment. Thus, in the end, the IDF
invested more than 375,000 pounds for transit camp improvements –
an impressive sum in those days.

EDUCATIONAL ACTIVITIES AND INFORMATION DISSEMINATION

The IDF guideline for educational and information dissemination
activities in the transit camps was anchored in the spirit of Zionist
ideals. This ideology guided the senior command throughout the
operation. The IDF was now being mobilized to shape the educational and cultural world of the immigrants in accord with State
needs, and this was the very same IDF that had attempted to find
solutions to the material distress of the immigrants. The soldiers,
through orders of their commanders and instructions from the
headquarters of the chief educational officer, viewed the teaching of
Hebrew, the information dissemination programmes, the lectures

and the festive occasions as a guaranteed method both of drawing the inhabitants of the transit camps closer to Israeli society and its culture, and also of creating the new Israeli. Those involved in this undertaking, however, were not aware of the problems entailed in the discontinuity of identity among the immigrants. For example, they failed to perceive the slight inflicted on the deeply engrained pride in their culture brought by the immigrants from their countries of origin. More to the point, the soldiers did not understand these problems. The soldiers initiated festival celebrations, Israeli folkdance evenings, and joint events for the transit camp and neighbouring settlement youth – all in complete accord with the cultural mould familiar to them and with complete faith that this was the right way. And like the people in the Education Ministry and its Cultural Department, they, too, clashed with communal religious practices and traditions, and got caught up in disputes, which ultimately led to the curtailment of the IDF's educational activities and information programmes in the transit camps.

Theatrical productions were among the cultural activities initiated by the army for the transit camps. They were military-organized productions in every sense of the word. An article in the IDF weekly, *BaMahane*, entitled 'Theatre in the Transit Camp' testifies to this:

> In the early hours of the evening, thousands of immigrants began to wend their way to the natural amphitheater ... They sat on the benches that the army brought for them. From time to time army transport vehicles arrived packed with men, women and children. The many thousands of spectators sat down to watch the show.[29]

The show itself, 'In the Plains of the Negev', dealt with a kibbutz during the War of Independence, a topic not familiar to the immigrant audience. The actors, of course, delivered their lines in Hebrew and many spectators did not understand them, not to mention that for many, this was their first time at a theatre performance. Before each act, someone stood on the stage and explained the outline of the plot in Yiddish and Arabic – and thus, thousands of immigrants were able to understand a little of what they were seeing. Nevertheless, one may suppose that they did not derive great pleasure from this theatre presentation. However, the feeling of the education officers, as reflected in the *BaMahane* article, was one of satisfaction; the naivety, perhaps the paternalism, revealed in retrospect after many years, did not bother them.

The IDF labelled the orders for the Operation to assist the transit camps as 'secret' and even as 'top secret', for fear that any announcement regarding the entry of the IDF into the transit camps would be interpreted as an admittance of incompetence on the part of the Government and bodies of the Jewish Agency. Once the activities actually began, it was not possible to hide the Operation, and within a number of days, large newspaper-headlines in all the Israeli newspapers reported on it accompanied by detailed articles.

Thus, for example, *Ha'aretz* declared in its edition of 21 November 1950: 'Reserve Forces of the Army Will Be Diverted to the Transit Camps'. Under the headline was an article telling about the mobilization of 200 doctors and hundreds of nurses for reserve duty in order to supply medical aid in the transit camps. In addition, the article detailed the undertakings of the Engineering Corps and the plans for building special camps for 1,500 children. In these camps, the newspaper told its readers, the army would assume full responsibility for the material well-being and education of the children for a period of three months. With regard to the 5 to 12 year olds who could not be taken out of the transit camps because of their parents' objection, it was reported that special huts would be built for them by the IDF and that they would be directly cared for by female soldiers.[30]

The following headline appeared in *Al Hamishmar*: 'The Defence Army Will Look After 37 Out of 108 Transit Camps'. The accompanying article described the IDF assistance plan in detail and emphasized in particular that IDF commanders would be responsible for managing the 37 transit camps and co-ordinating all the activities of agencies attending to immigrants.[31]

Contrary to fears that the entrance of the IDF into the transit camps would be perceived as a reflex response of the Government and the Jewish Agency to the fact that they could not supply the appropriate civilian manpower, it now became apparent that the action itself, and the dedication of the commanders and soldiers to the different tasks in the transit camps, actually contributed to the raising of public morale, especially among the immigrants. Ben-Gurion viewed the operation and the public response to it as a justification of his general outlook regarding the IDF as a central bearer of statist pioneering, and also as the body which could realize central national tasks. On 26 November 1950, a short time after the start of Operation Transit Camps, the Prime Minister visited the Furadis transit camp, then under the aegis of the Navy. The next day he sent a long letter to the Chief-of-Staff, Yigael Yadin:

> The central objective of our generation is the in-gathering of the exiles, and all the forces of the State and the people during this period must be harnessed for this supreme effort. But our public, and perhaps also the best among it, has not yet realized its significance, its content, its requirements, difficulties and dangers ... The army by itself cannot do this job, but without the army, it will not be done. And within the army, greater participation of the female soldiers is necessary because primary attention is needed here for infants, children and women – the home and the mother. And only a woman is capable of this.[32]

Ben-Gurion then addressed the problems of absorption of the Yemenite immigrants. He liked that group because of certain qualities they exhibited, especially their capability for solidarity (the Yemenites, he claimed again and again, are lovers of labour, do not seek out life in the city, exhibit a distinct link to Israel's tradition and even a grasp of the Hebrew language). He was also sensitive to their fears, stemming from the adverse influences of distress experienced in their country of origin.

> The first thing that must be done after arrangements for more efficient organization and hygienic conditions in the camp are attended to, is care for the children (including infants) and one must begin from the beginning: body cleansing, washing, elimination of lice, boils, trachoma. Better nutrition ... clothing and proper footwear for the winter ... special care for babies. It is possible and it is our conscientious obligation to reduce the mortality rate among Yemenite children to the level reached among the veteran population. Here, motherly care, which is still in the hands of the female soldier and the volunteer, is principally required ... Women must be taught to read and write Hebrew. The chasm between men and women in the Yemenite community is terrible, but it is possible and necessary to close slowly that chasm.[33]

Ben-Gurion emphasized that the soldiers must act in a tender-hearted manner, setting a personal example, without showing disrespect for the feelings and customs of the immigrants in general, and the

Yemenite immigrants in particular. Beyond this, he made it clear that the army's entrance into the transit camps was intended as a rescue operation preceding the influx of many volunteers, and added: 'From the security vantage point, our army has been called upon to be an advance party – building a nation and building a country, and the road before us is very long.'[34]

At the end of his letter, Ben-Gurion made the following affirmation:

> It is clear to me that the new reality demands that we find new forms and instruments for expressing the pioneering aspiration; I see the army as the primary framework – not the only one – for exercising the pioneering capacity of youth, and this framework must generate pioneering energy to all strata of the nation and its youth. The transit camps are the primary anvil for the pioneering hammer, and if this succeeds – and it must not be allowed not to succeed – the army will infuse many strata of the population with its pioneering spirit as well as generate from within the pioneering tension which will allow it to be the initiator and also the creator in the field of settlement and making the desert bloom.[35]

Operation Transit Camps was supposed to end in March 1951, but its recorded successes – certainly compared with the state of the camps beforehand – aroused a great many requests for the IDF to continue its activities after the winter season. For example, the head of the Area Council for Upper Galilee wrote to the Ministry of Defence on 23 March:

> We are increasingly fearful of what might occur the day after should the army wind up its caretaking operations. The transit camp at Kiryat Shemona numbers more than 3,000 persons. The majority of the personnel, who were brought in with great effort to look after the inhabitants of the transit camp, are comprised of army people. Discontinuing the work of the soldiers, and especially the female soldiers, will bring a halt to most of the services provided for the camp residents and its children and will lead to widespread suffering until these services are renewed ... Our petition is addressed in particular to the soldiers of the Women's Army Corps and Nahal, upon whose work is dependent the continued care of the children and infants.[36]

This was not the only request. On 5 April the head of the Settlement Department of the Jewish Agency, Levi Eshcol, wrote to the head of the Operations Department at GHQ, Yitzhak Rabin:

> In accord with yesterday's telephone conversation, I hereby confirm our request that the army also remain over the summer in the following locations: Elkosh, Rabasia, Dir el-Hawa [moshav]; Givat Ye'arim, Aminadav, Ora, Luzim, Muhraka, Hulikat and Breir. These places are in addition to the list of eight locations in which there was an agreement between the army and the Sick Fund to continue the army's medical treatment.[37]

In fact, several days prior to this it was decided that the army would remain in the transit camps beyond the appointed termination date, to the satisfaction of all who expressed concern. The letter of Minister of Labour, Golda Meir, to the Deputy Chief-of-Staff, Mordecai Macleff, sent after this decision, emphasized her feelings of joy and relief, and those of many bodies in the Establishment.[38]

During April 1951, orders for IDF units were promulgated which authorized their entry into immigrant 'absorption settlements' and assigned responsibility for their management in three areas: administration, social affairs and security. This operation, it was made clear, was intended to be a continuation of the assistance given to the transit camps during the winter. Its objective was to raise the morale of inhabitants living on the frontier, to strengthen their stamina and to improve the security situation on the frontier. The order stated:

> In the majority of these absorption settlements the IDF operated within the framework of 'Operation Transit Camps', functioning as a stimulating and encouraging factor for camp residents and kindling faith in its abilities. Our objective is to continue with this Operation in the most essential locations … The IDF will assume full responsibility for the management and organization of the absorption settlements that will be included in this Order, and the representative settlement institutions on location will be subordinate to them.[39]

The detailed duties assigned to the IDF in the absorption settlements on the frontier included:

1. Command, that is, supreme local authority.
2. Organization of local defence and military training of the residents in preparation for their assuming local guard duty.
3. Implementation of social care via the Women's Army Corps.
4. Care of nurseries.
5. Routine treatment by the Medical Corps and preventive medicine.

The operational order divided the settlements among the various commands, but every command was required to check whether there were any additional settlements within their area which needed aid, and to send recommendations to GHQ requesting responsibility for them. Thus, an additional link was added to the chain of army activities among the new immigrants. This assistance answered true security needs and helped to consolidate the immigrant agricultural moshavim.

On 25 July the IDF promulgated an Order parallel to that governing activity in absorption settlements which related to the continuation of activities in problematic transit camps:

> The great influx of immigrants, which was larger than planned, confronted the Absorption Department of the Jewish Agency with severe problems that could not be solved through its own organizational apparatus. A lack of social cohesion, a non-existent public life, and discipline comprised the principal problems. Consequently, the sanitary situation of the transit camps is very poor and the public mood subdued. In addition, there is a shortage of suitable personnel to operate the existing institutions established in the camp. The army has been asked to enter a number of transit camps and take over responsibility for their organization.[40]

In this operational framework, Northern Command received responsibility for six transit camps: Beit Shean, Tel Adashim, Kabri, Zichron Ya'akov, Hadera and Wadi Ara. Central Command was responsible for three transit camps: Ramat HaSharon, Skia 'A' and Skia 'B'. Southern Command was assigned two transit camps: Zarnuga 'B' and Beersheva. The tasks assigned the units were not new. A majority were similar to those mentioned in the previous orders, but the emphasis was directed towards social and cultural assignments, ranging from Hebrew lessons to a general effort at improving the health of family life in the transit camp and enhancing the integration of immigrants into Israeli society.

In light of this shift in orientation, the head of the Adjutant-General Branch, GHQ, General Shimon Maza, added a special series of instructions as an appendix to the operational order. The introductory statement read:

> The objective of the educational activity in the transit camps is to inculcate appropriate public and social notions among the new immigrants, to foster their connection to the country, to explain the basic problems of the State, and in this way to bring about their integration and absorption.[41]

Within this framework, the IDF began to publish a daily newspaper written with Hebrew vowels (points and dashes below consonants to facilitate pronounciation). The paper was distributed in all the transit camps and was used as a teaching aid in Hebrew language instruction. An army group undertook language instruction in each transit camp; in addition, salaried civilian teachers were also engaged in each camp for 110 hours per month. The instruction groups were also required to show a movie once a week to camp residents, and civilian instructors were to utilize the opportunity to engage in information dissemination among the audience. The lectures touched on different topics, such as geography, history of the Jewish people and of Zionism, security problems and social problems of the State of Israel.

The bulk of the burden was assigned to Nahal, the Engineering Corps, Gadna and the Women's Army Corps, but following the earlier effort, suitable reserve soldiers were also mobilized and special permission was granted to mobilize female reserve soldiers as doctors, nurses and caretakers for families and children. Through a call-up the army Rabbinate added its own instructors to this number; they were sent both to children's and transit camps in order to reduce conflicts with religious families as much as possible.

In July 1951 a Survey Committee was appointed for the transit camps with the participation of representatives from the IDF, Ministry of Labour and the Absorption Department of the Jewish Agency. The Committee's report, which was presented to the Deputy Chief-of-Staff in September 1951, following field trips and an inspection of 119 transit camps and 31 work camps, was extremely detailed. The report included a survey of the dismal situation, taking account of the objective problems arising from the unplanned waves of immigration. In the opinion of those who conducted the survey, many problems stemmed from the mistaken decision taken by absorption bodies to establish transit camps comprising a heterogeneous population based on countries of origin. As a result of this decision, there were many inter-communal tensions, frictions, disturbances and instances of violence which more than once required the intervention of law enforcement officers. The report stated that:

> the immigrants are not rooted in a Jewish way of life and are removed from any Zionist education, in contrast to previous waves of immigration, and thus their demands are more forceful. The policy of the Absorption Department to establish mixed camps for different Jewish communities was the source of tensions, feelings of deprivation, disparities in living standards, habits and languages ... It appears to us that this process is undertaken too early and many complications could have been avoided if the transit camps had been comprised of immigrants from a single community.[42]

The committee warned about omissions in the area of education and culture, on the shortage of teachers, equipment and suitable buildings for study. 'There is no activity being conducted among the youth, no public life; an atmosphere of boredom permeates the transit camp [and] the hardship of everyday life has become a bleak routine.'[43] In addition, the committee pointed to insufficient preparation for winter with respect to housing, a water system, a drainage system, access roads, interior streets, sanitary institutions, supplies, communication equipment and means of transportation. Harsh criticism was levelled at the health clinics in the transit camps, particularly the shortage of medical staff and the defects in everything connected to preventive medicine.

The committee ranked the transit camps according to three levels:

1. Twelve camps in which the army would have full responsibility and the entire civilian apparatus within the camps would be subordinate to military command.
2. Fifteen camps in which the army would begin operations in the winter season and provide assistance in defined areas: information dissemination, care of youth, medical matters and the like (in these areas the army teams would operate in restricted fields assigned to them in co-ordination with the Absorption Department.

3. Ten camps in which the army would provide one-time help preparing them for winter.

The committee also recommended continuation of IDF activities in the children's camps and in the medical treatment camps for children.

In the meantime, in preparation for the winter of 1951/52, the Absorption Department requested army help in 54 transit camps and 3 labour camps (at the 3 levels mentioned above), and not the 37 camps designated by the report of the Survey Committee.

The concerns of Jewish Agency personnel were formulated in the following manner:

> The principal problem facing the Absorption Department is control over the inhabitants of the transit camps. The majority are immigrants from Iraq and Kurdistan and are considered difficult cases with regard to discipline; they are rebellious, have inferiority complexes, and strongly feel that they are the butt of discrimination. Because they don't know the language, contact between workers in the Absorption Department system and immigrants is carried out by a number of mediators, drawn from among the immigrants who lack leadership skills ... The Jewish Agency regards the entry of the army into the transit camps as unavoidable in order to guarantee an authoritative presence and a framework for organizing normal life.[44]

In accordance with this, the IDF in the end acquired full command responsibility for 24 transit camps comprising 15,000 immigrant families.

In the order for Operation Transit Camps (1952), command authority for the IDF groups in the transit camps were defined as follows:

1. All the bodies operating in the transit camps, absorption settlements and children's camps will appoint commanders to each of the transit camps and the other camps.
2. The authority of the appointed commanders will be:
   i) Command responsibility in regard to those caretaking matters for which the army is responsible, as stipulated in this order.
   ii) Authority to instruct the civilian staff in these same transit camps on how to carry out the stipulated duties assigned to the army in the same transit camp.[45]

As in the instructions of July 1951, the tasks of national and Zionist education for transit camp residents, the raising of morale, organization, discipline and internal cohesion headed the list. Preparations for winter were pushed to the end of the list.

Additional clauses in the order outlined the tasks of the various commands. The Northern Command received full responsibility for two transit camps and the setting up of a children's camp for 300 children of school age, with full care for them for a period of three months. The Central Command received responsibility for six transit camps and five absorption settlements, in addition to responsibility for the children's camp in the Schneller compound. The Southern Command received responsibility for ten transit camps and one absorption settlement. The Eighth Command was responsible for six transit camps, for a children's camp with ringworm patients, and for the establishment of a children's camp at Rosh Ha'ayin. The Air Force was responsible for the establishment of a camp for 400 children at the Tel Nof site. The Navy received responsibility for setting up a children's camp for ringworm patients. Gadna was fully responsible for the complete care of 300 children at a camp set aside for medical screening. Nahal received responsibility for organizing youth in the following camps: Be'er Ya'akov, Ramat HaSharon, Migdal-Gad 'A' and Beershevea. The Israeli police received responsibility for the Migdal-Gad 'A' transit camp, subordinate to the authority and general responsibility of the IDF.

A number of exceptional disturbances and outbursts of violence left no other option but to deploy the Army Police. This was done on the basis of a standing order calling for employment of force only if there was a danger of harm befalling the military staff in the transit camp. Any intervention of the military police in the transit camps required the permission of the area commander, and was to be given only after all other means had been tried to calm the situation and solve the problem. 'It should be remembered', according to the Transit Camps Order (1952) 'that the deployment of the Israeli Police in the transit camps is an option which must be avoided as far as possible, and should only be resorted to in cases of clear (physical) danger to military personnel in the transit camp.'[46]

The rains in mid-December 1951 were very heavy. Dozens of transit camps, of all types, were severely damaged. Hundreds of tents collapsed and dozens of huts and structures were destroyed. IDF soldiers evacuated thousands of residents, adults and children, in military vehicles, quite often at great risk to their lives. The report of the Adjutant-General Branch, GHQ, Operations Branch, on the situation in 20 camps, gives a gloomy and unpleasant picture:

> Skia 'B' – the entire tent area has been flooded (the drainage is not working) and it is necessary to evacuate the children and part of the families from there. All the children have been concentrated in the huts within the transit camp and are receiving full care (including food) from the army. Rehovot – the entire transit camp has been flooded and 800 families affected and harmed. All the children, women and elderly have been evacuated by IDF soldiers. Holon – this transit camp was badly damaged. Approximately 80 tents and some of the tin shacks collapsed. Three hundred children and 25 families were evacuated to the town of Holon. All the children were taken out by military transport and were gathered together in a transit camp under the supervision and full care of the IDF. A Company from Brigade 5 was sent to reinforce the local army team. Petah Tikva – many tents collapsed, and the entire area was flooded. The children were gathered together into huts by the army; the army is providing care.[47]

The Chief-of-Staff, Yigael Yadin, was quick to tour the stricken camps that week. He took with him all the branch heads of the General Staff. Following his rounds of the camps, detailed instructions were issued to augment assistance and release equipment, food and everything required in a time of emergency. In a letter sent by Yadin to Ben-Gurion, he claimed that IDF soldiers performed well beyond their military capacities and added:

> I repeat my suggestion that you declare a state of emergency until all the tents are replaced (or at least those in the transit camps which were singled-out as suffering from the worst conditions) by huts. This must be carried out quickly even if it means temporarily halting work in building the country. It is difficult for me to describe the importance of this step for the Government in order to relieve the distress of the tent inhabitants and avoid exploitation of the situation by hostile elements.[48]

The difficult struggle against the severe weather during the winter of 1951 did not prevent the teams from continuing to carry out, in a serious manner, their organizational and educational tasks among the immigrants. The weekly and monthly reports of the brigades clearly reveal the investment and devotion of the soldiers, especially the female soldiers in caring for youth, children and infants. These documents survey educational and information dissemination activities, organization of parties, field trips and strengthening of the social framework. The written material reveals, for example, that information dissemination activities of the IDF soldiers curtailed the opposition of many parents to sending their children to kindergartens and public schools. This came about because of increased parental involvement in what was taking place. Some of them even took upon themselves public responsibility and joined the different committees which the IDF teams formed in the transit camps.

A characteristic report from Brigade 16, in February 1952, describes the situation in the moshavim of Aminadav and Ora:

> Aminadav: offering Hebrew lessons, conducted visits of youth to the Bezalel Museum and government and public institutions. The club continues to operate and they are attending to its repair. Employment – afforestation and preparation of the land area for permanent settlement. Ora: they continue to build, and to grow vegetables. Field trips have been conducted. The club house is operative and Hebrew is being taught.[49]

A letter that was sent by the residents' committee of the Be'er Ya'akov transit camp to the commander of the Armoured Brigade responsible for the camp provides testimony of the extent to which the IDF influenced life in these camps. It was written following rumours that, at the end of the winter, the army team would depart.

> In the last few days a rumour has swept our camp … to the effect that the army is going to leave the camp at the end of March. This rumour has caused us not a little concern. Before the soldiers arrived at our camp, there was real corruption here. But since the army gained control over the camp, almost all the troubles have been eliminated. It is the army which has imposed order, wiped out the daily fights in the lines for bread, meat, vegetables and fish … guarded the rooms which were evacuated by their owners and prevented squatters from entering them forcefully. It was the army which took care of several matters in the schools and kindergartens in our camp. Army personnel attended to camp cleanliness. And what deserves admiration was the time when a fire broke out in the camp. If it had not been for their assistance several disasters might have occurred. In case a pregnant woman

was in labour in the late hours of the night, army personnel immediately offered their help and brought her to the hospital (there is no Magen David ambulance in the camp). And there are more activities which cannot all be described in this paper.[50]

And of course, at the conclusion of this letter, the transit camp committee asked for a confirmation of the continuation of army activities in the camp.

Operation Transit Camps (1952) was completed at the end of March 1952. At its termination, the Chief-of-Staff, Yigael Yadin, wrote a brief letter of summation to IDF commanders and soldiers:

> Out of an awareness of its national and pioneering value, and the importance of our security of the ingathering, integration and rootedness of immigrants, for the second time we accepted the task assigned to us by the State of Israel. We wanted to extend a brotherly hand to these new Israeli citizens, who are still located in transit camps and are exposed with the coming rains to suffering and danger. The devoted, enthusiastic and attentive care for the immigrant children should especially be cited ... The Supreme Command is proud that you fulfilled this Operation as befits the Israel Defence Forces.[51]

As the winter of 1953 approached, again the Israeli Government and the Jewish Agency requested that the IDF be called in to help. The orders and the instructions were clear and even routine. The Area Commands and the various territorial brigades did not wait for orders. On their own initiative, they began preparatory work for the winter and sent out teams to study the situation on the ground. The full IDF order, which was promulgated only at the end of December 1952, delegated full responsibility to the army for 31 transit camps and absorption settlements. As a result of the reduction in the number of transit camps – from 1 January 1952 to 1 May 1955 the number of immigrants living in these camps dropped from 157,000 to 88,000 – and the improvement in the living conditions of many camps, various military bodies accordingly reduced the scope of their caretaking. While assistance in the field of logistics and maintenance indeed declined, the requests for help in the social and human spheres increased. And this was not by chance. The population which remained behind in the camps comprised for the most part those who did not manage to find work and housing outside the camp; it also had difficulties handling problems in the areas of education, sanitation, and the like. Lacking work and frustrated, this population became filled with bitterness and anger which found expression more than once through harmful action against Jewish Agency personnel. A report presented by the acting officer of the Adjutant General Branch, GHQ, of Southern Command, Major Herzl Schechterman (soon to become General Herzl Shafir), stated: '... a portion of the transit camps do not require special material assistance and are not in danger of being flooded. On the other hand, there is a danger of riots (especially after the great increase in the number of jobless)'.[52]

IDF soldiers also continued to attend to these problems with a focus upon medical care for children and educational activities among youth.

ACTIVITIES OF GADNA IN THE TRANSIT CAMPS

Gadna was one of the key instruments which the security establishment and the IDF wielded in their assistance operation for the transit camps. Gadna headquarters constructed a complete programme in the camps for children aged 13 years to 18 years on the assumption that these children were not in school, not working and that their educational and cultural level, as well as their physical fitness, were deficient. The declared goals of the programme were to:

- organize the transit camp youth in a military training and education programme
- foster gradual development of their physical and mental fitness with the creation of a background and basis for multi-faceted education
- facilitate acquisition of basic concepts and values associated with Israeli life
- inculcate social and spiritual identification with the State and its functions.[53]

Senior officers in Gadna thought that these goals would be attained through youth clubs formed in all the transit camps. These clubs would serve as meeting grounds and activity centres for different age groups in the camp. A staff of officers was supposed to operate in each of these clubs, in co-operation with teachers and civilian instructors, in such areas as drill exercises, gymnastics, track and field events, quasi-military exercises, archery, camping, field trips and treks. These activities were to be supplemented by programmes of information dissemination and education in the following topics: social concepts in youth society, the geography of the land of Israel, history of settlement, defence of the Yishuv and the struggle for independence, the War of Independence, vision in building and developing the State, the role of youth in the State. In addition, Hebrew was taught three times a week, (reading, writing and composition); arithmetic, (the four basic calculations – addition, subtraction, multiplication and division); Bible study and Jewish history; general history; and popular science.

Another aspect of the initiative focused on learning Israeli songs and dances, participating in theatre groups and creative drama, attending evening reading sessions of Israeli literature, and social games. While indulging in the many cultural activities, the immigrants would acquire an awareness and feeling of personal and public responsibility and develop democratic institutions within the camps. The initiators of these programmes hoped that they would foster the building of a 'new Israeli', the offspring of a unified Israeli society, rather than members of a community that happened to immigrate to the land of Israel.

Gadna commanders often consulted with educators at universities and Youth Aliya (a rescue operation to bring youth who had lost their families in the Holocaust), but it quickly became apparent that these sources had little relevant experience. What remained was operation on the basis of trial and error. At first, they conducted programmes which had enjoyed success among urban youth from the veteran population, but this did not work out. A good example of this was the initiative to round-up high school students for instruction in a transit camp. When this operation was announced, 75 per cent of the school youth in Jerusalem signed up, but when work began few remained. And it was not long before even many of those who did remain gave up. Commanders encountered difficult problems in the transit camps situated in the Jerusalem corridor and ceased all their activities there. Beyond this, the shift in emphasis of Gadna activities to the immigrant youth required a reduction of Gadna activities in the high schools, much to the discontent of some of the instructors.

Another Gadna experimental effort consisted in using local transit-camp youth who had been trained in Gadna squad commander courses as counsellors. This also ended in failure. The new squad leaders exhibited a lot of good will and warm care towards their squad members, but the latter were unwilling to accept their authority. According to the commander of Gadna, Colonel Akiva Atzmon, 'their common communal background "did not produce a respectful relationship"'.[54]

Operational difficulties in the transit camps gave birth to Operation Rootedness. The basic idea of this operation was to take youth of both sexes, between the ages of 13 years and 17 years from transit camps throughout the country and bring them to special Gadna bases for a month. There they would be subject to quasi-military discipline and would acquire basic cultural habits. The originators of the programme hoped that the framework would permit them to assess the health of their trainees and improve it if necessary, by inculcating habits of hygiene and cleanliness equivalent to that of the veteran population (this meant, in practice, spraying with DDT and shearing the hair as protection against ringworm and lice). In addition, morning hours would be devoted to Hebrew lessons, mathematics, Bible study and geography; the afternoon would be taken up by sport and military training; in the evening, there would be dissemination of information sessions and presentations to acquaint the youth with Israeli ways of life. Captain Ephraim Barzilai, a well-known educator, whose personality and principles were an outstanding example to thousands of instructors, was appointed officer of Operation Rootedness. Meir Gottesman served alongside him as officer in charge of immigrant education.

The mobilization of transit camp children into the Rootedness Camps is a story in itself. At first, Gadna Headquarters organized a unique course for instructors of three weeks duration. The majority of its participants were female soldiers. Graduates of this course were sent in groups of three for a number of days to each transit camp in order to 'sell the idea' of Rootedness Camps. Each trio brought a pup-tent and pitched it in the centre of the camp. This was sufficient to establish a basis for communication. Many camp members invited the 'guests' to stay with them in their 'more spacious' tents. This led to more direct intercourse, free of tensions, with the parents and the youths themselves.

The first two Rootedness Camps opened respectively on the 15 and 20 of November 1950. The camp at Sheikh Monis took in 180 children from the Tel Aviv area and the camp at Nes Tziona accommodated 120 children from Jerusalem and the southern part of the country. Girls comprised about 20 per cent to 25 per cent. Many children arrived at the camp insufficiently dressed, and even without shoes, and consequently the matter of apparel became an order of first priority. Later, instances of theft, fighting and undisciplined behaviour occurred. The instructors had to deal with these incidents with restraint, in an educational fashion, exhibiting patience and forgiveness.

During the first stage, Gadna Headquarters was in charge of the Rootedness Camps. When the number of youths surpassed 600, management was transferred to subordinate units of Gadna. At this stage, camps established at Damun on Mount Carmel, at the Schneller compound and in the Valley of the Cross in Jerusalem, in addition to Migdal-Gad (to become known as Ashkelon) and at Masmia, had already been included in the operation. By July 1952, 3,500 youths had passed through these camps. Forty of these youths stayed for an additional three months in a student instructors' course, on the assumption that they would undertake this type of task in the transit camps afterwards. But at this juncture another problem suddenly emerged. Most, if not all, of these instructors desperately wanted to leave the camps and go to the agricultural schools, and thus Gadna did not derive the hoped-for benefit from them.

Following Operation Rootedness, Gadna succeeded in forming about fifty Gadna clubs in the transit camps during 1952. The budget for maintaining these clubs came mainly from the Ministry of Defence and in part from the Jewish Agency. The majority of club counsellors, 70 per cent, were young female soldiers. For a brief spell they lived in tents within the transit camps. Bullying of the young female soldiers, which sometimes erupted into violent attacks, forced the termination of these living quarters.

It should be noted that every summary of Gadna transit-camp activities notes that the young instructors were not only caught up in the complex physical and psychological problems which were imposed on the immigrants in their distressed condition, but also found themselves victims of the attitude which the latter had toward the 'establishment' – a lack of trust, disrespect and even hatred toward the system, which was regarded as haughty and alienated (and not once in fact proved to be so). Gadna instructors, who bore the new Israeli culture, a secular Sabra (Jewish youth born in Israel before and after the establishment of the state, in contrast with youth who arrived via migration) culture, and who denied the diaspora culture and sought to free themselves from the dictates of religion and tradition, were regarded by the immigrant parents as part of the establishment and spreaders of heretical ideas. This orientation, of course, did not make it easier for them.

The accusation of heresy eventually turned into an accusation of anti-religious compulsion and aroused negative responses, not only among residents of the camps. In the beginning, indeed, there was an effort, in the spirit of the outlook that guided the army after the War of Independence, to refrain as much as possible from infringing upon religious feelings. Detailed orders forbade activities on the Sabbath and religious holidays, as well as smoking in public and the use of army vehicles on these days. Other instructions concerned the special status of females in social activities. Because most of those engaged in this effort were secular-oriented soldiers infused with a Zionist-secular consciousness, it was easy to find instances of non-conformance to all of the above orders.

Already by November 1950, the Minister of Welfare, Rabbi Yitzhak Meir Levine, had sent a telegram containing a hint of protest to Ben-Gurion:

> I request that you see to it that the operation which the IDF is undertaking in the transit camps will not aggrieve us from the religious point of view. I hope that you will make all the arrangements to ensure that the enterprise will place you in an honorable light as one who stands guard against anyone who would impinge, directly or indirectly, upon the religiosity of those who are loyal to the Torah of Israel.[55]

This telegram was sent following complaints from ultra-orthodox bodies regarding the intervention of army officers in the transit camps in education matters and on the cutting of hair side-locks on the basis of health considerations. Another telegram quickly followed. On 27 November 1950, Benjamin Mintz, leader of Poalei Agudat Yisrael, directed a complaint to the Prime Minister and the Chief-of-Staff:

> At the Agudat Yisrael settlement of Jessir beside Faluja, the army made its appearance in order to proffer help, as stipulated in the agreement between the Jewish Agency and the army. Contrary to the duties that the army received, the commanders began to intervene in instructional matters. The captain asked the men to assemble and proceeded to lecture against unplanned births on economic grounds; the army doctor announced to our instructor

that because of the lack of cleanliness he would order the side-
locks of the residents cut. In response to the protest, the
instructor replied that the location was under military authority
and he will do what he likes.[56]

In another instance, residents from the Kessalon transit camp
complained to the Minister of Welfare, Rabbi Levine, that IDF
soldiers were trying to distance them from their faith. They stated
that IDF soldiers drove girls and boys, including married young
women, together in the same vehicle to a Gadna camp and exposed
them to bad ways. In addition, they complained that the soldiers
violated the Sabbath and smoked in public, boys danced with girls at
the club, and so forth.

When Gadna inaugurated Operation Rootedness, HaPoel
HaMizrahi, who were veteran political partners of Mapai and of
Ben-Gurion, in what was known as 'the famous historical alliance',
also entered the picture. They demanded that this enterprise be
placed under the control of the rabbinate who would see to it that a
religious and traditional spirit prevailed. A letter to Hapoel Mizrahi
activists enunciates a clear course of action:

> It has been decided to inform all religious immigrants who fear
> for the fate of their sons, that they should prevent the participa-
> tion of religious youth in this enterprise as long as the religious
> character of the camps is not assured, and as long as no religious
> command is appointed for them. For your attention: At present,
> the IDF has no legal authority to obligate the youth to join
> Gadna. In bringing the above to your notice, we request that you
> make all the arrangements to prevent youth from departing for
> this enterprise until we announce differently.[57]

At the same time, a letter from the religious parties was sent to Ben-
Gurion demanding that the IDF be instructed to halt its intervention
in the fields of education and culture in the camps, that these areas
be left to the institutions authorized to deal with them, and that the
religious feelings of the camp residents be taken into consideration.

Ben-Gurion's public response to the claims of the religious bodies
was to mobilize the Military Rabbinate Corps and its reserve soldiers
to the transit camps operation. The funds required to finance 5,000
days of reserve duty were taken from the Ministry of Welfare
budget.

Soldiers from the Chief Army-Chaplain's unit were called up in January 1951 and sent to the Tel Nof children's camp. However, this did not bring an end to clashes between the IDF and religious bodies in the field. In several places, rumours spread that the army had fed residents of the transit camps non-kosher food, poured gasoline into the ritual baths in order to keep the women from attending to their monthly purification rites, and undertaken every possible action to distance Jews from their religious faith. At the Jessir camp the following declaration was publicized: 'Residents of Jessir camp. Remember that the army is Amalek [has evil soldiers] and we are at war with them. Do not allow the female soldiers to come into your huts for fear that they will have bad influence upon your children.'[58] The local teachers opposed every activity of the army, even the distribution of toys to the children, and censored the books that the soldiers brought. Pages that the teachers thought were improper were torn out of books such as *Dr Doolittle* and other children's stories of this genre.

A great many accusations regarding the behaviour of the army in the Jessir transit camp reached the plenary of the Knesset. As a result the Minister of Labour, Golda Meir, and the Minister of Welfare, Yitzhak Meir Levine, were appointed as 'An Investigatory Committee for Examining the Behaviour of the Army in the Jessir Transit Camp'. The two ministers visited the camp on 20 December 1950 and discovered that an army doctor had ordered the shaving of side-locks and beards; an army officer had spoken out against enlarged families; and there were cases of forced undressing of Yemenite women for general disinfectant spraying (carried out by male soldiers). The two ministers concluded from their investigation that the Chief-of-Staff must forbid soldiers from having any communication with residents of the camps, adults and children alike, on matters pertaining to religion, or try to influence in any way whatsoever their religious outlook. Another instruction stated that only women could engage in spraying of women and young girls.

Ben-Gurion also continued to handle other complaints about anti-religious compulsion by military bodies operating in the camps, and tried to the best of his ability to reduce tensions over this matter. Nevertheless, he also made sure that the IDF and Gadna continued their educational and cultural activities, and in this way prevented from the start any attempt to create military units based on religious orientation. The suggestion to divide Gadna into two – a secular and a religious unit – was rejected outright.

In November 1951, Elik Shomroni, head of the Youth and Nahal Branch wrote to the Prime Minister:

> As you know, courses of military training and education are now being conducted for transit camp youth at Gadna bases. Until now we have managed to graduate three classes which embraced more than 400 young men and women. This undertaking is being run in the transit camps amidst hard-line hostile propaganda by religious groups.[59]

Four days later the Government fell, following a Knesset vote on the issue of religious education in the transit camps.

There is no doubt that the campaign of religious bodies against the army conducting educational and information dissemination programmes among the immigrants in the camps significantly hampered any realization of the great expectations attached to this undertaking. It also struck at the very heart of the idea of converting the army into the principal arm for building Israeli society. Nevertheless, the words of Deborah Hacohen are true to their mark:

> Despite this, the contribution of the IDF in bringing about a personal encounter among all the immigrant diaspora communities and between them and members of the veteran Israeli community was considerable. In the army camps, wide and comprehensive contacts were established between immigrant inductees and veteran citizens that barely occur in the civilian sector of a fledgling state during its first years of existence. In this manner the IDF assisted in lowering the barriers between different parts of the population.[60]

Army assistance to the transit camps continued for three years, from the winter of 1950/51 to the winter of 1952/53. Throughout this period, command of field operations was placed in the hands of lower-echelon officers holding ranks as low as second lieutenant (lowest officer class) and occasionally even sergeant (enlisted person). Some of them were reservists called up especially for the operation, among them educational personnel specializing in social work, who requested these commander assignments in the transit or children's camps. They undertook responsibility in all areas of camp life and were involved well beyond what was stipulated in the orders of General Headquarters and the military ranks. Clear evidence for this may be found in different documents citing the numerous voluntary activities initiated in the camps.

Thus, for example, some units established a special assistance fund for the transit camp operation and managed to raise substantial sums. The Air Force established a fund 'for purchasing vital and useful supplies for children who cannot obtain them and cannot get them through army supply channels'. At one of the maintenance units of this corps, the soldiers were asked to volunteer their spare time in the mass production of toys for transit-camp children. Soldiers from brigade headquarters/district 11 of the Southern Command decided to set aside a portion of their meals – eggs, margarine and other served portions, for the camp residents.

Letters and angry reports from camp commanders to the headquarters to which they were subordinate cite difficulties encountered by them at different stages of their work in the transit camps. The most basic topics are referred to: food supply (including milk products for children); clothes and shoes; problems of medical services and care for children; housing matters and improvement of living conditions in the tents, tin shacks and wooden huts. In the report of Second-Lieutenant Miriam Calderon, responsible for female soldiers stationed in the transit camps under the authority of the 11th Brigade, it was stated:

> Camp commanders are complaining about the lack of supplies. They are complaining about the fact that they presented an equipment list for tools and materials a number of times and never received anything. There is a feeling in the camps that they are totally cut off and there is nobody to help them … The girl soldiers look after the children and try to teach them. There is no civilian teacher on location, nor is there a kindergarten teacher. There are 36 children there of primary school age and the female soldiers cannot fulfill the role of teacher. A teacher has been promised for the camp. With regard to studies for the children, there are no textbooks, no chairs, writing paper, pencils, etc., and no blackboard. Whom should we address in this matter?[61]

A report of the Control Committee, which inspected the situation in the Hulikat transit camp in November 1950, spoke of education and supply matters. It read:

There are 60 primary school children in the transit camp, 19 in the kindergarten. There are 2 teachers at the location. There is no school building – they learn at the synagogue. The studies are confined to Hebrew and arithmetic. They have not yet received writing material and textbooks. Furniture for the school has not yet arrived.[62] … Fresh vegetables and milk products are unavailable. Food supplies arrive once a month, except for bread, which is delivered daily. Clothing and footwear are in short supply and most go barefoot without the possibility of changing clothes even once a week. The children walk about barefoot and naked.[63]

But the following reports indicated the beginning of improvements in all the areas, especially in matters concerning the children. These reports mention the establishment of kitchens and the distribution of food and milk to the children on a daily basis, and also the opening of a nursery for children of ages two years to seven years. In addition, a report notes the distribution of clothing and footwear, mainly from army storehouses.

A great many reports talk of clean-up operations conducted every week in the transit camp without the camp residents themselves helping the soldiers, and it is noted that this behaviour produced indignation and anger among the soldiers. Reports from the Nahalat Yehuda camp in March 1952 tell of a serious clean-up operation with the participation of dozens of Gadna soldiers from the 11th Brigade, a group from the Medical Corps and a group of barbers. The author of the report notes that a group of army police, also called in for this operation, was left with nothing to do. 'The clean-up operations were conducted without any interference and with the co-operation of camp residents.'[64]

During the course of these undertakings, several reports were written about the morale of soldiers serving in the transit camps. Some of them, especially at the beginning, mention disappointment and frustration in light of the impossible assignments confronting them. According to a report from Southern Command written in January 1951:

The general enthusiasm of the soldiers following the announce-ment and explanations of the commanders which previewed the work in the camps declined in part when they arrived at the location. In a number of transit camps, principally in the Negev district, army groups experienced numerous difficulties in the first days both in terms of the objective conditions and because of a lack of manpower; the majority of male and female soldiers were not suitable for the task.[65]

As work continued, there was substantial improvement in the spirit and morale of the soldiers serving in the camps. On the other hand, lack of clarity pertaining to areas of responsibility, and lack of co-ordination with the civilian bodies, continued to contribute to frustration and bitterness during the first stages of the operation. These negative orientations, however, gave way to a sense of respon-sibility and pride that it was the IDF that was assuming the task of absorbing immigrants. One fact bears witness to this: in an inspec-tion of hundreds of weekly reports from transit camp commanders and different headquarters, there is no trace of a lack of motivation to continue with the mission.

General enthusiasm reached such a high pitch that the acting-general for the Southern Command, Colonel Joseph Eitan, correctly reminded his soldiers:

> From time to time, articles appearing in the press with regard to army activities in the transit camps create a false and undesir-able impression by stressing the capability of the army in contrast to the helplessness of the civilian institutions that operate in this field. Comments of this sort harm the standing of the IDF in the eyes of the public and its institutions, especially since the army has assumed only part of the burden for managing the transit camps.[66]

Looking back, that was indeed the case.

1. M. Sicron, *The Immigration to Israel 1948–1953* (Jerusalem: Central Bureau of Statistics, 1957); M. Sicron, 'Mass Immigration – its Dimensions, Characteristics, and Influence on the Israeli Population Structure', in M. Naor, *Immigrants and Transit Camps 1948–1952* (Jerusalem: Ben-Tzvi, 1987), pp. 31–52.
2. For selective immigration policy, see note 7.
3. M. Naor, *Immigrants and Transit Camps*, pp.31–52.
4. M. Kachinski, 'The Transit Camps', in M. Naor, *Immigrants and Transit Camps*, p. 70.
5. The Jewish Agency, Absorption Department, *11 Years of Absorption: Facts, Problems and Numbers* (Tel Aviv: The Jewish Agency, 1959), p. 10.
6. Arieh Gelblum, a series of 15 articles on transit camps and the situation of immigrants in *Ha'aretz* beginning from 13 April 1949.

7. On the disputes over the dimensions of the immigration, the demands to restrict it and to establish selection and regulatory criteria, see Y. Raphael, 'Mass Immigration in Terms of its Dimensions, Characteristics, and Influence on the Israeli Population Structure', in M. Noar, *Immigrants and Transit Camps*, pp. 19–30.
8. L. Eshcol, *The Birth Pains of Settlement* (Tel Aviv: Am Oved, 1958), p. 219.
9. For details regarding the methods of immigrant absorption in the transit camps and documents connected to absorption activities, see D. Rozen (ed.), *Transit Camps and Immigrant Settlements* (Jerusalem: Ministry of the Interior, 1983), pp. 101–2.
10. Report of the Inter-Ministerial Committee for Co-ordinating Social Services in the Transit Camps, under the signature of D. Riban, secretary of the committee, in D. Rozen (ed.), *Transit Camps and Immigrant Settlements*, p. 171.
11. Ibid., document 37, report from the Co-ordinating Body meeting of 7 February 1952, p. 145.
12. Ibid., document of Dr G. Yoseftal of 8 December 1950 to the Director of the Interior Ministry.
13. Z. Zameret, *Days of the Melting Pot: Investigatory Committee on the Education of Immigrant Children (1950)* (Sde Boker: Center for Ben-Gurion Studies, 1993).
14. S. Yoram (ed.), *Giora Yoseftal: His Life and Work* (Tel Aviv: Mapai, 1963), p. 139.
15. IDFA 247/55/11, Meeting of the Committee for Transit and Work Camp Matters, 21 January 1950.
16. BGA, Transit Camps File, Conversation between Golda Meir and Yigael Yadin, 6 November 1950.
17. IDFA 119/754, Operation Transit Camps Order, 17 November 1950.
18. Ibid.
19. BGA, Ben-Gurion Diary, 28 June 1949.
20. N. Ro'i, 'Medical Corps', in A. Kfir and Y. Erez (eds), *The IDF and Its Corps: Encyclopaedia for Army and Security* (Tel Aviv: Revivim, 1982), p. 112.
21. IDFA 119/754, Galei Tzahal, 24 April 1951, contents of a conversation broadcast on army radio.
22. *Absorbing Immigrants: The IDF and Mass Immigration at the Beginning of the Fifties*, research collection published by Air Force Headquarters, Planning and Organization Department, Branch for the History of the Air Force, 1990.
23. *HaBoker*, 4 April 1951.
24. BGA, Transit Camp File, 'Operation Transit Camp – Religious Children's Camps', letter from Colonel G. Shoken, acting Head of the Manpower Branch, to the Chief-of-Staff, January 1952.
25. Ibid. The dictum is from Proverbs 13:24.
26. BGA, Transit Camp File, Social File 5, Engineering Assignments, engineering appendix to the operation order, 17 November 1950.
27. IDFA 247/11/53, Transit Camp Order, Central Command, 13 November 1950. Operation order of the Central Command which went out on 13 November following discussion and instructions given at a meeting of commanders on the same day.
28. Ibid.
29. 'Theater in the Transit Camp', *BaMahane*, 26 July 1951.
30. 'Army Reservists Sent to Help Transit Camps', *Ha'aretz*, 21 November 1950.
31. *Al Hamishmar*, 1 November 1950.
32. BGA, Transit Camp File, Social file 5, Personal letter from Ben-Gurion to Yadin, 27 November 1950.
33. Ibid.
34. Ibid.
35. Ibid.
36. IDFA 119/754, Letter from Upper Galilee Area Council to the Ministry of Defence, 22 March 1951.
37. Ibid., Letter of Levi Eshcol on 5 April 1951.
38. BGA, Transit Camp File, Social file 5.
39. IDFA 119/7/54, Operational Command: 'Consolidating Absorption Settlements in the Rural Village', 10 April 1951.
40. BGA, Transit Camp File, order of General Staff Branch, GHQ/Operations: 'Caretaking in Absorption Transit Camps', 25 July 1951.

41. Ibid., 'Caretaking in Absorption Transit Camps', Headquarters/Adjutant General Branch, Headquarters', 15 August 1951.
42. IDFA 127/7/54, Committee for the Transit Camps Survey, 9 September 1951.
43. Ibid.
44. IDFA 119/7/54, Document of the Jewish Agency: 'Consolidating Absorption in the Transit Camps', October 1951.
45. BGA, Transit Camp File, order of General Staff Branch, GHQ/Operations: 'Operation Transit Camps 1952', 26 June 1951.
46. Ibid., order of General Staff Branch, GHQ/Operations: 'Assistance to Transit Camps through the Military Police', November 1951.
47. Ibid., report of General Staff Branch, GHQ/Operations: 'The Transit Camps following the Storm', 17 December 1951.
48. Ibid. Transit Camp File, Letter of the Chief-of-Staff to the Minister of Defence: 'The Transit Camps following the Storm', 17 December 1951.
49. IDFA 247/11/55, Reports of Brigade Headquarters 10 and Brigade Headquarters 16, February 1952.
50. IDFA 247/11/55, Letter from the Be'er Ya'akov Transit Camp residents' committee to the commander of the Armoured Brigade, Southern District, April 1952.
51. BGA, Transit Camp File, 'Order of the Day for Termination of Operation Transit Camps', Order of the Chief-of-Staff, 31 March 1952.
52. Ibid., Document of the General Staff Branch, Southern Command: 'Transit Camps 1952', 3 December 1952.
53. D. Dayan, *Yes, We are the Youth – A History of Gadna* (Tel Aviv: Ministry of Defence, 1977), p. 159.
54. CZA 9602. Protocol of the Knesset's Education and Culture Committee, Report on the Work of Gadna, by A. Atzmon, Commander of Gadna, in his submission before the Knesset Committee on 23 July 1951. Atzmon's remark requires some decoding. He was implying that leadership drawn from 'their own' did not carry the importance for local youth that an elitist, IDF-trained military leadership could provide. There was also a communal or ethnic division implied in this preference since most, if not all, the military leadership was Ashkenazi.
55. BGA, Transit Camp File, telegram from the Minister of Welfare, Rabbi Levine, to the Prime Minister, D. Ben-Gurion, 22 November 1950.
56. Ibid., telegram from B. Mintz, secretary of the Histadrut Association of Poalei Agudat Yisrael, 27 November 1950.
57. Ibid., letter from the Defence Department of Hapoel Ha'mizrahi to instructors in the transit camps, 3 December 1950.
58. BGA, Transit Camp File, Letter from the commander of the Jessir transit camp, Sergeant M. Goldring, to the commander of reconnaissance unit 17, 9 February 1951.
59. BGA, Transit Camp File, 'Operation Rootedness – Gadna', letter of A. Shomroni to the Prime Minister and Defence Minister, 11 February 1951.
60. D. Hacohen, 'The IDF and Immigrant Absorption', in M. Noar, *Immigrants and Transit Camps*, pp. 115–27.
61. IDFA 4/435/53, Miriam Calderon Report, 28 November 1950.
62. IDFA 4/435/53, Report of the Controller Committee, 13 November 1950.
63. Ibid., 11th Brigade, 13 November 1950.
64. IDFA 16/435/53, Report from the Rehovot Block Headquarters, Operation Garbage, 10 March 1952.
65. IDFA 21/1011/53, Southern Command, Transit Camp Progress Report, 5 January 1951.
66. Ibid.

Chapter 5

IDF Activity in Education and Culture

The effort to engage the IDF as the central carrier of statist pioneering could not, of course, overlook the field of education. Indeed, without widespread and dispersed educational activities both within and outside the framework of the IDF itself, it would have made no sense to turn the army into an agency with tasks extending beyond the field of direct security. Ben-Gurion's guidelines left no doubt whatsoever about the role of the army in this regard: 'Our army has a mission not only during times of war – but also, and perhaps especially, during times of peace. It must mould the character of our youth, and through them, the character of our people.'[1]

The initiation and operation of educational activities by the nascent IDF was enveloped in a profusion of concepts and slogans coined by the fragmented labour movement from as early as the days of the second Aliya. Ben-Gurion's inspirational rhetoric contributed not a little to this vocabulary. Expressions were derived from a variety of sources, among them visions of the prophets of Israel, the various shades of socialist Zionism, doctrines of revolutionary social change and theories of radical economic reform.

With the formation of the State, two central ideas stood out above all the others, and they were in essential contradiction to each other. On the one hand, there was the idea of the Jewish State as a supreme value in itself. On the other hand, there was the idea of a 'melting pot', which would forge all Jewish inhabitants coming from such diverse diaspora communities as the European Holocaust survivors and the immigrants from Islamic countries. It was expected that they would fuse into one collective body that would respond to the basic needs of the State's existence. Without being explicitly stated, this entity was to be created in the shadow of the governing elite, possessing a marked Ashkenazi-secular culture, opposed to the Jewish Diaspora culture rooted in religion and tradition, and anchored in the *Weltanschauung* held by the political ideologues in Mapai.

Ben-Gurion spoke in this vein on different occasions. One of the famous instances was at a meeting with writers and poets whom he invited to his house in March 1949 (it was at this meeting, as far as is known, that the term 'melting pot' was applied to the Israeli context).[2] Many of the best contemporary minds in education also thought along the same lines. At a convention of educators at Beit Berl College, under the patronage of Zalman Shazar, the first Minister of Education and Culture and one of the leading intellectuals in the Labour Movement, people spoke clearly about the centrality of the state and the need to channel the entire education system in accord with it.

At one of the central presentations, a leading educator, Dr Veiziger, noted:

> there is nobody who has suffered more than we, the Jewish people, because we did not have this instrument to guarantee our existence. And because we lacked this form for organizing our social life, because of this, it seems to me that if we speak of education, that is about values for whose sake we are educating the youth, then at this stage, educating on behalf of the state should be seen as the 'supreme value' which conditions all other values. Surely this is not the only value; there are other educational values, but their importance depends on the extent of their contribution to reinforcing this value.[3]

Ya'akov Niv, who was at this time the chief inspector for the 'Labour stream' in the educational system, addressed the same matter at this convention:

> Education for citizenship means all the instruments and all the forces are directed toward it, so that the future generation will know and feel that this is its homeland. It is here that this generation lives, and for this homeland it is prepared to sacrifice its life.[4]

Zalman Shazar summed it up: 'Youth must be educated to place themselves at the service of this society of which we dream and for which we fight.'[5]

Later, Elad Peled was to write about this.

> Behind these slogans stands the viewpoint that says that the 'founding fathers', members of the first, second, and third immigration waves abandoned the tradition of their fathers' home and created a new culture. The immigrants who arrived in the country after the State was founded were also to behave in the same manner. 'Negation of the Diaspora' is not only the negation of the Eastern-European Diaspora, but also negation of the entire Diaspora, whether it is Eastern Europe, South Yemen or North Africa. Negation of the Diaspora also naturally means the erasure of any difference among Jews originating in the various Diaspora communities and the eclipse of their Diaspora origin.[6]

And Moshe Lissak stated:

> In contrast to nostalgic descriptions, which are in fashion today, the traumatic feeling tied up with immigrant absorption among the close-knit faction which managed it was quite palpable. It is not surprising, then, that they tossed around all kinds of ideas which largely expressed disappointment with the human calibre of the immigrants and very deep fears as to what might happen in the future. And all that out of a deep responsibility that translated itself into a feeling of generalized patronage for the immigrants in general and for the immigrants from Islamic countries in particular.[7]

The debate over how to convert the slogans 'formation of the character of youth' and 'the character of the nation' (Ben-Gurion's formulations) into reality during the first years of the State is developed below on the basis of a variety of sources including discussions, articles, speeches, minutes, orders, lectures, debates, methodological material and archive documents.

On the basis of this material three principal areas will be analyzed. The first area embraces the framework and tools which the army constructed in order to cope with basic problems: Hebrew language instruction; elementary schooling for soldiers and high school education for commanders; instruments and programmes for ongoing information dissemination; inculcation of battle mores; and knowledge of the country. The Educational Corps facilities and various other units of the IDF served as forums for their delivery and operation.

The second area encompasses instruments and educational activities operating outside the regular army framework and is directed towards the public at large. This category includes: teaching and information dissemination among the civilian population; information dissemination and propaganda through the communication media of the IDF (the weekly publication *BaMahane,* other army organs and the IDF radio station, *Galei Tzahal*); army involvement in state events including the central ceremonies on national holidays; and performances of the army entertainment troupes.

The third area focuses on educational and sociological aspects of core army experiences during the early fifties, with an eye to the influence and significance of army service for youth who passed through the IDF ranks during these years. In retrospect it is possible to examine what the IDF contributed to Israeli society in the way of character formulation in its initial years.

THE ARMY FRAMEWORK AS AN EDUCATIONAL FRAMEWORK

Commanders of the Hagana, and those of Etzel and Lehi as well, were aware of the great importance of information dissemination and education for convincing subordinate ranks of the 'justness of the course' (and by direct inference, of the justness of the policy and political considerations of the relevant leadership). The Information Department of the Hagana had already been instituted in the thirties, organizing courses and seminars and publishing written material for the public – books, pamphlets and proclamations (including booklets on the 'Tradition of Heroism' of which thousands of copies were distributed), and the professional journal *Ma'arachot*). The principal people involved on the information side of Hagana activities were the editors of *Ma'arachot*, Eliezer Galili (who continued to edit this publication after the establishment of the IDF) and his right-hand man, Gershon Rivlin; Eliezer Livne, editor of the journal *Eshnav*; Katriel Katz (who became government secretary and a senior diplomat); the poet, Aharon Ze'ev (who became the Chief Education Officer of the IDF); and Ahuvia Malchin (who became head of the IDF's Information Dissemination Branch). In 1947, a new instrument was placed at their disposal. Hagana headquarters decided to convert the journal edited by its Tel Aviv Section, *BaMahane*, into a national organ and turned responsibility for its publication over to its Department of Information Dissemination. This newspaper began to appear in February 1948. With the official formation of the IDF, *BaMahane* became its weekly publication.

The information system of the Palmach, under the direction of Arnan Azaryahu and Zerrubavel Gilad, operated in parallel with the Hagana activities in this field. It was intended to enhance the unique spirit of the Palmach within the Hagana, and to ensure its full subordination to the Hagana command and to the civilian echelons which officially governed it. Palmach commanders, who derived considerable inspiration from the myths of the Red Army and the partisans in Eastern Europe during the Second World War, attributed great importance to *politruk* (conveyance of the moral and educational ethos of the organization to the rank and file) and wished to make it an essential part of each commander's functions in their service. 'We see cultural-ideational activity and the formation of patterns of life neither as light entertainment nor as luxuries, but rather as an indivisible part of the establishment of a mobilized defence-shield.'[8] The content of Palmach courses clearly reflected this orientation. They included lessons pertaining to matters of national security, geography and knowledge of the country, the scope of which matched those given at the end of the seventies at IDF officers' schools.

Moreover, from 1946 onwards, when the Palmach began to grow rapidly, its ranks became filled with young people possessing a low level of education and lacking a basic knowledge of Hebrew. This led to the development of an elementary school curriculum within its framework. Classes were conducted during a summer camp for new recruits at Kibbutz Ayalet Hashahar.

The importance of education and information dissemination expanded greatly with the outbreak of the War of Independence. The printed word served as a morale booster at a period when a bleak picture was being drawn of a war fought by the few, with a weapons and equipment disadvantage, facing many with a stockpile of weapons and equipment. The slogan 'it's not the tank but the man that will be victorious', written on the wall of the dining room of Kibbutz Nirim on the eve of the Egyptian army invasion, appeared therefore, not as a figure of speech but rather as applicable to every sector and front. The 'man' in this instance was he who was furnished with the proper spirit of battle, who learned to identify completely with the fighting nation and would realize his full potential from the strength of this identification. The question as to how one arrives at this, in due haste and efficiently, and what are the concrete activities that the military system must implement in this regard, was a real bone of contention among the various schools of thought in the fledgling army. These opposing viewpoints in the officers' ranks remained after the fighting had ended.

Many Second World War veterans from the British army regarded discipline as the key element. They claimed that a strict education designed to inculcate obedience of soldiers to every commander was the prime challenge facing the army. Most veterans of the Palmach, on the other hand, stuck closely to Zerrubavel Gilad's line, mentioned above, namely that cultural-ideational activity is an indivisible part of the defence force. The senior-ranking officer among them, Yigael Alon, who began the War of Independence as Commander of the Palmach and ended it as IDF Commander of the Southern Front, wrote on this matter: 'While technical exercises are intended to train and develop the body, technical knowledge on the other hand ... is intended to develop his independent thought and his rational understanding, to deepen his ideational consciousness, and to strengthen his spiritual stamina, what is called, "the fighting spirit".'[9] Alon was not averse to claiming that education of this kind was a matter touching the civilian system.

> The army will see itself as participating in the education of the citizen: this entails the ability to think in an orderly manner; to maintain order and cleanliness in matters pertaining to the body, dress, home, yard, and public institutions; honesty in social relations; exactitude, perseverance and tolerance, working together, and so forth. These are the characteristics and practical skills required for a person as well as a citizen, for a person as well as for a soldier, for society as well as for every military unit.[10]

A year before in an article entitled 'The People's Army – at the People's Service', which was published in Mapam's daily newspaper, *Al Hamishmar*, Alon wrote:

> The army has become part of our life experience, and an esteemed social factor ... we must see this phenomenon which is called an army as a kind of corridor which leaves a long-term imprint on a man's life and on the life of society. Therefore, we

consider it not enough for the army to be organized in sophis-
ticated brigades; rather it must school its people in education
for defence, education for pioneering, and for the creation of a
better and more just society.[11]

In a continuation of this line of thinking, he claimed that '"absorption
for defence" of new immigrants directly aids their social integration.'

The argument over army priorities and orientations was not
decided during the War. In March 1948, while the debate continued,
the Department of Information Dissemination was established at
General Staff Headquarters. This body, which was subordinate to the
Adjutant General Branch, was supposed to supply services in the fields
of education, information dissemination, schooling and entertainment,
for all the units except those of the Palmach, which fanatically stuck to
its own information dissemination system stationed at its headquarters. (Several months later, during the sharp confrontation over the
disbanding of the Palmach, this system was a key element of
contention between senior Palmach members, who pointed to the
importance of its autonomy, and Ben-Gurion and his supporters, who
claimed that this autonomy indicated undesirable intentions). Joseph
Krakovi (Kariv) from the Hagana Intelligence Service was the head of
its information department. He was acquainted with the elements of
propaganda because of his connections with underground radio
broadcasts. Krakovi bxegan to examine what was being done in the
field and to assign information and cultural officers at the battalion and
brigade level. At the same time, he prepared a proposal, which he
submitted to his superior commanders at the beginning of April, with
regard to the establishment of a cultural department. In this proposal
the department's objectives, its organizational standards, and the
structure required for its operation were spelled out. The Cultural
Department replaced the Information Department and in May became
the Cultural Service, the father of the Education Corps.

Commanders of the Cultural Service defined the educational
goals of the new army in the following words:

> To cultivate the spirit of the Jewish army through the propagation
> of Zionist goals [as found in] the basic values of the Zionist
> movement and the Hagana from their inception; [the offering of]
> language instruction, geography, and the basics of popular science
> for those who need it; the use of free time in the camp for cultural
> enjoyment, the cultivation of artistic values and sports activities.[12]

The designated tasks in the light of these goals included:

* preparation of lectures on current events;
* setting up seminars for intellectually-oriented information dissemination;
* publication of newspapers, monthlies and pamphlets containing material on cultural affairs, language and literature;
* publication of army unit leaflets for cultivating social and cultural life;
* special broadcasts for the units;
* organization of theatre groups, bands, choirs and art exhibitions;
* sending performing artists and films to army units;
* encouraging public songfests and publishing song books;
* establishing local and central libraries;
* supplying daily, weekly and other newspapers to army units;
* setting up courses for learning Hebrew;
* setting up courses for geography and popular sciences;
* organizing teachers and their training, upgrading young teachers and counselling them;
* organizing clubs in army units in order to foster an *esprit de corps*;
* care for wounded soldiers and soldiers in distress or difficult economic circumstances.

Some of the activities provided by the Cultural Service concentrated on soldiers inducted from abroad (Gahal) – more than 20,000 immigrants who were survivors of the Holocaust. Immediately after their arrival, they were sent to army units where they joined the IDF in the midst of battle. Most of the Gahal contingent entered the country after the declaration of independence on 15 May 1948. From the earliest stages it was clear that these soldiers had need of special welfare and cultural services and it was also clear from the beginning that the ability to supply these services was limited. The Gahal Department for Cultural Services consisted of only seven people. There were two English speakers, and one speaker in each of the following languages: Yiddish, Romanian, French, Bulgarian and Hungarian. The bulk of the work, therefore, fell on the information officers in the field.

Two information officers from the fighting units stood out from all the rest: Benny Marschak from the Palmach's Harel Brigade and Abba Kovner from the Givati Briagde. Both had been indoctrinated by *politruk* and their standing was immeasurably higher than their colleagues in the other brigades.

Benny Marschak was a veteran member of the Palmach, a member of kibbutz Givat Hashlosha, who made sure that he was never far from military action. In the Harel Brigade he acted not only as an information officer but also as the commander of a heavy- mortar unit and the confidant of the Brigade commander, Joseph Tabenkin. Uzi Narkiss, one of the senior officers of the brigade, testified with regard to his methods, which were generated by personal example:

> He called upon exceptional moral courage and pulled us time after time out of despair. I will point out one example, which occurred during one of our lunches at the Fefferman House at Ma'ale Hahamisha. While the chef was splattering food from a pot onto the plates of those in line, bombs suddenly began to whistle through the empty air. Everybody quickly sought shelter but Benny jumped out of nowhere, plate in hand, and roared out: 'Everybody line up! The bombardment will not frighten us. We are, we are the Palmach!' People took their place again in line. The bombardment continued.[13]

Alongside his indoctrination work aimed at raising morale and disseminating information, Marschak was also involved in issues concerning battle ethics and purity of arms. He played a major role in building an educational system for immigrants within the brigade framework and saw to it that Zionism was pounded into them. He devoted efforts to drumming up troupe entertainment and bringing performing artists, with whom he had personal connections, to the front lines. As would be expected, he was among the most forthright opponents of the dismemberment of the Palmach.

The poet Abba Kovner came by his duties in the Givati Brigade following his leadership in the ghetto uprising in Vilna, his military exploits with the partisans in German-occupied territories of the Soviet Union and his central role in the flight of Jews from war-torn Europe to Palestine (1944–47). In the brigade he edited a leaflet entitled 'A Battle Page' whose formula was toughly worded in rhetoric reminiscent of the Red Army. Some of his articles bore the following titles: 'Anglo-Farouk Dogs Beneath our Wheels'; 'Soldiers, on to battle! To the bitter end! To the moment of decision, on to victory!'; 'Six Million Souls Who did not Survive are Calling Us from the Earth: the Great Revenge will Arise'. Some time later, Shimon Avidan, Givati Brigade Commander commented that 'these pages, which were presented to the units' soldiers in their most downcast hours, were on a par with weapons.

Their military value was equivalent to the value of an experienced and proud unit. The letters on the page had the power to block the gaps that death tore in their ranks.'[14]

In the general reorganization of the army after the War of Independence, there were no successors of the calibre of Benny Marschak and Abba Kovner. Toward the end of 1949, in the framework of the overall reform in the structure of the IDF, and the resulting cutbacks in its service apparatus, cultural services were also drastically reduced. Whereas until March 1949 there were 746 officers and soldiers employed in these services, after the cutbacks the number stood at the much lower figure of 350 officers and soldiers. Initially, the positions for cultural sergeants in the units were cut; following this, there were cuts in the number of educational officers assigned to battalions. Finally, headquarters staff, as well as the budgets of the Cultural Service, were adversely affected. Beyond the desire to effect cost savings, these steps were rationalized by a new policy directive, which made the commander an agent of education and information dissemination. This expedient rendered superfluous cultural service personnel in the field.

The drastic cuts brought everything to a low ebb. Ben-Gurion's Diary entry of 22 October 1949 notes one of the outcomes of this:

> Joseph Krakovi came – he wants to leave the [Cultural] Service. Tired out by this work. The cultural workers have no standing, they have canceled the cultural officers and their duties have been assigned to the local commanders. I explained to him the importance of the educational activities in the new army and the great powers that this would require. The entire first year would be devoted to education: learning the language, a basic education, agricultural training, and learning a vocation. There is a need for a minimal dictionary (800–1,000 words), which every soldier who does not know Hebrew must learn, a minimum of Jewish history in a shortened version, geography of the country, profound knowledge of the contemporary history of the Jewish people, and a minimal social grounding.[15]

But Krakovi agreed to continue for another few months only.

At the beginning of April 1950, Lieutenant-Colonel Aaron Ze'ev replaced Krakovi. The official title given to his appointment was Chief Educational Officer. It was Ze'ev who laid the foundations for the operation of the educational system in the IDF. In a document formulated a short time after he began his duties – A Platform for Educating IDF Commanders – Ze'ev declared:

> Only a soldier who is deeply rooted in his homeland, in his nation's past, in its culture and its future vision, can have the feeling of bearing a mission which, if absent, will not permit him to reach the same level of internal discipline, volunteerism, courage, and self-sacrifice demanded of every soldier under the new battlefield conditions.[16]

Ze'ev divided his headquarters into three sections: Counselling and Information, Education and Entertainment. In addition, headquarters had direct control of the IDF radio station, Galei Tzahal, and the journal, *BaMahane*.

With the termination of the war and the demobilization of veteran soldiers, the information and education problems of the IDF began to appear in a different light. In the first place, the relative numbers of immigrants in the fighting units rose, and many found difficulty in adjusting to the rigid and demanding military framework. This resulted in a worsening of the problems of morale and discipline. Under these circumstances it was clear that the main educational task would fall on the shoulders of the direct commanders and, hence, senior army ranks commenced discussions on the proper ways to cope with this.

During one of these initial discussions at the office of the Defence Minister in September 1949, the writer, Yizhar Smilanski, who served as an information officer in the War of Independence and was now a member of the First Knesset, stated:

> I maintain that seminars must be established for training every officer who comes into direct contact with people. In the same way that one trains oneself to become the commander of a platoon, so one must train oneself to manage the education of the soldiers under one's command. These seminars should teach the fundamentals of educational didactics, psychology, knowledge of the land of Israel, and especially human relations, tolerance and love of one's fellow man.[17]

As is well known, these seminars did not come into existence.

Another discussion, much broader in scope, was held at a conference of the Supreme Command of the IDF on 6 April 1950. It was devoted to the topics of discipline, morale and education in IDF units. Ben-Gurion opened this conference with the following statement:

A commander of the Israel Defence Forces who is not aware of the ingathering of the exiles, of the value for our security and our future of this ingathering of the exiles, of the cultural patterns contained in the ingathering of the exiles, of the needs entailed in the ingathering of the exiles, of the difficulties of the ingathering of the exiles, who does not first of all educate himself to absorb the people and, before turning him into a mortarman, a sniper or a pilot, make of him a Jew and a son of Israel, a citizen of the State, a citizen of the homeland and a comrade and root out the German, the Moroccan, the Yemenite element in him, and imprint in him the cradle of tradition of the Jewish people and the new values that we are creating – such a commander will not succeed in his task even if he is the best soldier and the most dedicated commander.[18]

At this same gathering, the Chief-of-Staff, Yigael Yadin, made remarks that were later published as a newsletter for young IDF commanders:

The most important thing in a combatant is his will to fight and his courageous spirit. And it is here that your most important duties in the area of military training and education reside. The educational tasks that we must undertake are clear: to turn every Israeli (old-timer and new-comer) into a combatant, and every soldier and combatant in the army into a citizen – an active participant in the efforts of building and creation; to build cohesive military units which are strong and daring; to fashion the IDF into a mighty power capable of sacrifice in the protection of the State of Israel and capable of annihilating every aggressor; to educate units and the individual soldier to be prepared to come to the assistance of the nation in any diffi-cult rescue endeavor which the army calls upon them to do, whether it be settling or developing the country, or absorption of immigrants … We still lack the perfect citizen and it is our obligation to form him while simultaneously educating him as a soldier. Thus, in addition to the task which all other armies must undertake, that is, the fashioning of soldiers from citizens, we must also make citizens of our soldiers. More accurately, we must create rooted Israeli citizens – lovers of their homeland – and combatant soldiers, out Jews from the entire Diaspora who are not yet full citizens nor soldiers.[19]

As a background to these challenges, the head of the Adjutant General Section, GHQ, General Shimon Maza, presented the following data to the conference attendants: only 400 out of 6,000 (approximately 7 per cent) soldiers inducted from the end of the war (April 1949 to April 1950) were native born and high school graduates. Moreover, 30 per cent of those who served in the infantry units were native-born Israelis with only basic education and the remainder were immigrant soldiers who did not speak Hebrew and had no cultural or social roots in Israel. Many were still adversely affected by absorption and welfare problems.[20] Several speakers were more or less aware of this reality and shed light on it from different perspectives (although none of them disagreed with the educational function of the army in the face of the mass immigration and its accompanying problems). For example, Moshe Dayan, general of Southern Command stated: 'I am certain that this proportion is far less than anyone expected. The soldier learned Hebrew, he is brushing his teeth, but you should check out [whether they possess] those very terms that we define as culture.'[21] The commander of the Golani Brigade, Colonel Abraham Yaffe, agreed with Dayan's criticism and claimed that the educational achievements of forming the future soldier/citizen were far removed from the set goal, given the abundant means allocated to the subject. The Adjutant General Section spokesman, Lieutenant-Colonel Menahem Chodorovsky (who later went by the name of Menahem Savidor and became speaker of the 10th Knesset), one of the few attendants at the gathering whose roots were not embedded in the mentality and pathos of the Labour Movement, was even more extreme: 'I want to say to lieutenant-colonel Ze'ev [the Chief Educational Officer] that not only has he become slightly out of touch with reality in bringing to the fore ideas and ideals in the unit, but the Israel Defence Forces in its current composition is very far from being an army which will go into battle for the sake of an idea.'[22] Other speakers emphasized that the level of motivation in the various home-front commands and in the service units was even worse.

The only solution in the opinion of the majority of speakers was to change priorities regarding the mobilization of the country's native-born population. It was stated repeatedly that only when the native-born – those who had received educational training and had the capability of introducing their soldiers to the Hebrew language, Israeli culture, knowledge of the country and battle traditions – were appointed field commanders, would the hoped for change come about. At the same time, it was evident to all those present that they themselves must carry a considerable proportion of the burden, and this acknowledgment may have been the greatest contribution of that convention towards education in the IDF.

The lack of native-born junior commanders led to a meeting of Ben-Gurion, the Chief-of-Staff, Yigael Yadin, and the generals Mordecai Macleff and Shimon Mazia with the leaders of the settlement movements. At this meeting, which took place on 11 May 1950, it was stipulated that these movements work shoulder to shoulder with the military. They were asked to approve the signing up of dozens of officers who were members of their kibbutzim and moshavim for an extended period of army service. In addition, they were to induct dozens of additional officers to the standing army for a number of years. Ben-Gurion's central assertion in this discussion was that:

> A large part of the army is comprised of immigrants, people who do not know Hebrew, who are not familiar with the country, and do not know a lot of things which a Jew who lives here should know. For this reason, the need for native-born officers has become even more urgent. And the army now is not only a factor in the security of the country but is also becoming a prime factor in the absorption of the immigrant into the domestic life of the Yishuv, in the instruction of Hebrew and the country's geography, and so forth.[23]

THE INFORMATION DISSEMINATION SYSTEM

From the very start, the Counselling and Information Section was primarily assigned the task of training commanders in all matters pertaining to leadership, human relations and the care of the soldier as an individual and of the military unit as a group. The basic assumption was that the commanders' loyalty to the underlying values of the nation, their identification with the values of democracy and their acceptance of the authority and the laws of the State were of the utmost importance, and thus could be conveyed to their soldiers. The involvement of the commanders in the problems of Israeli society, through their in-depth study of ideological and spiritual matters, was intended to raise their personal level, to increase their confidence and to provide them with tools for education and leadership. This was the starting point for an educational training programme fashioned for all levels, from squad commander courses up to courses for senior commanders. The programme encompassed a variety of subjects:

military society and its problems; the individual as the basic factor in combat operations; the essence of army morale, its components and causes; government institutions; the nature of military leadership; the responsibilities and tasks of the commander as social leader of his unit; relations between the commander and his subordinates; and, finally, methods of military and social information dissemination as an educational tool. An additional area of officer instruction included topics such as getting to know Israeli culture, problems of the Jewish people and the State, and political science and current affairs. A considerable number of hours were devoted to the history of Zionism and the history of the military struggle in the War of Independence.

Commander training courses employed both oral teaching (at conventions, instruction days, commander soirées and courses at the IDF Agricultural Training School) and the use of written material (information booklets, newspapers and periodical information newsletters). The implementation of commander training programmes actually began during the War of Independence. Commanders were given leave from the battlefront for a few days and taken to the Rutenberg Centre in Haifa for a series of information sessions. After a while these programmes were transferred to the Sereni House at Kibbutz Givat Brenner. At the same time, the IDF Teaching Centre was established at Camp Marcus, located in the Rutenberg Centre. Over the years, selective topics from sociology, psychology and management, taught with an emphasis on their application to military realities, were added to the commanders' educational programme.

Beyond the training of commanders, the IDF Information wing was assigned the task, unchanged to this day, of working with all soldiers with the intention of attaining the following goals:

- enabling the soldier to know and understand the purpose of his actions
- developing basic characteristics of the 'good' soldier
- conveying a feeling of being part of the entire IDF system and the enhancement of soldier pride in anything connected to the IDF, to the unit and to the Corps in which he serves
- instilling IDF battle norms and a tradition of heroism drawn from the period before the creation of the State
- heightening national consciousness, love of country and the acquisition of characteristics of good citizenship;
- encouraging soldiers' interests in current affairs at home and abroad.[24]

The Information Officer sent to field units received standing orders which included an added emphasis on activities among the civilian population. As early as March 1948, an order determined that field officers 'have the obligation to undertake information dissemination among the civilian community using all publication materials.'[25] From the beginning, this directive concealed a desire to bring to the public's attention the political line of the senior civilian echelon, to raise morale and create a heightened motivation for volunteering and responding to army needs. At the end of the War of Independence, these functions came to be regarded as an inheritance of the army in the challenging framework of absorbing immigrants and in the building of a new society.

The Culture Department and the bodies which came into existence in its wake, built an information programme for new recruits as well as an information programme for all IDF field soldiers, reserve units, service units and commands. The information programme operating during the period of basic training was designed to ease integration of the new recruits into the IDF as well as make clear to him his obligations and rights. Commanders were required to give ten information sessions during the two-and-a-half months of basic training. The period of army service following this contained four subdivisions, each of six months. In each of these time divisions, the soldiers were exposed to 25 information sessions. The commanders were responsible for conducting these sessions, which took place in platoon and company frameworks. According to a standing order, the commanders were required to read their soldiers selected passages from the army journal *BaMahane* once a week. In addition, 'the squad commander was required to read from the newspaper *Omer* [written with Hebrew vowels for easier reading comprehension] on a daily basis to those soldiers who were unable to read or understand the paper by themselves'.[26]

Commanders were required to devote seven discussion sessions during the first six months to the history of the Hagana, the 'stockade and tower' undertakings, the Holocaust, the period of rebellion involving Lehi and Etzel, and the Palmach's struggle against the British. Eight additional sessions were devoted to familiarizing soldiers with the IDF. During the remainder of their compulsory army service, soldiers received information describing in general terms the War of Independence and its various military campaigns, as well as lectures on the Middle East.

The IDF information dissemination programme also prepared the soldier in advance for his demobilization. Shortly before the end of his service, the soldier was invited to information sessions which dealt with the State and various public authorities, civilian obligations and rights, democracy and elected government, the struggle for economic independence and other economic matters. These sessions had, for their main objective, the channelling of demobilized soldiers towards the productive sector of the economy, whether in agriculture or in industry.

The oral information-dissemination programme was based upon lectures by commanders, attuned to the outlook of the commander in his capacity as educational officer, and by civilian lecturers. The latter were registered in a pool organized for the education system by Dov Harari, a member of Kibbutz Beit Oren. Harari was the first person in the IDF assigned responsibility for information dissemination matters and, already at this stage, questions arose regarding the political undertones of the entire operation. Those responsible for the information programme had to make sure that appointed lecturers would not exploit their professional standing by taking positions on controversial subjects connected with their lectures. However, this directive was not fully upheld. Those lecturers who were affiliated with the settlement movements, or branches of the Government and the Histadrut, regarded lecturing as part of their 'mission', and comprised equally of information and propaganda. This approach meshed with the IDF's information system which relied upon films from the Information Centre, a body which also did not especially attempt to distinguish between what was information and what was propaganda.

Additional tools in the information effort included excursions and organized visits. Some trips were designed to familiarize soldiers with the topology and history of the country. They entailed tours of the various fronts in the War of Independence, and visits to cultural institutions, settlement projects at kibbutzim and moshavim, and historical museums such as Yad Vashem, the Ghetto Fighters' Museum, and the Golomb House (later to become the Hagana Museum).

The written information material included, first of all, the distribution of daily newspapers to all IDF units. New immigrants received Hebrew newspapers in which the Hebrew consonants were accompanied by vowels for easier comprehension, as well as foreign language newspapers. Thus, for example, the Gahal Department of the Cultural Service saw to the publication of the following weeklies: *LaHayal Ha'Oleh* (*The Immigrant Soldier*) in Hungarian, Bulgarian and

Czech; *La Degel* (*The Standard*) in Romanian; *'BaMoledet'* (*In the Homeland*) in French; *Unzerheim* (*Our Home*) in Yiddish; and additional newspapers in Italian and English. Following the end of the war, foreign language publications were curtailed and the distribution of booklets and newsletters written in easy Hebrew was expanded. With the stabilization of the IDF educational system, the following newspapers began to appear on a regular basis: *Ma'arachot, BaMahane, Bemahane L'Oleh* (a weekly Hebrew publication with vowels), *Bita'on Hayil HaAvir* (Air Force), *Niv Alumim* (Gadna), and *BaMahane Nahal*. In addition, the *Ma'arachot's* editors published military literature. Some time later, Tarmil Books joined the military press contingent, publishing pocket books from the more outstanding works in world literature and new Hebrew literature. As with the aforementioned military publications, Tarmil's books were also sold to the public at large.

BaMahane

The newspaper *BaMahane* was first published in the 1930s as a bulletin of the Hagana's branch in Tel Aviv. In 1947 it became the national newspaper of the Hagana and began to appear every two weeks. In February 1948, it was decided to publish it as the official information publication of the army. Chief-of-Staff Ya'akov Dori, appointed the writer, Moshe Shamir, as its first editor. During the time of the military engagements in the War of Independence, *BaMahane* brought its readers reports from the battlefield describing campaigns which liberated the Negev and the battles for Jerusalem.

The newspaper did not confine itself to military topics, but rather sought to provide for the general needs of its soldier-readers as individuals. Hence, its content contained a variety of cultural, artistic, sports and literary articles and reports, as well as overviews of world news. The newspaper also published material sent in by army units, thus giving the soldiers a forum for expression and offering its readers a picture of military life. The educational thrust of *BaMahane* could be seen in its publication of battle accounts and stories of bravery from the War of Independence, as well as many stories from the history of Zionist settlement (including extensive and detailed descriptions of the Ha-Shomer organization, the Tel Hai battle, the period of the stockade and tower, and the like.) The paper also devoted space to poems and short stories from the creative 'Generation of 48', among them Chaim Heffer, Chaim Guri, Dan Ben-Amotz, Menahem Talmi and Natan Shaham.

This mixed newspaper content succeeded to such an extent that *BaMahane* became a serious competitor of the civilian *Dvar HaShavua* (the weekend magazine of *Davar*). Zalman Shazar, who was still editor of *Davar* (and who was to be appointed the first Minister of Education and Culture) contacted Josph Kariv and accused him of destroying *Dvar HaShavua*. Kariv's reply was short and to the point: 'During wartime, everything for the army; after the war, all civilian functions must be transferred to civilians.'[27]

After the disbanding of Palmach headquarters at the beginning of 1948, *BaMahane* published a headline on its front page: 'The Black Man Has Done His Work'. In the immediate wake of this article, Moshe Shamir, a member of the Mapam Party, was fired from his position as editor. Meir Avizohar, a member of the Young Guard of Mapai, who replaced him, had unassailable political credentials. After a short period, Avizohar moved to the information section and his position was taken by the poet, Shlomo Tanai, who edited *BaMahane* for four years. In the first years of the institutionalization of the IDF system, the weekly played an important supportive role in the formation of a regular army, a factor which also gave it, with the beginning of the retaliatory raids in 1953, a monopoly on the newspaper accounts which accompanied these raids. It was not by chance that the IDF's operative programme for 1953 and 1954 recommended extending the paper's circulation to the civilian population, in order to bring security matters to reserve soldiers and to the public at large.[28]

A similar orientation emerged in the information activities carried out at the new immigrant centres and transit camps, which included, among other things, an illustrated wall-newspaper called *HaHoma* (*The Wall*). This monthly publication began in April 1951 and was pasted in public places in new immigrant settlements. Its declared purpose was to provide 'education on security matters to new immigrants living in the settlements'.[29]

In retrospect, this was the source of the attempt to influence a broad public by means of special editions of printed material in advance of the solemn festivals. For the first New Year (the festival of Rosh Hashanah occurs in the early autumn) celebrated in the new Israeli State, the IDF designed a calendar which was accompanied by an informative text. Half-a-year earlier, on the eve of the Passover festival, a military Passover Haggada (the book read during the *Seder*, the Passover festive meal) was published, whose design and content were in the spirit of the times. Traditional formulations were revised and there were chapters on the revival of the Jewish people and its fight for independence 'in this time'. It appears that only the Cultural Service could produce a Haggada in this style because the Chief Military Rabbinate had not yet been established. In June 1948, Rabbi Shlomo Goren was appointed Chief Military Rabbi within the General Adjutant Section, GHQ, and from then on began to shape the religious observance patterns of the IDF. Following Goren's appointment, the Independence Haggada met its demise.

The Information and Teaching Sections at the Chief Educational Officer's headquarters ordered the Haggada for the fourth Independence Day celebration, in 1952. Its composition was assigned to the writer Aharon Megged, who was associated with a group of literary artists belonging to the 'Generation of 48'. Megged wrote the history of the War of Independence in the style of the traditional Passover Haggada and expanded, among other textual innovations, upon stories connected with the siege of Jerusalem, the battle for Degania and the 'thirty-five' who fell in the effort to relieve the siege on the Gush Etzion bloc south-west of Bethlehem. The Independence Haggada concluded with a chapter entitled 'The Twelve Blows' (a play on the Hebrew word *'macah'* which means both 'blow' and 'plague' in the authentic Haggada's recital of the ten plagues rained by God upon the ancient Egyptians, and also entails the meaning of 'military defeat') in which the author listed the names of the decisive military operations which the IDF had launched against its enemies. The editors provided the Haggada with a traditional design and included many photographs.

The secular press praised the initiative of the Independence Haggada and presented it as an important spiritual contribution to every family in Israel. The daily newspaper *Ma'ariv*, published a full version of the Haggada with the following account under the article's headline:

> The army has presented us with a very special gift in honour of this day, and we are proud of it. It proves that the army's strength is to be found not only in parades and acrobatics, in equipment, in martial strength and military corps, but also in its spirit. The Educational and Cultural Section of the Armed Forces has answered the call with a literary creation full of charm and the joyful pathos of authenticity. This is the Independence Haggada, a splendid integration of the old and the new, a story of the departure of this generation from slavery to freedom formulated as the departure from Egypt recited

over the generations. This Haggada of our past glory and present genius was composed by Aharon Megged to be used as background for today's festive meals in the army and is replicated hereby in the conviction that perhaps in the future it will become the festival's Haggada for the entire House of Israel.[30]

Within several days, religious circles came out against the Haggada publication and demanded that its reading in the army be forbidden. Their principle objection was that the author replaced the name of God, in a number of passages from the traditional Passover Haggada, with the name IDF. The worst profanity, cited in the religious newspaper *HaTzophe*, was the passage in which the commander rises and declares: 'And not by means of an angel, nor by means of a seraph, nor by means of a messenger did we strike the enemy and overcome him, but by the Israel Defence Forces.'[31] The original Haggada version concludes with 'but by the Holy One blessed be He …'.

Following the commotion over the Independence Hagadda, and out of a desire to avoid impinging upon the sensitivities of the religious soldiers, the Chief-of-Staff ordered its withdrawal from circulation. Many people among the public at large responded to this step by reading the Haggada on Independence Day, but this practice was discontinued in the following years.

Israel Army Radio (Galei Tzahal)

On 24 September 1950, the army radio, which took the name *Galei Tzahal* (IDF Wavelengths), opened its broadcasting with the playing of the national anthem and the reading of a passage from the Bible which described the victory of David over Goliath. The Prime Minister, Chief-of-Staff and senior officers were present at the opening ceremony. Ben-Gurion, in his congratulatory opening remarks, defined the goals of the radio station:

> The army broadcasts which begin operation today are intended to do two things: to serve as an instrument of security and defence by providing an efficient and rapid means of communication for mobilization and training, and for the rapid deployment of all regular and reserve Israel Defence Force Brigades on land, sea and air; it has the additional purpose of providing the army with a tool for educating youth and the nation and a cultural means for absorbing immigrants, helping them learn Hebrew, providing

them with knowledge of the geography and history of the country, unifying the tribes of Israel, forging a national will and instilling a sense of responsibility toward state-conducted activity [the Governmental policy of *mamlachtiut*], and glorifying the historical vision of the Jewish people for a life of labour, peace, justice, freedom and brotherhood. This strange mission of army broadcasting is part and parcel of the very essence and objective of the Israel Defence Forces.[32]

At the same ceremony, the Chief-of-Staff, Yigael Yadin, emphasized the national duties of the IDF in the absorption and the education of hundreds of thousands of new immigrants from around the world. The next day the newspaper *Davar* wrote: 'The reading of the Biblical passage about David and Goliath was deliberately chosen to indicate our position in the midst of hostile neighbours and the success of our army in the destruction of those who had evil intentions towards us.'[33]

With the opening of Galei Tzahal broadcasts, the struggle for the right of an independent army-broadcasting unit to exist, separate from the Voice of Israel, came to an end. In many respects, this struggle began in June 1948, when the broadcasting station The Voice of Defence became The Voice of the Israeli Defence Forces. This radio station was subordinate to the Cultural Service of the IDF, and its personnel tried to integrate entertainment, cultural and educational programmes into it, along with the regular news broadcasts. For example, the station broadcast performances of artists, forums on 'knowing the enemy', discussions based on unit newsletters, and a geographic corner. For budgetary reasons, all these programmes were condensed into a meagre time frame consisting of two daily broadcasts between 12:30 p.m. and 1:00 p.m. and between 7:30 p.m. and 8:00 p.m. In practice, these broadcasts were squeezed in between the regular programmes of the Voice of Israel and on its radio frequency. From the listeners' point of view there really was no difference between the two stations.

Steps taken to reduce the military establishment following the conclusion of the War of Independence provided the head of the Cultural Service, Krakovi (Kariv) with the opportunity to abolish the arrangement of separate broadcasting units. The Voice of Israel, on its part, promised to allocate an hour of broadcasting for soldiers and to place responsibility for its content with the Cultural Service. From this point on, the programme dealt mainly with information dissemination. Kariv's colleagues opposed his views and tried to fight for the establishment of a separate army radio station.

Following the appointment of Yigael Yadin to the post of Chief-of-Staff, Lieutenant-Colonel Aaron Ze'ev, head of the Information and Education Section, put forward a proposal to establish a radio station. Ze'ev was appointed Chief Educational Officer in April 1950. In a document directed to the head of the Adjutant General Section, GHQ, in July 1950, he stated that the suggested station would involve itself, among other things, in the teaching of elementary Hebrew, improvement of the Hebrew language for those already familiar with its basics, diffusion of general knowledge, information dissemination about the IDF and its problems and study of the State and its institutions. The last two topics would be presented in popular and intelligible language. In addition, he mentioned that the radio station would allow soldiers to express themselves on the airwaves, transmit experiences of their units, and broadcast what the IDF was doing in general.

In the end, Chief-of-Staff Yadin adopted the idea and obtained the needed authorization from Ben-Gurion. The Signal Corps and the information and cultural apparatus of the IDF took preparatory steps for the establishment of the radio station. On 7 July 1950, *Davar* published a notice on this matter. Among the readers of this announcement was Ze'ev Schiff, Government Secretary and Director of the Prime Minister's Office who was responsible for the Voice of Israel radio. He immediately wrote a letter to Ben-Gurion:

> I must take issue with this project both on the grounds of its procedure and of its content itself ... As long as the Government has not come to a decision on the matter, there is a need for basic investigation as to whether there is a justification for duplication of this type of service, whether the needed manpower exists for it and whether there isn't unnecessary financial expenditure in this duplication which stands opposed to the savings orientation in the use of treasury funding which the Government has prescribed.[34]

Ben-Gurion responded to the letter by setting up a three-man committee comprised of Gershon Agron (head of the information service), Dr Mordecai Soliali (manager of the Voice of Israel, and Lieutenant-Colonel Aharon Ze'ev, and asked them to present their conclusions within ten days. Members of the committee were required 'to examine the army's request to have special broadcasting for army needs, to investigate the relations between civilian and military broadcasts, and to place the proposals before the Prime Minister'. The two civilian members of the committee arrived at the conclusion that the army's needs could be supplied through programmes prepared by the Information and Cultural Section of the IDF in three-hour long daily broadcasts on the Voice of Israel. In a minority opinion, Ze'ev claimed that the army had the right to independent broadcasting. One of the principal objectives of the broadcasts, he wrote, was to give the army in all its units the feeling of unity and perfection. 'The army does not need a special radio station', he wrote, and in an attempt to take the sting out of the budgetary constraints he added:

> It can carry out its broadcasting within the framework of the Voice of Israel through the assignment of a special signature, *Galei Tzahal* – Israel Defence Forces Broadcasting. This would prevent the public from feeling that the State's broadcasting apparatus had turned into a military radio station. Because the army has an internal transmitter for its internal needs and its staff workers are not working full time, the army could use this transmitter in order to cut down on expenses and maintain the morale of the aforementioned team of workers ... The programmes of army radio will be in constant contact with broadcast programmers of the Voice of Israel, to coordinate the joint parts of parallel programmes.[35]

Ben-Gurion in fact adopted the minority opinion and on 7 September he brought the matter up for governmental decision. The next day all the newspapers proclaimed: 'At a Government session yesterday, it was decided to establish a broadcasting service for the IDF in coordination with the Voice of Israel.'[36]

The new radio station gave the IDF tremendous power for information dissemination and propaganda, given the limited scope of communication and equipment, especially electronic communication media in those years. Several years later, the following remarks were made in regard to the operative programmes of the Manpower Section:

> The broadcasts will continue to serve two central goals:
> 1. education and information dissemination for internal military consumption (including the army reserves);

2. Cultivation of awareness of security problems and high regard for the IDF amongst the civilian population in general and amongst youth – the future soldiers – in particular.[37]

The Chief-of-Staff was directly involved in the supervision of radio programmes, and even before broadcasts began, the appointments of two station managers were cancelled. The first appointee, Shaul Hone, who was army reporter for *Davar*, formulated a rather weighty programme based on lectures for educating the soldiers, with additional programmes devoted to classical music. This aroused the protest of army educational personnel and Hone decided to return to his newspaper. The second candidate, Amos Eilon, offered a lighter programme, half of which comprised musical broadcasts, one-fifth talk programmes, and the remainder educational and informative programming through radio plays and quizzes. The head of Manpower and the Chief-of-Staff rejected this programme design. Yadin then issued instructions to expand the talk programmes at the expense of the musical programmes. Eilon responded by handing in his resignation. At the beginning of September, First- Lieutenant Tzvi Brosh (Boroshek), who became the first commander of the army radio station, entered the picture. He was in his early forties, and prior to his appointment had been part of the team which edited the weekly radio programme, 'Radio Jerusalem'. From the beginning of 1946, he had served as deputy manager of the news department for the Mandatory Government radio, and had been involved in the founding of the radio station Kol HaMagen HaIvri (The Voice of Jewish Defence) in Jerusalem. In May 1950 he joined the Information and Education Section at General Staff Headquarters.

The programme which he presented to his superiors was mainly military and contained many elements from the areas of education and information dissemination. The programme was also designed to raise the cultural level of daily life in the army units. On the day that broadcasting began, the head of the Chief-of-Staff's Bureau wrote to the head of the Adjutant-General Branch: 'The Chief-of-Staff has approved the programmes contained therein, although in his opinion they are not satisfactory in all the details. Efforts should be made to give the programmes a more military character.'[38]

In its first year of operation, the radio station's budget was small, amounting to 800 Israeli pounds (to finance the programmes only). The station broadcast for three hours per day and included education and information programmes, music and entertainment. Manpower allocation was officially budgeted for five people. The command responsibility was given to the Education and Information Section.

In autumn 1950, the largest army training exercise since the establishment of the IDF took place. Tens of thousands of reserve soldiers were mobilized. During the course of the exercise Galei Tzahal was required to broadcast for 12 hours a day, and in order to do so it called upon reserve staff from the Voice of Israel, including dozens of reporters who meandered among the units and reviewed what was taking place. The broad scope of the review and the 'live reporting' from the exercise area, pointed to the possibility of drastically expanding the station's information and educational activities and also supplied a springboard for expanding routine daily broadcasts.

Following the exercise, the staff allocation for Galei Tzahal was increased to 11 soldiers, and in addition a permanent staff of veteran radio personnel drawn from the reserves was formed. The latter were also employed in training young radio announcers who joined the radio station in the framework of their compulsory army service. The combination of 'citizens in uniform' and the regular soldiers carrying out joint activities and regular programming, has given a special stamp to the army radio station throughout the years. In practice, what was created was a combination of professional maturity which channelled the adventurousness and daring of a young generation of reporters. Thus, for example, it was possible to break into the area of foreign language hit-parade music which was so popular among the youth but was almost completely boycotted by the civilian broadcasting network.

The new spirit found expression in a congratulatory piece written in *BaMahane* celebrating the founding of Galei Tzahal:

> The 'Soldiers' Hour' on the Voice of Israel has been adapted to the level of the station's general listening public. This is not the case with Galei Tzahal whose standard of broadcasting is attuned to the educational and interest level of the average recruit in the IDF. The station's guidelines are not what should interest the soldiers but rather what actually interests them, and it will be examined by the extent to which it will succeed in drawing their interest.[39]

A survey of listeners conducted in the army in October 1950, a month after broadcasts began, indicated that most soldiers preferred musical to talk-show programmes. Military marching songs and entertainment programmes interested them more than broadcasts on Israeli and military history, geography of the country, history of the Hagana, and what was happening in Arab countries. The same survey found that only 10 per cent were regular listeners to the army station, 38 per cent were frequent listeners and 38 per cent were occasional listeners.[40] Results of this survey had practical implications for the broadcasting schedule. The percentage of music and entertainment programmes was raised to between 65 per cent and 70 per cent of the total broadcasting time. Moreover, Galei Tzahal, from its early beginnings, addressed its listeners in a freer, lighter and clearer fashion than the Voice of Israel, 'the big brother', broadcasting with impeccable decorum, and insisting on standard Hebrew and proper diction. The underlying assumption that the soldier listening to broadcasts was weary and lacked patience for lengthy talk programmes resulted in a 'sandwich pattern' of broadcast content which combined talk shows with songs and hit-parade tunes.

Expansion of the activities of the army radio station in its first years was also reflected on the financial side. While the radio budget for the first year of operation was only 800 Israeli pounds, in 1953–1954 the budget of Galei Tzahal stood at 13,000 Israeli pounds. Nine- thousand pounds were allocated to performing artists, payments to orchestras, preparation and staging of radio plays, and authors' and producers' fees. An additional 3,000 pounds was allotted for the purchase of phonograph records and the remainder for local recordings.[41]

During these years Galei Tzahal was the only alternative Hebrew radio station to the Voice of Israel. On this account alone, the army broadcasting station had a distinguished role in the formulation of basic social and national concepts, as well as in the formulation of the cultural world of many of the State's young citizens.

THE EDUCATIONAL SYSTEM

As in the information dissemination field, it became clear in the educational field that IDF activity was expanding beyond the limits of military service. Initially, this system was designed to improve the education of IDF soldiers who had not reached a sufficiently rudimentary level before they began their army service. But from the available data it becomes evident that the army became the main school for many immigrants, whether they were part of the regular or reserve forces.

The foundations of the educational systems in the country had their origins in the Hagana and the Palmach. On the one hand, Hagana commanders began to study English and Arabic, the history of the Land of Israel, and mathematics after they had been forced to cut short their regular studies in order to integrate themselves into the organizational apparatus of the military underground; they were also motivated by their desire for future integration into civilian life. On the other hand, Palmach inductees who came from disadvantaged neighbourhoods and lacked a basic education, were given Hebrew lessons, arithmetic, history of the Jewish people and basic excerpts in the history of Zionism, at a summer camp for recruits located at Kibbutz Ayelet Hashachar. With the establishment of the State and the absorption of 20,239 Gahal soldiers (up to March 1949), the need for educational activities within the army's ranks rose drastically, for at least one reason. According to Colonel Yehuda Wallach, Givati Brigade Commander in the early 1950s:

> Briefings in advance of military activities were not that easy. Squad commanders issued instructions for an operation while 30, 40 or 50 per cent of his soldiers did not yet have a full grasp of Hebrew. And the company commander, for his many sins, did not always speak Yiddish. As a result, a very serious communication problem arose, and afterwards, in the heat of battle, no one understood the orders.[42]

In other words, the teaching of Hebrew was carried out for tactical–operative reasons. Beyond this, teaching of Hebrew was a condition for absorbing the newcomers into the life of the units and Israeli society.

The harsh conditions of the war did not allow for the granting of the necessary facilities required for studies. However, from the start, regulations at the induction base for Gahal soldiers stipulated that every commander should be 'an officer who proves himself in battle, is proficient in pedagogical skills and exhibits exemplary human qualities'.[43] Following this, three brigades organized Hebrew classes: Palmach–Harel, Yiftach and The Negev; later Golani and Givati followed suit. The teachers were male and female volunteers who had begun work in the fortified strongholds and in the areas where the military units organized themselves during the period of the ceasefire. Teachers inducted into the Cultural Service during the summer school vacation joined them. They were sent to supervise six weeks of intensive studies in army units. Several months later, Abba Kovner declared in the *Battle Pages* of the Givati Brigade: 'Combatants Engaged in a Common Effort Must Speak Hebrew.'[44]

In the meantime, the senior command had come to perceive basic education, including Hebrew, not only as an auxiliary means for the integration of these soldiers into the army but also as a vital basis for their acculturation to the Israeli State. This outlook remained a cornerstone in the IDF's educational codex for many years. In a document on education in the IDF issued by the headquarters of the Chief Education Officer, its position was clearly stated:

> We still see elementary education and the first years of second-ary-school education as a most urgent matter. The reason for this is that for the poorly educated soldier, additional schooling and learning Hebrew constitute a vital matter which can tremen-dously influence his ability to adjust in Israel, find a respectable job following his military service and acquire a general feeling of identification with the State and its objectives.[45]

On 30 August 1948, Ben-Gurion entered the following note in his diary: 'The Labour Ministry has hired 250 teachers to teach Hebrew to soldiers. After the summer vacation, a unit for this purpose must be mobilized. There are tens of thousands of soldiers who are in need of Hebrew lessons.'[46] The establishment of this unit got bogged down in many difficulties, and a temporary solution for the problem, labelled 'Operation Hebrew', was proposed in March 1949. Its objec-tive was defined in a relevant Headquarters' order as the acquisition of a defined, minimal vocabulary within a short time by every male and female soldier who did not know the Hebrew language. The exact wording of the order stipulated: 'Every soldier in the Israel Defence Forces who does not know Hebrew – speaking, reading and writing – must learn Hebrew. Every unit commander is responsible for seeing that every soldier in his unit who does not know Hebrew devotes at least 6 hours per week to language study.' In practice, the order meant the acquisition of 1,500 words of basic vocabulary.[47]

Responsibility for this operation was assigned to the Educational Department of the Cultural Service. The Hebrew Studies Office of this department mobilized, as a supplement to the small headquar-ters' team, a number of language teachers and instructors whose task was to formulate a teaching programme in the army. The curricu-lum, instruction methods and textbooks were adapted to the special characteristics of the IDF. A teaching unit comprised of teachers holding the rank of sergeant, and headed by a supervisory officer, was sent to every brigade and independent unit in the army. Operational headquarters were established in the units themselves. Each of these headquarters included a unit adjutant, a cultural officer and an additional headquarters officer. Its main function was to place those who were in need of Hebrew lessons into groups of 15, according to their language level.

Some of the units organized their curricula in a concentrated manner. In other units, several hours of study were inserted into the training programme each day. A number of units organized a concentrated course for the jurisdictional area. Units that inserted the study programme into the daily training programme met with little success in contrast with the concentrated brigade school programmes.

The IDF published a number of reference books and dictionaries in connection with this operation. The core textbook was built around 1,100 basic words, which were built up with every lesson. Reading passages in the study books dealt with topics from the life experience of the soldier: immigration to the country, the city, the street, the camp, the family, the home, military training, the country's landscape, work and a profession.

Every lesson ended with a brief review of new vocabulary learned and simple, basic rules for irregular grammar and spelling. Supplementary material also included the *Essential Dictionary* in which the basic vocabulary was translated into different languages, according to subject, in 20 chapters. The dictionary contained 6,000 terms arranged in alphabetical order. Among the different topics included in the dictionary were 'the human body', 'at the office', 'the dining room', 'place and time', 'direction', and the like.

During the course of the first year of absorbing immigrant soldiers the Cultural Service, in co-operation with the Gahal Department in the Adjutant General Branch, GHQ, produced a string of newspapers in eight languages. In addition, they edited newsletters on a duplicating machine in foreign languages, parallel to the Hebrew newspapers sent to army units. For many Gahal soldiers, this printed information was their sole written link to what was occurring in the State.

Within the framework of 'Operation Hebrew' the Cultural Service began editing a newspaper with Hebrew vowels called *BaMahane LaOleh* which was a successor to the foreign language newsletters. This paper initially appeared three times a week, and in November 1949 began to appear as a daily. It included passages written in easy Hebrew employing vocabulary which the soldiers had learned in the Hebrew classes provided by 'Operation Hebrew'. The level was not high, and the Israeli press insisted on its improvement. *BaMahane* wrote:

> Now that *Bamahane LaOleh* has become the only remaining newspaper to service the soldier every morning, it must progress and quickly rise to be *the* voweled newspaper for immigrants. The army is the only body today which publishes such a newspaper while the new immigrants outside the army are in need of the foreign language press only during their first months in the country. Again the army has shown its advantage over all other societal bodies in its ability to absorb immigrants.[48]

Over the course of time it became apparent that despite the detailed orders which emanated from General Headquarters, and despite the readiness of different commanders to carry them out energetically, units encountered quite a few difficulties. These difficulties ranged from the granting of orderly study leave for immigrant soldiers to the allocation of suitable classrooms. To overcome these problems, the army operated command-area schools, as well as its central school for education. Hebrew was taught at Camp Marcus in the Rutenberg Centre in Haifa.

The command-area schools offered concentrated courses, lasting three to four weeks, to thousand of soldiers from field units. The study programmes included not only Hebrew language courses but also Bible study, history of the Jewish people, general history, arithmetic, the geography of Israel, general geography, the foundations of natural science and citizenship. Parallel to this, interested soldiers were offered the possibility of completing their elementary-school education through three months of studies at Camp Marcus at the conclusion of their service. Those who so desired could sign on for four months additional service devoted to secondary school education and preparation for pre-matriculation exams. From August 1948 to December 1949, 3,500 Gahal students, comprising 35 classes and 55 courses, studied at Camp Marcus.[49]

At the beginning of 1950 there were close to 4,500 students in the army study programmes. The estimated number of soldiers who required Hebrew study but did not study, because there was insufficient funding, was around 2,000. The change was a consequence of a change in the nature of the inductees. Immigration from Arab lands and North Africa changed the demographic structure of the entire society and of the IDF in particular. The central IDF School shifted from being an institution whose principal charge was the provision of Hebrew to Gahal soldiers to a school offering Hebrew and elementary education for soldiers in the regular army service.

At the start of 1950, courses of two weeks were offered. Between 170 and 200 soldiers participated in each course. The soldiers were divided into two groups: the first, French-speaking, for those who originated from Morocco, and the second in Hebrew, for those who came from Europe and understood the spoken language. During the year the IDF organized itself so that entire units could be transferred to a school, in order to make the studies more efficient. The central problems, arising out of the pupils' low educational level, stemmed from the instability of the teaching staff roster. The high turnover prevented the educational system from benefiting from the assimilation of lessons and teaching experience which would have accumulated through greater staff continuity.

In an interview in the July 1950 edition of *BaMahane* commemorating the second year of Camp Marcus, the commander of the school, Captain Shlomo Adiv, noted:

> Today, the overwhelming majority of soldiers are from Islamic countries. The goal: to make them partners in our heritage, our life, the nation's achievements and its culture – the landscape, the historical past, its experiences. The key, which is the common language, in effect bears the essence of the Zionist enterprise.[50]

Since the opening of Hebrew studies at Camp Marcus, 76 courses had been offered to 4,830 soldiers.

Table 1
Hebrew Studies at Camp Marcus

No. of Courses	Course/Participants	No. of Pupils
16	Those with basic Hebrew	1,234
15	French speakers	891
11	Yiddish speakers	810
7	English speakers	549
5	Bulgarian speakers	337
6	Hungarian speakers	333
3	Ladino speakers	143
2	Czech speakers	138
1	Yugoslav speakers	100
1	Headquarters and Information Officers (complementary course)	94
1	Squad Commanders	63
2	Gahal activists	61
5	Intensive Hebrew	44
1	Complementary (short)	33

Source: Multiple Sources

The arrangement for Hebrew lessons at the Marcus Camp was only part of the general system of language and basic education provision for all IDF units. Again it became clear, as it had during the absorption of Gahal soldiers at the height of the War of Independence, that lack of knowledge of Hebrew caused a tactical-operative problem. General Raphael Vardi took note of this in 1952 and 1953 when he was deputy commander of the Golani Brigade:

> The means of instruction and transmission of material was through interpreters who translated the lesson topics into Arabic or Yiddish. The absorption process took place through the learning of Hebrew taught by female soldiers trained as teachers. During military training, at least two hours per day was devoted to Hebrew instruction by these female soldiers sent from the Bureau of the Chief Education Officer.[51]

Soldiers who received basic Hebrew lessons in their unit were transferred in the second stage to the command schools for an additional period of study, where they improved their language skills and obtained a basic education. The first such schools were at Instructional Base 4, at Base Camp 782 and at Camp Marcus.

The problem of Hebrew-language proficiency continued to concern the IDF throughout the 1950s. In an effort to solve it, the IDF initiated Hebrew lessons for reserve soldiers in their residential areas during afternoon hours. They were usually located where there was a concentration of immigrants. The teachers received their salary from the IDF, which also supplied the necessary textbooks. Regional educational officers in the districts, in the battalions and the territorial commands meticulously monitored attendance. This monitoring involved even senior army staff up to the rank of Major General. A letter from the deputy commander of the Shomron Bloc to the Northern Command testifies to this high rank involvement:

1. I am aware that members of the Battalion who reside in Hadera attend Hebrew lessons once a week.
2. In addition, I would like to know whether Hebrew lessons are conducted in any of the nearby places such as Pardes Hanna, Karkur, Binyamina, and Zikhron Yaakov.
3. In accordance with this, the Battalion commander requests a report on progress in these lessons from their organizer.[52]

The initiative for teaching Hebrew to new immigrants in the military reserves also came from army units in the districts. Thus, for example, the Jezreel Bloc, which was included in Brigade/District 9, requested that the Northern Command open Hebrew classes in the boarding-school framework of the bloc and provide teachers and textbooks for the pupils. Many other examples may be found in the files of the various commands.[53] The entire operation continued for a number of years. The annual report of the Adjutant General Section, GHQ, Section for Individual Matters for 1955 to 1956 reveals that 2,000 reserve soldiers learned Hebrew that year through the instruction of military reserve teachers.[54]

As part of the effort to raise the level of officers and commanders, 15 courses were planned each year at the central educational base. Each course lasted from 14 to 18 days and involved about 500 officers. The educational programme for 1953/54 required that each officer complete his elementary school education, and every officer above and including the rank of captain complete a high school education. In order to accomplish this, 40 evening classes were opened in urban centres. These classes enrolled 1,200 regular army personnel, among them 300 officers bearing the rank of captain or above. The project cost 87,850 Israeli pounds, approximately 20 per cent of the IDF educational budget for that year.[55] In addition, officers in the standing army were given the opportunity to pursue academic studies, and 150 officers from field units obtained 10 months leave for these concentrated studies.

Another educational undertaking during this period was the allocation of 14 days devoted to information dissemination and education in a squad-commander course. This programme took the form of a continuing seminar intended to raise the educational level of lower-rank commanders. The seminar included geography lessons, Israeli history, the history of the Hagana, and the like. The command headquarters and the corps were obliged to offer identical courses to all the lower-rank commanders who were not commanders of squads. The studies at the headquarters and army bases were principally conducted during evening hours.

With the expansion of the studies programme the IDF had to produce appropriate textbooks. In 1952, Hebrew (part I) textbooks appeared for arithmetic and general history. Afterwards, the army published two additional volumes of texts for learning Hebrew, a general geography book and two history books, *The Jewish People* and *The Revival of the Jewish State*. In the field of Israeli geography, the IDF studies programme published the *Geographical–Historical Atlas*, a collection of articles entitled 'Every Place', and booklets called *Know Your Country* which presented overviews of different regions of the Land of Israel according to geographical–historical divisions. This material was also widely distributed among the general public.

In May 1951, in advance of the State's third Independence Day, the IDF published a *Dictionary of Military Terms* edited by Major A. Akavia and Saadia Goldberg, a member of the Hebrew Language Committee. The work of collecting material went on for 13 years, from the days of the Hagana, through the Jewish Brigade Group, and up to the first years of the IDF. Joining this effort were people from the fields of language and literature who worked in tandem with the army and the educational system. The dictionary included 6,000 terms in alphabetical order, in English. Alongside the English term was the Hebrew translation with detailed explanations whenever required. In the majority of cases, international terms were transliterated in the Hebrew but sometimes there were language innovations that embodied derivations from Biblical language. An example of this is the transfer of the Biblical term 'novice priests' to 'officer cadets' and 'air force cadets' (*pirchai ketzuna* and *pirchai ta'is* – literally 'flowering officers' and 'flowering pilots'). Another innovation was the term 'decentralization' (*bizur*) referring to a Hebrew root, *'bezer'* found in the Bible (see, for example, Daniel 11:24; Psalms 68:30). The publication of the dictionary gave writers, newspaper publishers, teachers, and other lovers of knowledge, a functional language tool that, up to that point, had been lacking in the new, Hebrew culture.

FEMALE SOLDIER TEACHERS

Like all the state and Histadrut bodies which dealt with the imparting of language instruction and basic education during the days of massive immigration, the IDF also encountered the problem of a lack of teachers. In the first stages following the War of Independence, 200 teacher-soldiers served in various IDF units. The majority were graduates of teachers' seminaries, and a few of them were men and women soldiers with capabilities and skills, who had graduated from high schools, and were sent to teach Hebrew and basic education in the army units and the immigrant and transit camps. Mainly Nahal and Gadna soldiers assumed teaching roles in the transit camps and the immigrant settlements. In order to prepare an extensive number of teachers to service the ever expanding needs for instruction, the IDF opened an evening seminar for teachers in schools and kindergartens in co-operation with the Ministry of Education.

The first seminary study courses began on 1 August 1950, with the participation of 25 female soldiers. The Education Ministry placed the teaching team and the facility of a Tel Aviv school at the disposal of the IDF, and this opened a period of fruitful co-operation which quickly doubled the capacity for training teachers. The seminary studies programme was similar to that of the teacher's seminary and was spread over 13 months. There were 14 hours of study per week and in addition the female soldiers had the opportunity to obtain practical experience. Graduates of the seminary received an elementary-school teaching diploma and became qualified teachers following additional examinations. All were native-born, high school graduates, who had obtained teaching experience in IDF educational operations in the transit camps.

Following the first evening seminars in Tel Aviv, similar seminars were opened in Jerusalem and Haifa. Following this, it was decided in co-ordination with the Education Ministry that all women who wanted to enter the teaching profession would be directly released from obligatory military service. They would study at civilian teachers' training colleges, but would report for duty to their reserve units and would be called upon to serve as teachers according to army needs. All these arrangements supplied hundreds of elementary school and kindergarten teachers to the elementary school system and to the educational system in the IDF. This created the opportunity to acquire a basic education and Hebrew proficiency for tens of thousands of children and adults.

In the years from 1948 to 1950 the educational and dissemination information programmes provided by the IDF, including 'Operation Language Instruction' were the largest and most important State operations in this field. No other national agency supplied the wealth of educational and learning activities which the army offered its soldiers during and immediately after the war. In the effort to cope simultaneously with narrow military needs and a broad security and social outlook, the latter received priority. The IDF regarded the absorption of immigrants as a national mission of the utmost importance from the individual, military and social standpoints. The absorption of immigrants from the Mediterranean and North African countries, in the years 1950 to 1953, was not easier than the absorption

of Gahal soldiers, but the IDF did not recoil from the task. The funda-
mental outlook that the IDF should take responsibility for completing
the basic education of each and every soldier and should guide him
into civilian life with a basis which would permit him to integrate into
society, was interwoven in all the educational activities and information dissemination sessions of the army. Part of this orientation was
also directed toward the reserve forces.

A number of sociological studies conducted in the seventies and
eighties firmly uphold the claim that the IDF fulfilled a central role in
the field of education among the new immigrant population (even if it
did not succeed in building the long-awaited bridge to Jews from the
Oriental communities and thereby lessen the inter-communal gap).
'The most successful contribution of the IDF,' according to Romani, 'was
immigrant absorption in the field of education, professional specialization and transmission of a Zionist ideology to Oriental Jewry.'[56] In
retrospect, this major achievement cannot be taken for granted.

NOTES

1. G. Rivlin and E. Prat (eds), *David Ben-Gurion: The Man and the IDF* (Tel Aviv: Ministry of Defence, 1986).
2. BGA, Meeting File, accounts of authors at a meeting initiated by the Prime Minister, 27 March 1949.
3. M. Veiziger, 'Education for Citizenship in the State', in *Conversations 'A', Education and the Test for the Ingathering of the Exiles* (Tel Aviv: Mapai, 1951), p. 31.
4. Y. Niv, 'Comments', in *Conversations 'A'*, p. 92.
5. Z. Shazar, 'Summary Remarks', in *Conversations 'A'*, p. 121.
6. E. Peled, 'Ideology and Political Power: Progenitors of Educational Policy', *Megamot*, March 1984.
7. M. Lissak, 'Ben-Gurion's Conception of Institution Building', in S. Avineri (ed.) *David Ben-Gurion: Portrait of a Leader in the Workers' Movement* (Tel Aviv: Am Oved, 1986), p. 114.
8. Z. Gilad (ed.), *The Palmach Book I* (Tel Aviv: HaKibbutz HaMeuchad, 1956), p. 484.
9. Y. Alon, 'Educating Combatants', *Ma'arachot*, 1950, p. 143.
10. Ibid., p. 148.
11. CZA S71/512; Y. Alon, 'The People's Army at the Service of the People', *Al Hamishmar*, 11 March 1949.
12. IDFA 794/50, Cultural Department, 'Cultural Services: A Definition of its Goal and Role' (n.d.).
13. U. Narkiss, *Soldier of Jerusalem* (Jerusalem: Ma'arachot, 1991), p. 98.
14. IDFA, 'Battle Pages', Givati Brigade.
15. BGA, Ben-Gurion Diary, 22 October 1949.
16. A. Ze'ev, 'Education of the Commander and its Objective – Proposal for Discussion', in *Education and Morale in the IDF*, General Headquarters Publication, Chief Education Officer, 1956.
17. BGA, Topical File, Education and information in the IDF, Y. Smilanski, 'Cultural Activity in the IDF', discussion 19 September 1949.
18. D. Ben-Gurion, lecture at the conference of the Supreme Command, 6 April 1950, in *Education and Morale in the IDF*, p. 24.
19. Ibid.

20. Ibid. See the remarks of General S. Maza, the Head of the Adjutant General Section, GHQ, in a discussion of commanders on 6 April 1950.
21. Idem, General M. Dayan, at a meeting of the General Command, 1950.
22. Idem, Lieutenant-Colonel M. Chodorovsky, at a meeting of the General Command, 1950.
23. BGA, File of Meetings, Meeting with the Prime Minister/Minister of Defence, D. Ben-Gurion, and officers of the General Staff with deputies of the settlement movements, 11 May 1950.
24. *Education in the IDF*, booklet edited by the General Staff/Chief Education Officer (n.d.).
25. IDFA 840/49, File ג -161, Standing orders to the Information Officer, 5 March 1948.
26. 'Information – Standing Rules', in *Education and Morale in the IDF*, 1956.
27. A. Shalev, 'The Education Corps', in *The IDF and its Corps*, p. 167.
28. IDFA 171/55/65, Working Programme for 1953–54, Adjutant General Branch, GHQ.
29. IDFA 173/52/55, Document from the headquarters of Northern Command, Information Officer and Manpower and Personal Administration of the Command Brigades on the matter of *The Wall* – wall-poster journal intended for distribution in new immigrant centres.
30. *Ma'ariv*, 30 April 1952.
31. *HaTzophe*, 8 May 1952.
32. Précis of the Ben-Gurion speech in the morning papers the day after the first broadcast: in *Davar* and *Ha'aretz*, 25 September, 1950.
33. *Davar*, 25 September 1950.
34. R. Mann and T. Gon-Gross, *Galei Tzahal All the Time* (Tel Aviv: Ministry of Defence, 1991), p. 17.
35. Ibid., pp. 17 and 19.
36. See *Yediot Aharanot, Davar* and *Ha'aretz*, 8 September 1950.
37. IDFA55/65/171, Working order of the Adjutant General Section for 1953–54, ch. 7.
38. IDFA, Galei Tzahal file, Document from the office of the Chief-of-Staff to the office of the head of the Adjutant General Section, GHQ, 24 September 1950.
39. 'Galei Tzahal for Greater Cohesiveness', *BaMahane*, 1 October 1950.
40. R. Mann and T. Gon-Gross, *Galei Tzahal*, p. 35.
41. IDFA 55/65/171, Budget detail of the annual working programme.
42. Y. Wallach, 'Gahal, Mahal and a Common Language', in *The Contribution of Immigration in the War of Independence* (Tel Aviv: Yad Tabenkin, 1992), p. 44.
43. IDFA 852/51/1453, Appendix for correcting the central army training camps. From the head of the Adjutant General Section, GHQ (n.d.).
44. Original copy in the author's house.
45. *Education in the IDF*, published by the General Staff, Chief Education Officer (n.d.),p. 4.
46. BGA, Ben-Gurion's diary, 30 August 1948.
47. IDFA 930/520/52, General Headquarters 6/41, Operation Hebrew, 17 March 1949.
48. S. Shimon, 'The Voweled Newspaper Replaces the Foreign Language Press', in *BaMahane*, 13, 24 November 1949.
49. *BaMahane*, 16–17, 5 December 1949.
50. 'Two Years for the Army's Elementary School', Ba*Mahane*, 47, 20 July 1957.
51. Personal interview with General Raphael Vardi (Reserves), 15 September 1993. General Vardi was one of the Gadna commanders in the Tel Aviv area at the beginning of the War of Independence, and then commander of a battalion in the Givati Brigade. At the end of the war he continued his command duties in this brigade and his last position was head of the Manpower Section.
52. IDFA 55/173/52, Education File, Northern Command, letter of deputy battalion commander 926 to the Officer of Education and Information Dissemination, Northern Command, pertaining to Hebrew lessons, 6 March 1951.
53. Ibid., letter of the Manpower and Personal Administration Officer, brigade 9, to the officer of Education and Information Dissemination, Northern Command, 22 February 1951.
54. Ibid., 55/65/1014, Annual Operative Report, Adjutant General Section, GHQ, Individual Soldier Bureau, for the years 1955 and 1956, on 15 April 1956.
55. Ibid., 55/65/171, Working educational programme of the Adjutant General Section, GHQ, for 1953 and 1954, ch. 11, p. 11.
56. M.M. Roumani, *From Immigrant to Citizen: The Contribution of the Army to National Integration in Israel* (Beersheva: Ben-Gurion University of the Negev, 1979).

Chapter 6

The Gadna – Its Activities and Educational Role

Young men and women were integrated into the security activities of the Yishuv almost from its beginning. The legendary Abraham Shapira, for example, began to be involved in the guarding of Petah Tikva at the age of 14; Mordecai Yigael and Tzvi Nadav joined the Ha-Shomer organization at the age of 17. At the turn of the twentieth century, dozens of lesser-known teenagers took up guard duty in the various *moshavot* throughout the country. At the time of the establishment of the Reali School in Haifa, its founder and first principal, Dr Arthur Biram, purchased a number of weapons and hid them under the coal heaped on the roof of the workers' kitchen in Haifa. They were intended for use in time of need (and until such emergency he secretly trained his students with them). Among students of the first years of the Gymnasia Herzliya, founded in 1910 as the first Jewish high school in Palestine, the idea of being inducted into national service was widespread, and this included participation in the activities of the HaShomer.

From the time of its establishment in the early 1920s, Hagana youth training groups became acquainted with communication and semaphore tasks. Shaul Avigur initiated the spread of these activities in 1933, and the uprisings of 1936 to 1939 brought additional expansion. Even before the uprisings, Biram introduced 'extensive physical education' into his high-school curricula. Teachers raised objections that this would have the effect of 'militarizing' the youth. Biram's curricula included foot drill, scouting, various useful sports and martial arts (for example, jujitsu and hand-to-hand combat).

In June 1939, the Department of Education of the National Council of Palestinian Jewry adopted the essence of Biram's physical education programme and decided to put it into effect in every high school within its jurisdiction. The 'extensive physical education' programme, as it was called, defined its goal as 'the preparation of youth for security duties through raising of his awareness and physical fitness'. Following the uprisings and with the clouds of war gathering on the international horizon, the programme no longer generated any objections. Even the Mandatory Government praised these activities and approved them. The programme was quickly expanded to night schools and the youth movements.

Hagana headquarters regarded the extensive physical education programme as a convenient basis for expanding the training of youth, and began to formulate ideas for youth regiments (the name was then abbreviated to Gadna (that is, *GiDudai* [regiments] *NoAr* [Youth]). In November 1940, the first version of the Youth Order was promulgated. It stated, among other things, that: 'It is the duty of the organization to see to it that the basics of defence education in the schools and the youth movements are integrated into Zionist and humanistic education of the Hebrew youth in the country.' The Youth Order added that 'extensive physical education' programmes should commence amongst children from the age of eight. Although the programme involved open and recognized – that is to say, legal – activities, nevertheless the order determined that:

> teaching 'extensive physical education' ... will be done by order of the organization and through constant contact with it ... [That is, in subordination to an officer of the general staff acting as] general supervisor over 'extensive physical education' in the schools ... The instructors and the commanders will be authorized for their tasks by the general staff following suitable training.[1]

On the holiday of Lag B'Omer (15 May 1941), the Command Council of the Hagana promulgated an additional Youth Order which was stamped for the first time with the name Gadna. It depicted youth battalions along the lines of the combat corps, with each unit embracing 500 youth. The Hagana General Staff then proceeded to form a Youth Office and appointed a Chief Officer for Youth (to whom youth officers in all the areas, regions, territories and cities were subordinate). This officer (who was also responsible for the extensive physical education programme) was directly subordinate to the Chief-of-Staff. Youth between the ages of 15 and 18 years were eligible for Gadna service, which entailed 1,200 hours of pre-army training. Exercises included field training, long marches, martial arts, orienteering, rifle and pistol practice and grenade tossing. In addition, activities inculcating the national heroic tradition were integrated into the training programme. Many of these activities were conducted jointly with the youth movements and in the framework of the extensive physical education programme. For example, Gadna ranks marched in festive parades during the Hanukah holiday (to mark the heroism of the Maccabees), on Tel-Hai day (which was celebrated more than once as Hagana Day) and on Lag B'Omer (which was connected to the rebellion of Bar Cochba and which was in fact the birthday of Gadna). In addition, marches and pilgrimages were carried out – both in the Gadna framework and in the framework of the youth movements connected to the Hagana – at sites associated with Jewish heroism: Massada, Gush Halav, Yodfat and Tel-Hai.

Youth activities in the Gadna framework expanded as the Second World War drew to a close. In 1945, almost 40 per cent of the Jewish youth in the country between the ages of 14 and 18 were in its ranks.[2] This situation greatly aided the Hagana in projecting its prominence, but at the same time it also contained an element which shed light in an uncomplimentary way on the true power of the organization. The majority of the Gadna youth were not exactly authentic combatants.

GADNA AND ITS ROLE IN BEN-GURION'S EYES

David Ben-Gurion first began to voice his opinion on Gadna and its mission at the well-known 'Seminar' proceedings during the first months of 1947. He did this with a sense that the Yishuv's human resources were limited, as well as from fear of the magical attraction which groups beyond his control and influence – principally the Etzel and Lehi organizations – might have on youth. At the beginning of April 1947, he wrote in his Diary:

> Youth – not to establish a new youth movement in the conventional manner – which formulates its own *weltanschauung* and determines a position regarding current and enduring questions about the nation and society, but rather a framework of youth subservient to the nation. There is no hope that the pioneering youth movements will embrace all youth. 'Splinter groups' [Etzel and Lehi] recruit and seek out lower age groups – they

begin at age 12. We must do the same. A minimum of military training, field trips, learning about the country, quasi-martial arts, information sessions (on illegal immigration and the like), Zionist education, leaflet distribution by the children, newspaper reporting, contributing to local agricultural production, and service in the entrance ranks of the Hagana. It will embrace both working youth and students, mainly in the distressed neighborhoods. A framework of authority, obligation and command – [which will embrace] all school children from age 12 [and those] who are not attending school. Youth will be allowed to join other youth associations – but care should be given over time to preventing conflicts between the general framework and the youth organizations.[3]

A month later he wrote the following in his diary, as part of the lessons learned from the 'Seminar':

Should the budget structure be examined and changed in order to:
1. expand the youth framework;
2. improve the combat forces;
3. advance the [Palmah] Brigade?[4]

And almost alongside this he added: 'Should youth frameworks be expanded and their content enriched?' On 18 June he wrote, without employing question marks: 'Gadna must be expanded in order to embrace school youth from the lower grades as well, and from youth outside the school system.'[5]

Following the War of Independence and the absorption of hundreds-of-thousands of new immigrants, and in light of the difficult problems confronting the young State, Ben-Gurion turned to Gadna as one of the important state instruments for carrying out pioneering tasks. One thing stood out clearly: there were 100,000 youth between the ages of 14 and 18 years in the country and only 20,000 of them were studying in high school or vocational schools. Many of the remaining 80,000 had received no education – Hebrew or general – and were cut off from the heritage and culture of Israeli society. Gadna thus appeared to him as a body which could address this issue. At this time he claimed:

The great historical destiny of Gadna is to educate youth, whether they are studying or working, or whether they are street children given over to idleness and ignorance and also perhaps to a life of crime. To make of it a central lever for the moral, cultural, and social change which must come about in this motley and highly fragmented Yishuv – to refine and blend them into an historical unit, with one will, and desire, and language, and strength, and instinct, and creative passion – in other words, to turn them into a people.[6]

In an article he explained that 'the intention is not to transmit to this youth a pre-military education, but rather an education in basic human and Jewish values, familiarity with the country, order and cleanliness, brotherly feelings, mutual respect, patriotism, values of the Hebrew and pioneering nation.'[7]

Ben-Gurion's opinion on this strengthened and he continued to praise the importance of Gadna in the coming years, even while the educational activities of Gadna were the subject of criticism among factions of the General Staff and their vital role was questioned in light of budgetary considerations. On every one of these occasions, he rejected the demands for cutbacks by relying upon educational arguments.

THE STRUCTURE AND ORGANIZATION OF GADNA

On 12 September 1948 the Order for the Structure of the Gadna was promulgated. It stated: 'The youth battalions of the Israel Defence Force will be an independent unit, which bears the name, Gadna.' This order also contains a special section in which the leading statement specifies that 'in order to safeguard the pioneering element in settlement, a special framework within Gadna will be organized for it. This framework ... will be called "Fighting Pioneer Youth", or Nahal [the Hebrew acronym].[8] In its initial phase, Gadna also included Nahal (and a few referred to it as 'Gadnahal'). The first commander of this corps was Lieutenant-Colonel Elhanan Yishai, one of Ben-Gurion's most loyal followers. The above order created the legal basis for youth activity under IDF command and in co-operation with the education system through the schools.

Gadna's pattern of activities at the start was dictated by the army's conceptual framework and the Hagana heritage but it quickly became apparent that there was a need for far-reaching innovation. Elhanan Yishai noted that:

A large part of Gadna's activity was devoted to education, love of country and a familiarity with its paths and byways … The special conditions under which the Jewish people live here forced us to employ a quasi-military framework … to educate for the defence of the State according to the contingencies of mood and whenever necessary.[9]

Gadna was organized on a national basis with divisions into urban and rural areas. Every area established a command headquarters for instructional and educational undertakings. The Gadna units themselves were organized in a military way – squads, platoons, companies and battalions. The junior commanders were youth, trained in special courses, principally courses for squad commanders held once a year, with the participation of 1,800 recruits. IDF officers were in charge of them – they numbered 150 at the beginning of 1949. At the same time, 24,000 out of 44,000 youths between the ages of 15 and 17 years joined the ranks of Gadna.[10] Special frameworks within Gadna were formed, including Gadna airforce and naval units. However, the main effort was centred upon educational and pioneering activity.

In the summer of 1950, the Prime Minister called a joint meeting with the Education and Culture Minister, representatives from General Headquarters, the Defence Ministry and the Education and Culture Ministry, at which it was decided on a common and integrated activity for Gadna through the country's school system. Physical education, weapons training, other military training and lectures on military and security matters were placed at the centre of this programme. The programme consisted of six hours per week scheduled within the general school studies curricula. Another obligatory element in the programme consisted of nine days of marching and 14 days of work per annum in the framework of Gadna national service. To this were added extra-curricular activities in different subjects. All expenses belonging to these additional activities were paid for out of the education budget.[11]

Several months later, the Supreme Command issued the following instructions:

1. Gadna (Paramilitary Corps) constitutes a framework for training and pre-military education of Israeli youth from age 14 to 18.
2. The aim of Gadna is to prepare and educate youth who have joined its ranks, to create a sense of urgency in regard to building

the State, and to be on call at any moment to defend it. This will be brought about in the following five ways:

i) educating youth to love and dedicate themselves to their country and the Jewish people and instilling in them a feeling of concern and willingness for building the State and contributing to its security;
ii) developing the physical strength and endurance of youth, assisting in the improvement of their health, and contributing to their physical capability;
iii) developing openly-acknowledged disciplinary habits among youth;
iv) channeling the training of its recruits to the military-related vocations of the IDF corps, in line with planning and instructions of General Headquarters;
v) spotting gifted youth who have the potential to become commanders and rapidly developing them along this path.[12]

These instructions were principally realized through a programme for high school students spread over four years of study and included:

- foot drill and arms drill – 52 hours
- quasi-martial sport – 100 hours
- gymnastics and male sport exercises – 52 hours
- gymnastics and female sport exercises – 72 hours
- topography – 48 hours
- information dissemination – 48 hours
- boxing for males – 60 hours
- archery – 60 hours.[13]

Apart from this, and in tune with the supreme-command instructions concerning military-related vocational training for the soldiers, Gadna initiated an extra-curricular system of soldiers' circles in the schools, run in a voluntary fashion. These circles met once or twice a week, in the afternoon. In the beginning they encompassed the following topics: airforce, communication, artillery, armoured vehicles, engineering, intelligence, scouting and medics. Their training also included courses crammed into the days of summer vacation.

In the 1952 airforce course devoted to gliding studies, which even reached the stage of solo flight, about 800 students out of the 14,000

candidates were chosen to proceed. The results of medical examinations eliminated many at this first cut. Only 14 attained their wings
and thus qualified for solo flight. Moreover, in a very short time it
became clear that these airforce-training programmes were of no
military value, and that their contribution to the corps of airforce
pilots did not justify the effort. Only a tiny fraction of the graduates
from these programmes became pilots, and opinion was widespread
that they would have become pilots in any case. Gadna – Navy
opened its programme during the summer months in co-operation
with the Zim Shipping Line and its recruits boarded the ships of this
company. It was soon discovered that attaching Gadna youth to
sailors and professional ship crews brought about negative educational results and the entire initiative was cancelled. From this point
on, the Gadna summer courses focused upon sailboating, mainly in
the framework of the fisherman's school at Kfar Vitkin. The number
of recruits in this field reached 420 in 1952. In addition, a course was
conducted at Tantura in which 85 young men and women participated. Gadna succeeded in obtaining 16 boats for their training
programme.

The communication programme in Gadna ran nine-day courses
during the holidays throughout the year and imparted knowledge
about all the IDF communications equipment, radio and telephone
operators. More than 300 youth participated annually in these
courses. The Chief Communications Headquarters, which was
involved in the programme's content and implementation of the
courses, took charge of directing graduates, at the time of their
induction, to the Communication Corps.

The corps-orientation activities of Gadna in other fields – in
particular, armoured vehicles, engineering and artillery – were the
least successful. Youth were not particularly enthusiastic about
becoming involved in these types of activities and the majority of
relevant frameworks were cancelled in 1952, after operating for only
one year.

Even when the Gadna training programmes proceeded according to plan, it seems that their educational significance within the
school system was negligible. Youth were not particularly excited
about them and many parents actively sought to exempt their
children from the training marches, fearing that overexertion would
harm their health. In his appearance before the Knesset's Education
Committee, Mr Artzi, principal of Ohel Shem high school in Ramat
Gan, pointed out that:

The truancy surrounding Gadna activities, through different and unethical means, has turned into a worrisome phenomenon. As you know, any pupil whose health situation is doubtful is forbidden to participate in Gadna activities and marches. But on the other hand, every instance of evasion on false pretenses and inauthentic documents and the like must be prevented. There is no doubt that this behavior brings demoralization in all its senses.[14]

It seems that he slightly exaggerated in his statement, at least in relation to the extent of the phenomenon, but at the same time it also appears impossible to deny its existence.

YOUTH COMMUNITIES – A COMPREHENSIVE STATE YOUTH MOVEMENT

The second commander of Gadna, Colonel Akiva Atzmon (who served in this post from 1950 to 1954) generated comprehensive educational programmes and sought to turn Gadna into a Government youth movement. It appears that Ben-Gurion did not have reservations about this initiative. His confidant, Elik Shomroni, who headed the Youth and Nahal Branch, supported it fully, and made mention, time and again, of the shortcomings of the youth movements in light of the new conditions created with the establishment of the State. At the heart of the idea broached by Atzmon were several findings raised during an inspection of the system under his command. In written documents, he observed that:

1. Gadna activity embraced not more than 25 per cent of the youth between the ages of 13 and 18.
2. The manpower available for Gadna was limited in number and even more so in quality. The very gym teachers and instructors that worked part-time did not consider it a mission but rather a matter of income alone, and did not whip up enthusiasm among the youth for voluntary activities and pioneering ventures.
3. The Gadna training hours inserted into the school curricula did not make room for outdoor training and cut off every tendency for creating an educational atmosphere which would match the tasks set for the Gadna.
4. Discussions and lectures on manual labour and the work ethic, without connection to the action itself, was valueless. The participa-

tion of youth in pioneering tasks was the sole solution to the problem of recognizing the needs of the State and identifying with them.

5. The mood in Israeli society – in which the black market, profiteering, political incitement and all the rest of the political diseases dominated – did not allow real educational activities to take place.

Atzmon thus came to the general conclusion that the Gadna must go out to the desert, literally, to youth communities which would be built within a five-year span in the wasteland landscapes, far from the urban centres. Every young man and woman studying in a high school or vocational school, proposed Atzmon, would be obligated to go out to these communities twice a year for a period of 45 days. The time allocation for activities was: farming and occupational trades – 28 days; study, sport and relaxation – 6 weekends; field trips and training – 11 days. (In the annual summation report: 56 days of work, 22 days of training and marches and 56 hours study about the country and its heritage.) Activities of this sort, during four years of study, were designed to make youth acquainted with all areas of the country.

The communities were to be established, according to Atzmon's proposal, in four places (two of which were not exactly in the desert): the area of Mount Meron in the Upper Galilee; the Carmel, in the northern Negev (close to the town of Ashkelon of today); and the Arava (where Atzmon dreamed of establishing 7–8 farms, from Ein Gedi to Eilat). Atzmon also called for the training of 1,000 counsellors in special courses; these counsellors would run the youth communities and their first task would be the absorption of 15,000 immigrant youth for a month-and-a-half in these communities. In other words, he wanted to double and triple the number of immigrants under Gadna care in the framework of Operation Taking Root.

One of the important aims of Youth Communities, in Atzmon's opinion, was education for citizenship and democracy. Thus, he planned to entrust all youth who passed through the portals of these communities with most of the management tasks, and emphasized that this would involve elections, discussions and activation of institutions that would learn to bear responsibilities. Another important aspect was the economic–productive element. Work carried out by the youth in the communities would bring in enough income to cover daily expenses and even bring a return on part of the investments. In the Mount Meron community, for example, the following economic areas were scheduled: a vegetable garden, fruit orchards, tobacco, hay and cereal crops, cowsheds, hen-roosts, a nursery garden, a canning factory, a metal workshop and smith workshop. Of course, the realization of the programme depended upon widespread reform in the schools (including the teacher-training institutions) and in the youth movements. All these bodies were called upon to change the content as well as the patterns and schedules of their activities, and to adjust them to the basic idea and needs of Youth Communities. However, implementation of this grand demand was never put to the test. The Youth Communities programme remained an idea on paper and the required reforms were never seriously discussed.

The Education Committee of the Knesset debated Atzmon's proposal at two special sittings, but many of the speakers in this debate rejected it outright. They regarded it as contributing towards a dangerous and superfluous militarization of youth; they also opposed it from basic political considerations. Opposition political parties saw the establishment of a State Youth Movement as an imposition of the ruling party upon youth, as a sort of threat directed against all the other parties and to their own youth movements. Mapam circles (which were still united in the Young Guard and Achdut Ha'avoda) naturally raised all the contentions which had been heard since the struggle over the disbanding of the Palmah. In the debates in the Educational Committee, Knesset member Dr Elimelech Rimalt (from the General Zionist Party) said:

> I support state education for the youth but with two reserva-
> tions: no military education – because I am not a militarist. With
> all due respect to it … you see, it is the army which educates
> people to kill the enemy, and a soldier who does not know how
> to do that is not a soldier … Anyway, I cannot educate people,
> who are situated in a military framework, in humanitarian
> values.[15]

Knesset member Dr Abraham (Adolf) Berman (Mapam Party) saw the new programme proposed by Atzmon as 'an anti-pedagogical and anti-socialist revolution'.[16] This was also the opinion of Knesset member Moshe Oonah (HaPoal HaMizrahi Party), who compared the programme to education in ancient Sparta and called for the strengthening of the youth movements through their educational and pioneering undertakings.

The struggle against the Atzmon proposal in particular, and in fact the desire of Ben-Gurion to turn the Gadna into a general State youth movement, even found expression in the youth movements close to Mapai. Evidence for this appears in the correspondence between the secretary of the Working Youth Organization (Noar Ha'oved, which was at the time the largest youth movement) and Ben-Gurion. Alexander Barzel, secretary of the Working Youth (and himself a member of Mapai), called upon Ben-Gurion to leave the education of youth and the formation of a human and pioneering character in the hands of the youth movements. These movements, wrote Barzel, continued to remain faithful to voluntarism and to the belief in free will and thus rejected the intervention from above in areas which were theirs by nature. In the concluding section of his letter, Barzel took issue with the depiction of the military framework as containing educational worth:

> Great anxiety envelops those who undertake the education of our youth, in face of the well-based rumors regarding the army and its leaders' desire to turn Gadna into a state youth movement … the problem before us is not whether military training is required today, but rather whether it is appropriate to give Gadna – which carries out military training – the form of a youth movement with all its regalia … Our enterprise is based on voluntarism. We have not yet ceased to believe in the value of the free will of Hebrew pioneering, which enfolds the whole Zionist effort – immigration, settlement, defence, and state service up to today. To the extent that we lose this value in our lives, we will lose the conviction that our goal can be achieved. We have not yet clarified for ourselves whether we really want an identification between the state and the educational authorities in it, not to mention whether this should occur between the army and the educational authorities. Our political situation, of course, requires constant alert and military preparedness. Pre-army education is requisite, obligatory for all youth, even from age 13. Obligatory pre-military training: Yes! A compulsory and comprehensive youth movement: No! [The sentiments in the original].[17]

Ben-Gurion's reply to this letter was anchored equally in principled and political arguments. 'Several of the youth movements are poisoning the youth spirit; marching with the red flag and singing the Internationale does not pardon the betrayal of 'Maki' [Israel Communist Party] youth, and a large portion of Mapam youth.' Later, he added, in a reprimanding note:

> You rely upon the voluntary efforts of a number of instructors to bring about a youth movement. I rely upon the working people of the state – they are a decisive majority and will remain a decisive majority in the population of the State: they will be loyal to its historical destination ... The habits, the opportunities, the directions and the concepts to which some of the youth counselors adhered before we had this blessed and powerful instrument of a state ... do not match the needs, the possibilities and the opportunities of the present day.[18]

Ben-Gurion could not refrain from confirming at the beginning of the letter that 'to my great regret, there is still no possibility of creating a general and obligatory framework for youth sponsored by the state'. He, too, recognized the impossibility of establishing a State youth movement. And indeed, it did not come about.

GADNA ACTIVITIES AMONG THE NEW IMMIGRANTS

Despite the objections from all sides of the political spectrum to Gadna's monopoly, this body was nevertheless compelled to expand its activities to youth in the poor urban quarters and the transit camps, and even to concentrate on this particular population. The justification for this demand, which did not meet with any real opposition in the political arena, was seemingly 'objective'. The target population constituted 80 per cent of the youth population who were not organized in any other educational activity framework. Yet it appears that this was exactly the root of the matter. Youth movements abstained from coming to grips with the 'problematic' population and thus were prepared to leave it almost entirely to a State agency – to Gadna – despite the fact that it was 'militaristic'.

This activity (see chapter 4) was most problematic and more than once involved difficult encounters with the youths' parents. It even happened, now and then, that Gadna counsellors were violently expelled from the transit camps.

The initial activity programme focused upon organizing youth activities in the transit camp clubhouse. This facility could serve as the centre for a platoon of 135 to 150 cadets. The club-house was supposed to be in a cabin located in the heart of the transit camp and was intended to allow those who came to it to spend their time in 'educational' pursuits, suitable to their age and anchored in the basic aims of Gadna. The activities including singing, dancing, theatre and practical work – but above all activities involving dissemination of information. The objective of these activities was to develop a sense of responsibility, a feeling of partnership and self-discipline and a cultivation of the basic values of a democratic society. Core subjects in Hebrew, arithmetic, the Bible and history were inserted between all this.

All the direct educational activities were to be carried out in classes of no more than 15 young men and women. Lessons were scheduled twice a week. Once a month there was a gathering of platoons and companies for concentrated activities and festive parades. Gadna headquarters allocated a full staff complement at company level for each clubhouse: a company commander and his second, three platoon commanders and nine squad commanders. The majority of this staff – sometimes up to 70 per cent – were female soldiers. In the beginning they lived in tents in the transit camps, under the same difficult conditions that were the lot of the inhabitants. However, after several assault incidents, there was no choice but to withdraw them from the camps.

The command staff of each clubhouse was augmented by four teachers, a singing instructor, a dancing instructor and an instructor for practical work. During 1952, about 50 Gadna clubhouses were erected in the transit camps. Budgets for their activities came from the Youth Branch of the Defence Ministry and the Immigration Department of the Jewish Agency.

Despite the goodwill and the large investment by Gadna headquarters, the entire initiative generally met with failure, and even abject failure (despite registering local successes here and there; at the Rosh Ha'ayin transit camp, for example, activities embraced more than 400 youth after one year). In the first place, Gadna did not succeed in creating a bridge between transit camp youth and youth of the veteran citizens. For example, when Gadna commanders tried to enrol Jerusalem youth as instructors in the transit camps, they found that only a few responded, and even they did not persevere. On the other hand, the attempt to employ youth from the transit camps as counsellors, even though they received training in courses given for commanders, also came to nothing: 'to the youth of the camps, their "pedigree" did not seem great enough to command their allegiance.'[19]

In view of these difficulties, Gadna began to operate Taking Root Camps. Several thousand youth passed through these camps and for many this was the real gateway to Israeli society – sometimes to the extent that it created cultural clashes with their parents.

The activities of Gadna among the youth in the poor suburban quarters were carried on through the Gadna houses, which were established in relevant population concentrations – mainly in the neighbourhoods and quarters inhabited by new immigrants. The number of youth who participated in this framework stood at close to 6,000, the majority between the ages of 13 and 17 years. The entire operation was directed by a committee composed of representatives from Gadna headquarters – the chief medical officer, the chief education officer and an officer responsible for looking after youth in the distressed suburban areas. The Cultural Department of the Ministry of Education and Culture was also a partner. Instruction for these youth was drawn from male and female teachers, mobilized for reserve duty, who were taken out of the area in which they had regular work.

The scope of these activities was very far from responding to the needs, especially in light of the fact that Gadna was almost the only state agency which came to the assistance of this sector. An article by Kalter[20] which was written in 1951, indicates that the army (that is, Gadna) served as a last-ditch reservoir for preventing the descent of youth from distressed areas into the world of crime. The writer did not forget to indicate that this reservoir could not cope with the heavy burden.

THE GADNA FARM AT BE'ER ORA

The pioneering side of Gadna's activities, once it had severed relations with Nahal, found expression in the establishment of a farm at Be'er Ora in Bir Hindis (that is, Be'er Tsalmavet) about 20 kilometers north of Eilat. The decision on this matter was made during the summer of 1950, and on 22 December of that year, the first contingent of kibbutzim youth had already settled in. They came from the Emek area – children from Tel Yosef, Ein Harod, Geva – and a group of immigrant children from Kvutzat HaSharon. They were the pioneers who began to shape the pattern of farm life at Be'er Ora.

Eight-thousand youth passed through the farm in its first year, many of them new immigrants and youth from distressed neighbourhoods. Each contingent, which spent two weeks on the farm, numbered about 100 youth. Ten days were devoted to work and guard duty on the farm (also to unloading cargo at the newly opened port at Eilat, paving the road to Eilat and the building of an airport) and the remaining days to excursions in the area. In the evenings, the youth participated in social and cultural programmes. In the first year, an extensive plan for planting eucalyptus trees on farmland and along the road to Eilat was drawn up, but the lack of available water prevented its realization. In lieu of this they resorted to setting up a tree nursery for eucalyptus, acacia and jujube. In addition, inspections and experiments were begun to develop a farm economy in the hope that it would be self-sufficient. Later, experiments were conducted in irrigation, using sewage water, and the enrichment of the soil through fertilization with organic manure. The results of these experiments contributed to academic knowledge but did not actually assist in the development of settlement at the farm.

The Gadna command coined the name Operation Blooming of the Desert for the entire undertaking. The Gadna commander, Lieutenant-Colonel Akiva Atzmon, even declared, with festive pathos, in *Niv Alumim*, the Gadna newsletter:

> Youth regiments are built on the basis of an integration of the pioneering and military ethos into a single spiritual blend ... We will build farms in the desert, on the model of Be'er Ora. We will plant forests on rocky ground, groves along the railway lines. We will create soil for the people from wasteland.[21]

In his view, Be'er Ora was the first swallow in the framework of Youth Communities, and following it three similar youth farms in the Arava were to be established. But the termination of the general plan eliminated the farm from the pioneering agenda. Three other farms were built in Afula, Beit Dagan and Ein Zeytim respectively but they did not last. In the last stage of their existence (1952 to 1953), these farms served as a station for growing vegetables for the IDF. Be'er Ora continued to serve Gadna as an educational centre for many years.

NOTES

1. A. Doron, 'Youth Order: The Gadna', in A. Kfir and Y. Erez (eds), *The IDF and its Corps* (Tel Aviv: Revivim, 1982), p. 114.
2. BGA, Ben-Gurion Diary, 7 April 1947, a review of Gadna, commanders, number of youth in area frameworks, training programmes, and extended future programmes.

3. Ibid., 3 April 1947.
4. Ibid., 2 May 1947.
5. Ibid., 18 June 1947.
6. D. Ben-Gurion, 'A Melting Pot Forges a People', in D. Ben-Gurion, *Army and Security* (Tel Aviv: Ma'arachot, 1955), p. 297.
7. D. Ben-Gurion, 'Our Generation's Operation and its Mission', *Eternal Israel* (Tel Aviv: Eyanot, 1964), p. 399.
8. See A. Doron, *Youth Order: The Gadna*, p. 120.
9. BGA , Subject File, Gadna, Security Values, Aims of Gadna; see A. Doron, *Youth Order: The Gadna*, p. 120.
10. BGA, Ben-Gurion Diary, 24 and 26 August 1949.
11. SA 5354 ג . File 1401, Document recording the summary of a joint meeting, signed by D. Ben-Gurion and directed to the Ministry of Education and the General Headquarters of the IDF, 28 August 1950.
12. SA 5434 ג , File 1401, Instructions from the Supreme Command, 15 November 1950.
13. SA 5435 ג , File 1401, Protocol 37, Meeting of the Education and Cultural Committee of the Knesset, 23 July 1952, report by the Commander of Gadna, Colonel A. Atzmon.
14. SA 5435ג , File 1401, Protocol 43, Meeting of the Education and Cultural Committee of the Knesset, 13 August 1952.
15. Ibid.
16. Ibid.
17. UKA, Section 8, Noar Oved V'lomed, Container 3, Central Institutions, File 2, Letter of A. Barzel to the Minister of Defence, 26 May 1953.
18. UKA, Section 8, 'Regimented Voluntarism', a term employed by Professor Lissak, which derives its sense from the deeds and words of Ben-Gurion in his statist activities connected to the organizing of 'voluntarism' in the areas of settlement, education and immigrant absorption. This orientation is expressed in the reply to a letter from A. Barzel, the Secretary of Hanoar Ha'oved: 'What the voluntary framework cannot do – although we indeed accomplished great things under the conditions of the previous period – the state with all its power and compulsion will do under our direction, and it will be under our direction – if we dare to direct the state in fulfilling its historical destiny.' Letter of Ben-Gurion, 2 July 1953.
19. SA 5435ג , File 1401, Protocol 37, Report of the Commander of Gadna.
20. UKA, Section 25, Series 25, Container 35, File 5; P. Kalter, 'Problems of Abandoned Youth and the Army's Contribution to Solving Them', in *Anthology of the Commander of Gadna* 12 (1951), pp. 4–8.
21. BGA, Subject File Gadna, Container 2, Operation Blooming of the Desert, in Gadna news organ: *BaMahane Alumin [In the Youth Camp]*, 22 (1952).

Conclusion

During the first years of the Israeli State, the IDF was a central partner in the formation of its social and physical character. Its involvement in the areas of settlement, immigrant absorption and education left its mark on Israeli society for many years to come and made concrete such sociological concepts as 'an army engaged in nation-building', 'melting pot', and 'a nation in uniform'. During this entire period, from May 1948 to December 1953, the IDF operated directly under David Ben-Gurion, Israel's first Prime Minister and Minister of Defence. Ben-Gurion acquired a special standing at the pinnacle of the regime. It was he who tipped the scales in most important decisions, including many operative decisions involving relations between the armed forces of the State and its domestic environment. It was he who created a broad security conception, by delineating IDF undertakings and commitments which went beyond narrow military goals. It was he who made settlement, education, immigrant absorption and the building of Israeli society an integral part of State security under the aegis of the armed forces.

In many contemporary developing states, the army emerges as the only institution which is built to conform with modernity. As an institution which employs advanced technologies, it is obligated to sustain and cultivate an organizational system which has the capacity to put into operation these technologies. It naturally follows that such a system requires, first and foremost, manpower possessing suitable skills. It is, therefore, not surprising that in these states the army is called upon to assume responsibility for organizing the basic frameworks of the State and society and for undertaking a series of non-military but vital roles in the economic, social and educational spheres. Later, as the State matures and develops, the involvement of the army in these processes gradually decreases. The Israeli State underwent a developmental pattern of this sort immediately after its establishment.

The young Israel, however, was not a classic type of developing state. The hard core of its population was closely tied to Western civilization, and at the time of its establishment the State contained legislative, administrative and national institutions which had already been carrying out governmental functions. With the influx of a large number of immigrants, a wide gap was created between the existing governmental systems and many of the newcomers, who came from areas which lacked a democratic tradition and had no basic Western education. A portion of the population was even illiterate.

This gap had an additional unique feature: in contrast to many states, the Israeli army was heavily engaged in security undertakings – the young State was under constant military threat and its existence could not be taken for granted – and strove to adjust its standards to these tasks. For this reason, and because there were heavy manpower constraints, the IDF had no choice but to invest a great deal of its efforts in the civilian population in order to improve the quality of its recruits.

Against this background Ben-Gurion formulated a conception that was both pragmatic and ideological. The IDF would participate in the formation of emergent Israeli society and, at the same time, it would fashion an image of the 'new Israeli'. This conception included ideas about the need for national renewal and awareness of the organizational and logistic potential of the army. It also contained elements of that tradition from the Workers' Movement and the Hagana, which justified a comprehensive mobilization of resources for changing social and national patterns. Many of those who disagreed with Ben-Gurion objected less to this mobilization than to the fact that it was Ben-Gurion, the man, who determined the aims of this mobilization in such a dominant manner, and imprinted upon them the stamp of statism as opposed to reliance upon political movements. From the moment that Ben-Gurion established the authority of the civilian over the military echelon, as well as his personal authority as political and security leader, his difficulties in directing the army to civilian tasks were no longer on the level of principles. The senior command was right to follow him in these tasks and co-operated with him to the best of its ability. Here and there, reservations could be heard regarding priorities, and sometimes the not unintentional delays in implementation that occurred, but the majority of the IDF commanders were convinced that it was their duty to operate beyond the narrow confines of the military framework. They well understood that the IDF, as a

State army not caught up in political, communal or religious divisions, and as an entity which bore the halo of victory in the War of Independence, was situated at the centre of national consensus. By virtue of this concurrence and approbation, it was clear to the leadership that there was no better agency than the armed forces for working among the immigrants and attending to other problematic fronts.

Furthermore, more than once it was IDF commanders who initiated their own suggestions in the spirit of Ben-Gurion's basic outlook of employing the army in nation building. An especially salient supporter of this approach was Yigael Yadin, the second Chief-of-Staff, who had an additional consideration. Fearing a second round of fighting, he was interested in preserving a large and strong military; IDF engagement in civilian activities allowed him to move in that direction. Moreover, in a certain sense, Yadin went farther than Ben-Gurion and sought to employ the IDF in explicitly civilian undertakings (paving roads, communication and educational matters, hospitals and hospitalization). It was quite ironic that, of all matters, it was this broad approach of Yadin's which brought him into confrontation with Ben-Gurion and led to the termination of his army career. Prior to this confrontation, however, Yadin was the most suitable Chief-of-Staff for carrying out the military–civilian intentions of Ben-Gurion. Thus, for example, it was Yadin who enthusiastically orchestrated Operation Name Change, which sought to supply Hebrew names to IDF soldiers and commanders. What would appear to many as a brazen invasion of privacy, appeared to the Chief-of-Staff at the time (and even more so to Ben-Gurion who was his superior officer) as a justified step in making a break with the past and thereby erasing 'traces of the exile'. This, too, was part of the effort to create a system of new values and contents which the IDF was required to convey to its personnel as citizens of the State.

The defence system and the IDF were dominant factors in determining the location of settlement in the Israeli State. The fortified settlements and settlement activities of the Nahal created facts in the frontier areas (and blocked infiltration) which would not have been accomplished had it not been for the IDF. Furthermore, the physical features of the settlements were determined because of the IDF's involvement in the planning processes and their establishment. Through a system of information dissemination and organization, at the conclusion of the war, the IDF recruited core groups of demobilized soldiers into settlements, thereby influencing the formative social fabric of a great number of kibbutzim and moshavim.

At the same time, the Nahal encountered a series of confrontations and even failures. For example, Nahal units in the 1950s did not integrate native-born and immigrant soldiers, a practice opposed to what was planned and declared. They consisted principally of new immigrants under the command of native-born Israelis. In addition, over time, the number of soldiers choosing agricultural training under the National Security Service Law declined, and there was a continuous and precipitous decline in the number of Nahal soldiers who chose the kibbutz as their life course. Nevertheless, from a general perspective, against the background of the period, Nahal was a military/civilian body drawn to pioneering tasks, absorbing youth of immigrant origin, and trying to integrate them into the Israeli social experience; moreover, it cultivated an enthusiasm for populating frontier areas, contributed to a feeling of security, uplifted morale and stood at the centre of national consensus. In a word, it played a significant role in creating a social–national ethos, and its importance should not be underestimated.

This aspect of Nahal blended with one of the principal aspects of the Defence Service Law, which obligated all youth, both male and female, to join the IDF. This law also clearly contained the imprint of Ben-Gurion's formulaic ideological/pragmatic mix; in practice, it created an additional stage in the educational system of the new generation. The routine activities, the order and discipline, the commitment and assignation of responsibility, and the social experience created in the units had a major influence on the maturation process of youth. It had an impact on their social behaviour, their national orientations and the development of their individual skills, and served as a preparation for civilian life. It is, indeed, easy to find negative and even dangerous motifs in the make-up of military life, but it is doubtful whether these are sufficient to outweigh the advantages as they panned out in the first years of Israeli sovereignty. In the circumstances of the time, the military system knew how to instil in many of the immigrants a sense of patriotism and a feeling of belonging to Israeli society. The IDF was the nation's most important socialization agent. Through its facilitating and interventionist role, immigrants acquired the concepts and the basic values of the society and the State (including a working knowledge of the Hebrew language and acquaintance with Israeli culture). Here, by virtue of a modern bureaucratic institution, built on the principle of achievement rather than ascription, immigrant horizons were opened to the possibilities of social mobilization and advancement. Moreover, for many immigrants, the IDF also served as an agent of modernization and entrance into a world of Western culture. The IDF provided them, for the first time, with the opportunity to gain experience with advanced Western technology and to learn modern Western ways of thinking and work. The army experience also eased their absorption into Israeli society.

IDF activities which took place outside the regular army ranks, both in the reserve units and in the immigrant settlement and transit camps, expanded the influential circle of its educational–social activities. Operation Learning Hebrew, carried out by female soldiers in places of immigrant concentration, not only resulted in the learning of the Hebrew language but also brought about the dissemination of citizenship studies, history and Zionism. The Gadna camps, children's camps and daily activities among the youth generation in immigrant conclaves provided many with the bases of Israeli citizenship and the common denominator for social and national identity.

The overall conclusion was quite removed from the initial expectations. The power of a dynamic reality overcame all the ideas woven into the 'utopia in uniform' framework. This utopia was unable to solve many of the difficult problems which swept through the State at its beginning. But it appears possible to affirm that in contrast to what occurred in other developing states, society in the Israeli State of the early 1950s was not at the service of the army. Rather, the IDF was called to the service of society and supplied its needs, and it did that without exercising extra privileges.

This involvement of the IDF in the early formation of the character of Israeli society helped crystallize the entire citizenry into one nation possessing those common national values which are essential in a liberal Western democracy.

Bibliography

ARCHIVES

Ben-Gurion Archives, The Ben-Gurion Research Center, Sede Boqer Campus

Ben-Gurion diaries
Ben-Gurion correspondence file
General archive material
Protocol files of meetings
Subject file: Gadna
Subject file: Nahal
Subject file: The IDF and Israeli Society
Subject file: Transit camps

Central Zionist Archives (CZA)

Demobilized soldiers – S12
Newspaper articles – S71
Office of Ben-Gurion – S44
Office of Berl Locker – S41
Office of G. Yoseftal – S42
Office of Levi Eshcol – S43
Protocols from Sessions of the Jewish Agency Executive
The Political Department – S25
The Settlement Department – S15

HaKibbutz HaMeuchad Archive – Yad Tabenkin (AKM)

Galilee Section

Palmah Headquarters Archive
Section 2: Testimony on Security, Society, Military Induction, Relations Abroad, Absorption, Immigration, Youth Immigration
Section 4: HaKibbutz HaMeuchad Congresses
Section 5: HaKibbutz HaMeuchad Council
Section 25, file 1: Elik Shomroni file
Section 25, series 23: Nahal
Section 25, series 23: Shalhin Battalion

Historical Branch: Research

Gadna file
Galei Tzahal file, Ben-Gurion files: 230/72/2156
General Staff Branch – GHQ, Operations: 7/54, transit camps file; children's camp file: 11/55
Medical Corps file
Office of Chief of the General Staff Branch – GHQ: territorial defence organization, settlement: 79/54; file 27
Rehabilitation of Demobilized Soldiers: 580/56
Welfare Service: 792/50/142

IDF Archive (the resources mentioned are only open files)

Adjutant General Branch files, GHQ: 1368/50/25; 782/65/1186
Department of Culture files 1794/50/1; 165/51; 794/50/183/15
Ministry of Defence files
Nahal files: 321/54; 231/54;1687/85
Settlement Committee file: 1116/57

Labour Movement Archive in the name of Lavon

The Agricultural Center – Sessions: 104 VI
The Eighth Congress: 307 VI
Hertzfeld Correspondence: 104-53-47 IV
Information Dissemination: 307 IV
The Moshav Movement – Council: 307 IV
Negev Undertakings: 307 IV
Security Committee: 307 IV

Israel State Archives

Immigration and Registration Branch files – section 73
Knesset files – section 60
Ministry of Agriculture files
Ministry of Defence files
Ministry of Health files – section 57
Ministry of the Interior files
Ministry of Religion files
Office of the Prime Minister files – section 43

NEWSPAPERS AND PERIODICALS

State Government and International Relations (Medina, Memshal v'Yahasim Benleumi'im)
Migvan
Kathedra
M'Bifnim
Niv HaKvutza
Zmanim

IDF Publications

BaMahane
BaMahane Nahal
Ma'arachot
Skira Hodsheet
Biton Hel Avir

Daily Newspapers

Ma'ariv
Yediot Aharonot
HaBoker
Ha'aretz
HaTsopheh
Davar
Al Hamishmar
Herut

THESES AND DISSERTATIONS

Bar-On, M. 'The Security and Foreign Policy of Israel in the Years 1955–1957', dissertation, The Hebrew University of Jerusalem, 1988.

Breaman, A. 'Examination of the Gadna as an Informal Education Organization', MA thesis, The Hebrew University of Jerusalem, 1984.

Cohen, D. 'The Policy of Absorption during the Period of Mass Immigration, 1948–1953', dissertation, Bar-Ilan University, 1985.

Drory, Z. 'Retaliatory Policy in the 1950s: The Role of the Military in the Escalation Process', MA thesis, Tel Aviv University, 1988.

Golani, M. 'The Sinai War – Political and Military Aspects', dissertation, Haifa University, 1992.

Kafkafi, E. 'Changes in the Ideology of the United Kibbutz Movement Ideology during the Cold War, 1944–1954', dissertation, Tel Aviv University, 1986.

Kenan, E. '"HaShomer HaTsa'ir" and the Mass Immigration', MA thesis, Tel Aviv University, 1989.

Markovitzky, I. 'Gahal: Its Activities, and Contribution during the War of Independence', dissertation, Haifa University, 1993.

Milch, Z. 'Mapai and Mass Immigration, 1948–1952', MA thesis, Tel Aviv University, 1988.

Shiran, A. 'Settlement from a Security Outlook: New Settlement during the War of Independence', MA thesis, Tel Aviv University, 1993.

Tal, D. 'The Development of Israel's Concept of Routine Security 1949–1956', dissertation, Tel Aviv University, 1993.

Yablonka, H. 'Absorption and Integration Problems of Holocaust Survivors during the Process of Formation of Israeli Society', dissertation, The Hebrew University of Jerusalem, 1969.

ARTICLES

Baki, R. 'Demographic Development in Israel', *Economic Quarterly*, vol. 2 (8) (1954).

Ginnosar, P. (ed.) *Studies in Zionism, the Yishuv and the State of Israel*, vol. 1, Ben-Gurion: University of the Negev, 1991, pp.170–90.

Greenberg, Y., 'National Security and Military Strength: Between Statesman and Military Commander', *Studies in Zionism, the Yishuv and the State of Israel*, vol. 1 (1991), pp.170–90.

Horowitz, D. and Kimmerling, B. 'Some Social Implications of Military Service and the Reserve System in Israel', *European Journal of Sociology*, vol.15 (2) (1974), pp.262–76.

Kimmerling, B. 'Determination of the Boundaries and Frameworks of Conscription: Two Dimensions of the Civil–Military Relations in Israel', *Studies in Comparative International Development: Transaction Periodicals Consortium*, vol.14 (1) (1979), pp.22–41.

Lintz, A. 'Military Industry in Israel', *Armed Forces and Society*, vol.12 (1) (1983), pp.9–28.

Victor, A. and Kimmerling, B. 'New Immigrants in the Israeli Armed Forces', *Armed Forces and Society*, vol.6 (1980), pp.455–82.

BOOKS

Adler, H. and Kahane, R. (eds) *Israel: Society in the Making*. Jerusalem: Akademon, 1978.

Alon, Y. *Sandscreen*. Tel Aviv: HaKibbutz HaMeuchad, 1958.

Arian, A. *Politics and Regime in Israel*. Tel Aviv: Zmora Bitan, 1985.

Atid, D., Kahonovitz, A. and Lifshitz, S. *Absorption of Nahal Groups in Settlements*. Rehovot: The Centre for Rural and Urban Settlement Research, 1975.

Avidar, Y. *The Way to the IDF*. Tel Aviv: Ma'arachot, 1973.

Avihai, A. *David Ben-Gurion: The Designer of the State*. Jerusalem: Keter, 1974.

Avineri, S. (ed.) *David Ben-Gurion: Portrait of a Leader in the Workers' Movement*. Tel Aviv: Am Oved, 1986.

—— (ed.) *Now or Never*: Beit Berl: Eyanot, 1989.

—— (ed.) *Chimes of Independence: Memoirs – March–November 1947*. Tel Aviv: Am Oved, 1993.

Bar-On, M. *Challenge and Conflict: The Road to Operation Kadesh, 1956*. The Ben-Gurion Research Center, Sede Boqer Campus, 1991.

Bar-Zohar, M. *Ben-Gurion*. Tel Aviv: Am Oved, 1977.

Ben-Gurion, D. 'The Labourer in Zionism', *From Class to Nation*. Tel Aviv: Davar, 1933.

—— *Vision and Way*. Tel Aviv, 1942.

—— *On the Campaigns*. Tel Aviv: Ministry of Defence, 1950–54.

—— *Army and Security*. Tel Aviv: Maarachot, 1955.

—— *Eternal Israel*. Tel Aviv: Eyanot, 1964.

——*When Israel Fought in Battle*. Tel Aviv: Mapai, 1969.

—— *The State of Israel Renewed*. Tel Aviv: Am Oved, 1969.

—— *Memoirs*. Tel Aviv: Am Oved, 1971.

—— *Uniqueness and Destination*. Tel Aviv: Ma'arachot, 1972.

—— *War Diary*. G. Rivlin, E. Oren (eds), Tel Aviv: Am Oved, 1982.

—— *On Settlement*. Tel Aviv: HaKibbutz HaMeuchad, 1987.

Begin, M. *The Revolt*. Tel Aviv: Ahiasaf, 1978.

Bein, A. *Immigration and Settlement in the State of Israel*. Tel Aviv: Am Oved, 1982.

Brenner, A. *The Mobilized Groups of the Palmah 1942–1948*. Ramat Eyfal: Yad Tabenkin, 1983.

Conversations A, The Testing of Education in the Ingathering of the Exiles. Tel Aviv: Mapai, 1951.

Conversations B, Youth in Israel: Reality, Problems, Roles. Tel Aviv: Mapai, 1951.

Dayan, D. *Yes, We Are the Youth: A History of Gadna*. Tel Aviv: Ministry of Defence, 1977.

Doar, Y. *Nahal Units Album*. Tel Aviv: Ministry of Defence, 1989.

Education and Morale in the IDF. Tel Aviv: Chief-of-Staff, Education Officer, 1956.

Eisenstadt, S. N. *Absorption of Immigrants: Sociological Research*. Jerusalem: Magnes Press, 1952.

—— *Absorption of Immigrants: The Ingathering of the Exiles and Problems in the Transformation of Israeli Society*. Jerusalem: Magnes Press, 1969.

—— *Society in Israel*. Jerusalem: Magnes Press, 1973.

Eisenstadt, S. N., Adler, H., Bar-Yosef, R. and Kahane, R. (eds) *The Social Structure of Israel*. Jerusalem: Magnes, 1969.

Eshcol, L. *The Birth Pains of Settlement*. Tel Aviv: Am Oved, 1958.

Gal, R. *A Portrait of the Israeli Soldier*. New York: Greenwood Press, 1986.

Galnoor, Y. *The Beginnings of Democracy in Israel*. Tel Aviv: Am Oved, 1985.

Gelber, Y. *The Emergence of a Jewish Army: The Veterans of the British Army in the IDF*. Jerusalem: Yad Izhak Ben-Zvi, 1986.

—— *Why They Disbanded the Palmah*. Jerusalem: Shocken, 1986.

Gilad, Z. (ed.) *The Palmah Book*. Tel Aviv: HaKibbutz HaMeuchad, 1956.

Ginnosar, P. (ed.), *Studies in Zionism, the Yishuv and the State of Israel*, vols 1–4. Ben-Gurion University of the Negev, 1991–94.

Ginossar, P. (ed.) *Immigrants in Israel*. Jerusalem: Akademon, 1969.

Golani, M. (ed.) *Settlement and Security: Lectures and Discussions*, Elazar Pages Series. Tel Aviv: Amikam and Tel Aviv University Press, 1981.

—— (ed.) *'Black Arrow': Operation Gaza and the Israeli Policy of Retaliation during the Fifties*. Tel Aviv: Ministry of Defence, Haifa University, the Herzl Institute for Zionist Research, 1994.

Guttman, E. and Dror, Y. (eds) *Political Regime in Israel*. Jerusalem: Magnes, 1961.

Gvati, H. *One Hundred Years of Settlement*. Tel Aviv: HaKibbutz HaMeuchad, 1981.

Horowitz, D. 'The Israel Defence Forces: A Civilianized Military in a Partially Militarized Society', in R. Kolkowitz and A. Korbonski (eds) *Soldiers, Peasants and Bureaucrats*. London: George Allen and Unwin, 1982: pp.77–106.

—— *Distress in Utopia*. Tel Aviv: Am Oved, 1990.

Horowitz, D. and Lissak, M. *From Settlement to State*. Tel Aviv: Am Oved, 1977.

Huntington, S. P. *Political Order in Changing Societies*. New Haven, CT and London: Yale University Press, 1968.

—— *The Soldier and the State*. Cambridge, MA: Vintage Books, 1975.

Ilem, Y. *The Haganah: The Zionist Path to Power*. Tel Aviv: Zmora, 1979.

Keel, I. *State Religious Education: Its Roots, History and Problems*. Jerusalem: The Ministry of Education and Culture, 1977.

Keren, M. *Ben-Gurion and the Intellectuals*. The Ben-Gurion Research Center, Sede Boqer Campus, 1988.

Keren, S. *Between Ears of Corn and the Sword*. Tel Aviv: Ministry of Defence, 1991.

Kfir, A. and Erez, I. (eds) *The IDF and Its Corps: Encyclopaedia of the Army and Defence*. Tel Aviv: Revivim, 1982.

Kimmerling, B. *Social Interruption and Besieged Societies: The Case of Israel*. Special Studies Series, Buffalo, NY: Council on International Studies, 1979.

Kolet, I. *Fathers and Founders*. Tel Aviv: Kibbutz Meuchad, 1975.

Koren, I. *The Ingathering of the Exiles and Its Settling on the Land*. Tel Aviv: Am Oved, 1964.

Levi (Levitza), L. *Nine Measures: Jerusalem during the War of Independence Battles*. Tel Aviv: Ma'arachot, 1986.

Lissak, M. 'The Israeli Defense Forces as an Agent of Socialization and Education: A Research in Role Expansion in Democratic Society', in M. R. van Gils (ed.) *The Perceived Role of the Military*. Rotterdam: Rotterdam University Press, 1972.

—— 'Paradoxes of Israeli Civil–Military Relations', in M. Lissak (ed.) *Israeli Society and Its Defense Establishment*. London: Frank Cass, 1984.

Lissak, M. and Kimmerling, B. *Army and Security*. Jerusalem: Magnes, 1985.

Lorch, N. *History of the War of Independence*. Tel Aviv: Masada, 1989.

Luttwak, E. and Horowitz, D. *The Israeli Army*. London: Allan Lowe, 1975.

Man, R. and Gon-Gross, Z. *IDF Radio All the Time*. Tel Aviv: Ministry of Defence, 1991.

Morris, B. *Birth of the Palestinian Refugee Problem, 1947–1949*. Tel Aviv: Am Oved, 1986.

Naor, M. (ed.) *Immigrants and Transit Camps, 1948–1952*, Edan Series 8. Jerusalem: Yad Ben-Zvi, 1987.

—— (ed.) *Youth Movement 1920–1960*. Edan Series 13. Jerusalem: Yad Ben-Zvi, 1989.

Ofer, Tzvi and Cover, A. (eds) *The Price of Power*. Tel Aviv: Ma'arachot, 1984.

Ostfeld, Z. *An Army Is Born*. Tel Aviv: Ministry of Defence, 1994.

Palmah Album. Tel Aviv: Kibbutz Meuchad, 1959 (opening remarks: Yigael Alon).

Pe'il, M. *From the 'Hagana' to the Israel Defense Forces*. Tel Aviv: Zmora Bitan, 1979.

Peri, Y. *Between Battles and Ballots: Israeli Military in Politics*. Cambridge: Cambridge University Press, 1983.

Perlmutter, A. *Military and Politics in Israel*. London: Frank Cass, 1969.

Rattner, I. *My Life and I*. Tel Aviv: Shocken, 1978.

Rivlin, G. (ed.) *The Tel Hai Heritage*. Tel Aviv, 1983.

Rosen, D. (ed.) *Transit Camps and Immigrant Settlements*. Jerusalem: Ministry of the Interior, 1985.

Roumani, M. M. *From Immigrant to Citizen: The Contribution of the Army to National Integration in Israel*. Be'er Sheva: Ben-Gurion University of the Negev, 1979.

Segev, T. *1949: The First Israelis*. Jerusalem: Domino, 1984.

Shalem, H. *To the Negev*. Tel Aviv: Yair, 1988.

Shapira, A. *The Army Controversy, 1948: Ben Gurion's Struggle for Control*. Tel Aviv: HaKibbutz Meuchad, 1984.

—— *The Zionist Dove's Sword and Its Power, 1881–1948 (Herev HaYonah HaTzionit V'HaKoach, 1881–1948)*. Tel Aviv: Am Oved, 1992. Translated into English as *Land and Power: The Zionist Resort to Force 1881–1948*. New York: Oxford University Press, 1992.

Sharett, M. *Personal Diary*, vols 2–5. Tel Aviv: Ma'ariv, 1978.

Shomroni, A. *Elik: Life Horizons*. Tel Aviv: Amalgamated Farming Cooperatives and Kibbutzim, 1958.

—— *Scythe and Sword*. Tel Aviv: Ma'arachot, 1955.

Shteptel, S. *Security Settlement and Its Linkage to the War of Independence, November 1947–July 1948*. Tel Aviv: Ministry of Defence, 1992.

Sicron, M. *Immigration to Israel: 1948–1953*. Jerusalem: The Central Bureau of Statistics, 1957.

Slutzky, Y. (ed.) *History of the Hagana*. Tel Aviv: Am Oved, 1972.

Sternberg, A. *Absorbing a Nation*. Tel Aviv: HaKibbutz HaMeuchad, 1973.

Tadmor, I. *Educational Concepts in Gadna*. Tel Aviv: University of Tel Aviv, 1976.

Tevet, S. *The Jealousy of David: The Life of Ben-Gurion*. Tel Aviv: Shocken, 1977.

Troen, S. I. and Lucas, N. (eds) *Israel: The First Decade of Independence*. New York: State University of New York Press, 1995.

Tzahor, Z. *Vision and Reckoning: Ben-Gurion between Ideology and Politics*. Tel Aviv: Sifriat Poalim, 1994.

Tzameret, Z. *Days of the Melting Pot: Investigatory Committee on the Education of Immigrant Children*. The Ben-Gurion Research Center, Sede Boqer Campus, 1993.

Tzur, Z. *The United Kibbutz Movement in the Settlement of the Country, 1949–1969*. Ramat Eyfal: Yad Tabenkin, 1984.

Victor, A. 'Israeli Armed Forces', in J. Morris and S. D. Westbrood (eds) *Civic Education in the Military*, vol. 11, California: Publications Inc., 1983: 99–122.

Weitz, Y. *My Diaries and Letters to the Sons*. Tel Aviv: Masada, 1965.

Yavlonka, H. *Foreign Brothers*. Jerusalem: Yad Izhak Ben-Tzvi, 1994.

Yoram, S. (ed.) *Giora Yoseftal: His Life and Activities. A Selection of Writings, Oral Conversations, Diaries and Letters*. Tel Aviv: Mapai, 1963.

Zweig, R. W. (ed.) *David Ben-Gurion: Politics and Leadership in Israel*. London: Frank Cass and Yad Izhak Ben-Zvi, 1991.

Index